94-78

P9-AOV-221

This book was
donated by:

"RETIRED"

MARY BLATZ

94-78

THE READING CORNER

GOODYEAR EDUCATION SERIES
Theodore W. Hipple, Editor
University of South Carolina at Spartanburg

CHANGE FOR CHILDREN
Sandra N. Kaplan, Jo Ann B. Kaplan, Sheila K. Madsen, Bette K. Taylor

CREATING A LEARNING ENVIRONMENT
Ethel Breyfogle, Pamela Santich, Ronald Kremer, Susan Nelson, Carol Pitts

DO YOU READ ME?
Arnold Griese

IMAGINE THAT!
Joyce King and Carol Katzman

THE LANGUAGE ARTS IDEA BOOK
Joanne D. Schaff

THE LEARNING CENTER BOOK
Tom Davidson, Phyllis Fountain, Rachel Grogan, Verl Short, Judy Steely, Katherine Freeman

LOVING AND BEYOND
Joe Abruscato and Jack Hassard

MAINSTREAMING LANGUAGE ARTS AND SOCIAL STUDIES
Charles R. Coble, Anne Adams, Paul B. Hounshell

MAINSTREAMING SCIENCE AND MATH
Charles R. Coble, Anne Adams, Paul B. Hounshell

NEW SCHOOLS FOR A NEW AGE
William Georgiades, Reuben Hilde, Grant Macaulay

ONE AT A TIME ALL AT ONCE
Jack E. Blackburn and Conrad Powell

THE OTHER SIDE OF THE REPORT CARD
Larry Chase

AN OUNCE OF PREVENTION PLUS A POUND OF CURE
Ronald W. Bruton

REACHING TEENAGERS
Don Beach

THE READING CORNER
Harry W. Forgan

A SURVIVAL KIT FOR TEACHERS AND PARENTS
Myrtle T. Collins and DWane R. Collins

THE WHOLE COSMOS CATALOG OF SCIENCE ACTIVITIES
Joe Abruscato and Jack Hassard

WILL THE REAL TEACHER PLEASE STAND UP? 2nd edition
Mary C. Greer and Bonnie Rubinstein

A YOUNG CHILD EXPERIENCES
Sandra N. Kaplan, Jo Ann B. Kaplan, Sheila K. Madsen, Bette K. Gould

THE READING CORNER:

IDEAS, GAMES, AND ACTIVITIES FOR INDIVIDUALIZING READING

Harry W. Forgan, Ph.D.
School of Education
University of Miami

Goodyear Publishing Company, Inc.
Santa Monica, California

ARCADIA
LMC

Library of Congress Cataloging in Publication Data

Forgan, Harry W.
  The reading corner.

  (Goodyear education series)
  1. Individualized reading instruction. I. Title.
LB1050.38.F67   372.4'147   76-28292
ISBN 0-87620-796-4 case.
ISBN 0-87620-795-6 pbk.

Copyright © 1977 by
Goodyear Publishing Company, Inc.,
Santa Monica, California 90401 and
Harry W. Forgan, Jr.

All rights reserved. No part of this book may be reproduced in
any form or by any means, except those portions intended for
reproduction by teachers for classroom use, without
permission in writing from the publisher and the author.

Y-7956-9 (p)
Y-7964-3 (c)

Current Printing (last digit):
10 9 8 7 6 5 4 3 2 1

Printed in the United States of America

Production Editor: Janice Gallagher
Copy Editor: Sherri Butterfield
Text Design: John Odam and Tom Gould
Cover Design: Tom Gould and John Odam
Illustrations: Joyce Kitchell, John Odam,
Tom Gould
(Appendix items 21 & 22 from concepts by Bonnie Striebel)

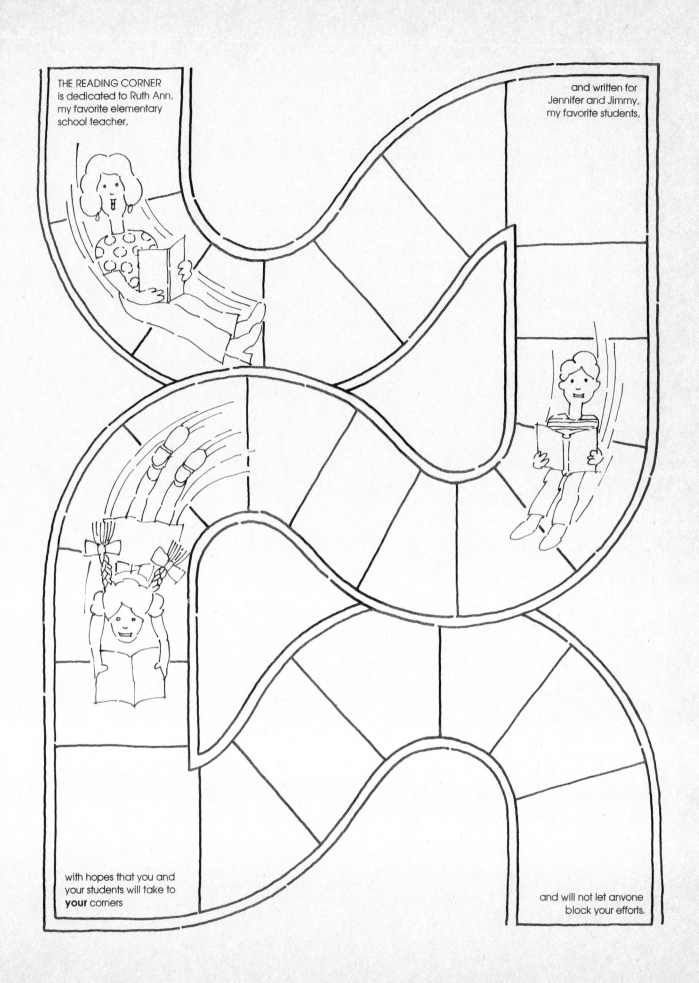

THE READING CORNER
is dedicated to Ruth Ann,
my favorite elementary
school teacher,

and written for
Jennifer and Jimmy,
my favorite students,

with hopes that you and
your students will take to
your corners

and will not let anyone
block your efforts.

CONTENTS

PREFACE

The first chapter in this book presents a step-by-step plan for individualizing reading instruction. Teachers are asked to know the reading skills, diagnose students' needs in reading, record the results of diagnosis, determine flexible groups, establish learning centers, develop schedules, instruct, and evaluate students' accomplishment of goals. Specific suggestions are provided to implement each one of these procedures.

The other chapters are devoted to each one of the broad skill areas in reading: prereading skills, word recognition, comprehension, and functional reading skills. Detailed descriptions of eight specific skills in each broad area are presented along with diagnostic devices to determine students' needs, ideas for introducing each skill in a teacher-directed activity, and learning center activities to help children practice each skill independently. *The Reading Corner*, then, is designed as a handbook for teachers who desire to meet individual needs of students in reading.

The Appendix is unique in that ready-to-duplicate skill tests, learning center activity sheets, letters to parents, record-keeping forms, and other time-saving devices are included. These Appendix items are numbered, and the numbers are used for easy reference when descriptions of them or directions for their use are given in the text. A symbol in the margin makes corresponding text passages easy to find. A list of these ready-to-reproduce materials by item number, including the page on which each is described and the page on which it appears, can be found with the Contents.

The elementary school teacher's task is one of the most difficult and challenging in the world of work. Teachers are given thirty children who differ widely in reading achievement and are expected to meet the needs of each one. There are few occupations that require the worker to handle thirty different tasks at one time while criticisms are shouted from the sidelines. The cries of teachers for aides, smaller classes, more materials, and planning time have been heard by some, but too many teachers find their task overwhelming. I hope the ready-to-duplicate materials in the Appendix, along with the ideas in the book, will assist teachers in performing the many roles necessary to provide for individual differences.

I wrote this book especially for the preservice elementary school teachers at the University of Miami and for the many teachers whom I have instructed in workshops. Both preservice and inservice elementary school teachers have responded enthusiastically to the ideas it contains. These ideas can be used in many different types of reading programs, from those that are completely individualized to those that follow the "three basic group" organization. Teachers need not jump on some methods bandwagon when using the suggestions in this book. Instead, they can select from a smorgasbord of ideas for testing, record keeping, and use those they find most tempting.

A book such as this would not be possible without the help and encouragement of many people. I especially want to thank the University of Miami students and inservice teachers who have helped me formulate my ideas and have encouraged me to put all of my handouts into a book. Marge Kelley, my secretary at the University of Miami, deserves a special word of appreciation for typing and duplicating the first drafts of some of the materials. George Mitchell and Ann Ebersole of the University of Miami Book Store made arrangements for publishing the field trial edition of the book.

The teachers and students at West Laboratory School on the University of Miami campus deserve special recognition for allowing me to field test many of the ideas. Louise Clement, Marilyn Durant, Sandra Murray, Dori Sutherland, and Joni Topolosky used many of the activities and provided valuable feedback. Bonnie Striebel provided the art concepts for Appendix Items 21 and 22. Janice Gallagher, Sherri Butterfield, and Dave Grady of Goodyear Publishing Company shared sound advice to make the book useful.

Most important, I want to thank my wife, Ruth Ann, for her continuous encouragement, for typing the manuscript and all my very rough copies, and for drawing the first illustrations. This book would not have been possible without her cooperation.

A SYSTEMATIC PLAN FOR INDIVIDUALIZED READING INSTRUCTION

A PANORAMIC VIEW OF THE SYSTEMATIC PLAN

In my education courses one phrase, "individual differences," was mentioned so many times I got tired of hearing it. It seemed every time an instructor or a student spoke, these two words were uttered. During my first week as a fifth grade teacher, I realized why this phrase was used so frequently. As I was administering a spelling test to my thirty-two students, I noticed one boy scribbling on the paper rather than writing the words, another student writing all the words before my even pronouncing them.

It did not take long to realize that children differed in reading achievement, too. Some children could not read the tables of contents in social studies and health textbooks that I tried to introduce in a most stimulating manner. A few students could not read the list of necessary school supplies; whereas, others in the same class were able to read popular novels. There were individual differences!

The first role a teacher performs in providing for individual differences in reading is that of *scholar*. Reading can be defined as a process of getting meaning from printed symbols. Yet, this definition is an oversimplification because many skills, some knowledge, and certain attitudes are essential to obtain meaning from the printed symbols. Some K–6 reading programs enumerate well over 400 distinctive reading skills and bits of knowledge. Teachers must be aware of the specific skills, knowledge, and attitudes required for reading so they can determine what different children know and can do. Detailed descriptions of the major skills and knowledge in reading are provided in this book.

The second role in providing for individual differences is that of *diagnostician*. Teachers must assess the differences in reading achievement among children in order to set appropriate objectives for each child. Ready-to-use informal skill tests that

can be administered quickly to groups of children are provided in this book.

The third role in this systematic plan for individualized reading instruction makes the teacher an *accountant*. It is necessary to record the results of diagnosis in order to organize the reading program so individual differences can be met. Record forms for keeping information concerning the reading needs and progress of children are provided in this book.

The fourth role in meeting individual differences requires the teacher to become a *sociologist*. This role is essential in that teachers commonly group children who have similar needs in reading. Even though children do differ, there will be some children who are ready to master particular skills or acquire specific knowledge at the same time. Rather than teaching the same skill ten times to ten different children, teachers are wise to have the ten children meet in a group for well-planned instruction. Ideas are presented in this book for establishing and instructing groups of children who have common reading skill needs.

The fifth role offers yet another responsibility, that of *interior decorator*. Teachers must establish an attractive environment in the classroom. This is usually done by setting up learning centers to store materials, equipment, and activities relating to a particular skill or content area. Learning centers are used to provide activities, materials, and equipment children can use independently to practice reading skills. Teachers then have more opportunities to meet with individuals and small groups while the children do meaningful and appropriate independent activities for skill reinforcement.

Suggestions for setting up learning centers, as well as ready-to-use learning center activity sheets and games, are presented in this book.

The sixth role requires the teacher be a *reservationist*, that is, to schedule the reading program. Teachers must determine when they can meet with various individuals in groups and what other children will be doing while they are working with certain groups. Suggestions for scheduling children are presented in this chapter.

The seventh role finally allows teachers to do their thing—*teach* the children. Teachers need a variety of instructional activities to help children accomplish the objectives and understand the importance of certain skills and knowledge. This book presents activities for introducing reading skills and knowledge, and ideas for helping students accomplish the objectives. We cannot assume that materials automatically teach. Many children need teacher-directed instruction.

The final step involved in providing for individual differences offers two more roles: being a *judge* and being an *informant*. Teachers must determine who is accomplishing the objectives and who needs more instruction. Evaluation or judging takes place during and after instruction. The teacher then becomes an informant in that parents, the principal, and others want to know how children are progressing. This chapter includes ideas for implementing these two roles.

The process of providing for individual differences is a circular process: it does not end. Teachers are continuously going around in circles as they perform these various roles. Figure 1 helps us understand why teachers sometimes get weary

Figure 1. Providing for individual differences keeps teachers going around in circles.

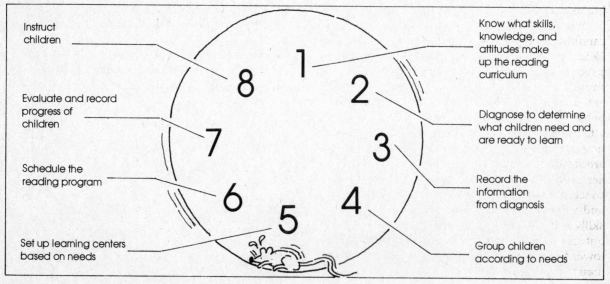

Instruct children

Evaluate and record progress of children

Schedule the reading program

Set up learning centers based on needs

Know what skills, knowledge, and attitudes make up the reading curriculum

Diagnose to determine what children need and are ready to learn

Record the information from diagnosis

Group children according to needs

and frustrated. The task of providing for individual differences is a never ending one. In fact, differences increase with effective instruction.

There are some teachers who are bound and determined to provide for differences and spend hours before and after school doing so. Generally it is not long before these teachers are tired, irritable, and stale because they have neglected their social and recreational lives. Conversely, to some teachers the job of providing for individual differences is so overwhelming that attempts are never initiated. These teachers may have exciting lives outside the classroom, but the children suffer because the instruction in the classroom is either too difficult or too easy.

Somewhere between these two extremes there are happy teachers who are satisfied because they are doing their best to provide for individual differences and yet have time to engage in social and recreational activities that enrich their lives as people. They realize the task of providing for individual differences is never complete and, in fact, not entirely possible because they have more than one student. At the same time, these teachers are aware that children do differ, and are committed to a "good day's work" to meet these differences.

If you are one of the satisfied teachers who is, in turn, helping students experience satisfaction by achieving rather than being frustrated or bored, this book is for you. It is designed to provide you with a smorgasbord of ideas to use as you perform the eight roles of a reading teacher. You are invited to select the most tempting and season to your taste.

ROLE 1: THE TEACHER AS SCHOLAR WHO KNOWS WHAT TO TEACH

Generally, the "reading skills" of which teachers must be aware are grouped under four broad categories: prereading, word recognition, comprehension, and functional reading skills. In this book each broad area is then divided into eight subheadings. In total then, we shall be dealing with 32 major skills in reading which are taught during the kindergarten through sixth grade levels.

I chose to group the reading skills into 32 broader and more inclusive categories rather than treating each skill and bit of knowledge separately. A group of 32 skills is simply more *manageable* than a group of 500. Management is especially important to teachers who must diagnose, keep records, select activities, and so forth for each one of the skills. Dealing with a group of 32 skills also makes reading more meaningful to children who are trying to integrate the skills so they can read.

When these lists of reading skills are examined carefully, one notices that many of the "reading skills" are actually bits of knowledge rather than psychomotor skills. For example, the consonant sounds are generally classified as reading skills. Yet, no skill is involved. Rather, there is a cognitive behavior of associating a symbol with a sound. No attempt is made in this book to correct this semantic error; however, you should be aware that you are dealing with skills *and* knowledge. Also, you are cautioned to pay attention to the third major concern involved in teaching reading: attitudes and values. It is important not only to teach the skills and knowledge that enable children to read, but also to help children develop positive attitudes toward reading by valuing it as a source of information and pleasure.

The *prereading skills* are those skills, knowledge, and attitudes that enable children to learn to read. These skills are prerequisites for learning to associate sounds and symbols and thus derive meaning from these associations. Before children can learn to read they must be able to

1. see differences in the letter forms
2. hear differences among the sounds in our language
3. remember sequences of letters and sounds
4. follow a printed line of symbols
5. have adequate speaking and listening vocabularies
6. have concepts or mental images from past experiences
7. show interest in words and books
8. learn the names of the letters

The second major skill area in reading is *word recognition*. The word recognition skills are the skills and knowledge that enable children to recognize words that may at first seem unfamiliar to

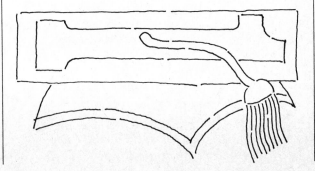

them. When teaching the word recognition skills, teachers help children

1. learn frequently used words by sight
2. learn the consonant sounds and the generalizations that concern consonants
3. learn sound patterns that appear frequently
4. learn the vowel sounds and generalizations that help children determine the sounds of the vowels
5. divide words into syllables and accent the correct syllables
6. use context clues to determine the meaning and pronunciation of a word
7. use structural analysis clues to determine the pronunciation and meaning of a word
8. use the dictionary to find the pronunciation and meaning of a word

The third major area of reading is *comprehension*. Comprehension skills are the skills and knowledge that help a reader get meaning from the printed symbols. Teachers help children comprehend by teaching them to

1. recognize the main idea of a selection
2. note the significant details in the selection
3. determine the sequence of events in the selection
4. draw conclusions concerning the information presented in the selection

5. evaluate critically what is being read
6. increase their vocabulary which in turn improves comprehension
7. adjust the rate of reading to the nature of the selection
8. develop oral reading skills so others can listen and comprehend

Another major area of reading is *functional reading*. The functional reading skills enable children to "read to learn" and to enjoy reading as a recreational activity. Teachers help children

1. read symbols and abbreviations
2. read maps
3. read tables, diagrams, and charts
4. use the different parts of books correctly
5. use reference materials
6. develop library skills
7. develop study skills
8. enjoy reading as a recreational activity

A description of "what children should learn" is provided for each one of the 32 skills mentioned above. This background information enables teachers to perform their role as scholars in that they will know the objectives of reading instruction.

No attempt is made in this book to list the 32 major skills in sequential order. When such lists are prepared, we find that not all children develop the skills in the same sequential order. An attempt is made to provide an array of reading skills which can be plugged into any reading program. Given this array of skills, teachers can diagnose to see what skills their students have or have not developed.

ROLE 2: THE TEACHER AS DIAGNOSTICIAN WHO DETERMINES STUDENTS' NEEDS

How can you determine which skills to teach the many different students in your class? This is the initial question you ask and continue to answer throughout the year because individual differences increase with instruction. Reliable and valid diagnostic devices are needed to pinpoint the specific skill needs of children. To know what skills to teach and what materials to use, it is generally necessary to determine students' reading levels. The informal reading inventory is the most widely recommended diagnostic device to determine the students' levels. You are advised to administer an informal reading inventory as soon as possible to

determine what materials the students can read independently, what materials should be used in instructing them, and what materials are too difficult for them to read. Remember, at the independent level students can generally recognize 99 percent of the words and comprehend 90 percent of what they read. The instructional reading level requires at least 95 percent word recognition and at least 75 percent comprehension. The frustrational reading level, which you will want to avoid, is evident when the children recognize less than 90 percent of the words and comprehend less than 75 percent of the material.

There are many commercial informal reading inventories available, such as the *Classroom Reading Inventory* by Nicholas Silvaroli. Most publishers of basal reading systems also provide an informal reading inventory with the series. More recently many school systems have developed their own informal reading inventories. You are encouraged to select an informal reading inventory that relates to (1) the backgrounds and interests of your children and (2) the reading materials most frequently used with the children.

This book provides *informal skill tests* to help you determine the specific skill needs of the students. An informal skill test is a test or checklist designed to measure the students' accomplishment of some particular reading skill. The results of the skill test can be used to determine if the children need instruction in that particular skill. Informal skill tests are very specific as compared to informal reading inventories, which measure more general skills. Skill tests indicate only whether the student has or has not developed the skills or knowledge the test measures.

The informal skill tests presented in this book are designed for group use. The ready-to-use diagnostic devices found in the Appendix are presented in game form whenever possible. Yet, suggestions are provided for analyzing the results

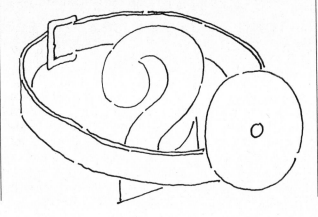

to determine the skill needs of students. You might keep in mind too that many of the learning center activity sheets included in the Appendix can also be used as supplemental diagnostic devices since they emphasize particular reading skills.

The first step in diagnosing, then, is to administer an informal reading inventory to find the children's levels. It is suggested that you administer the Comprehension Skills Test (Appendix Items 43-48) discussed in Chapter 4 and the Interest Inventory (Appendix Items 71 and 72) discussed in Chapter 5 to all the children. Other informal skill

APPENDIX ITEMS 43 – 48

APPENDIX ITEMS 71 AND 72

tests in this book can be selected on the basis of the children's instructional level. Use the guidelines listed in Table 1 to select the most important tests to give to different students. You are cautioned not to bore children by administering too many diagnostic tests in a short period of time.

It is important to determine some of the needs of the students and then begin teaching. As you teach, other skill needs will be observed. *Observation* is one of the most important and most useful diagnostic devices. You are encouraged to read carefully the "What Children Should Learn" sections so you will know what observations to make. Remember, children develop different aspects of the many reading skills at different reading levels.

In addition to determining the reading levels and reading skill needs of the children, you will want to gather information about factors that influence reading achievement. Table 2, which summarizes the diagnostic information you desire, can be used as a guide.

Table 1. Skill Test Selection Guide

If the Instructional Reading Level Is	Administer
Below preprimer or primer	The prereading skills tests in Chapter 2 to determine the prereading skill needs of the student: visual perception, auditory perception, visual-auditory sequencing and memory, visual motor perception, and names of letters.
First and second grade	Administer the word recognition skills test in Chapter 2: sight words, consonant sounds, sound patterns, vowel sounds, and structural analysis.
Third and fourth grade	Administer the syllabication/accent skills test, context clues test, and use of the dictionary tests found in Chapter 3, along with the symbols/abbreviations skills test and reference materials skills test found in Chapter 5.
Fifth and sixth grade	Administer the following skills tests from Chapter 5: parts of books, study skills, map skills, reading tables, graphs, and diagrams, and library skills.

Table 2. Diagnostic Summary

Information I Want	Methods of Gathering Information
Reading Levels	Use an informal reading inventory.
Specific Reading Skill Needs	Use the skill tests in this book and your observation of the children as you work with them.
Vision	Observation is the key. Does the child skip lines, lose his place frequently, appear irritable when doing close work, rub his eyes excessively, blink more than usual, hold his book too close or too far from his eyes (14 inches is average), squint frequently, have inflamed or watery eyes, complain of headaches or nausea following close work, tilt his head to one side and thrust his head forward when looking at something, or stumble frequently?
Hearing	Does the child cup his ear with his hand, complain of persistent earaches or buzzing or ringing in his ears? Does he tilt his head toward you when you speak to him? Has he had difficulty in learning different speech sounds? Has he had excessive draining or inflammation of the ear? Does he ask you to repeat directions frequently? Does he show attentiveness when others are talking?
General Health	Does the child appear healthy? Is the child's attendance regular in school? Does the child have any history of glandular disturbances or other physical handicaps on his health record in the cumulative file?
Aptitude	There are some standardized intelligence tests available. If you use them instead of looking at the IQ score, look at the subtests to see what factors of intelligence the tests measure. For an example, most intelligence tests measure visual memory or auditory memory. This information is more important to you as a reading teacher than the child's IQ score. As you observe, does the child ask questions that indicate he is thinking? How extensive is his vocabulary? Is he able to draw conclusions and make sound judgments? Does the child have a fairly good background of general information? Is the child able to see similarities and differences in concepts? Is there any record of the child's having had head injuries or prolonged periods of fever?
Language Development	Does the child have a good vocabulary? Does he use standard English correctly? Is English spoken in the home? Does the child make frequent spelling errors that indicate a lack of knowledge of sounds and sound patterns? Is the child able to listen and understand what he hears?
Background of Experiences	Observation and talking with children are again the most important ways to determine background of experiences. Some teachers also send a checklist of experiences home for parents to complete to indicate what experiences the child has had. You might ask the child if he has ever been to the beach, zoo, out of the state, etc. Ask the child if he has any books, magazines, or other reading materials at home. In talking with the parents you might note if they pressure him too much, or accept him as he is.
Social-Emotional Status	Does the child have many friends? Is he accepted by his peers? Does he have a positive self-concept? Is he able to control his emotions? Does the child seem happy? Is he able to concentrate long enough to complete a task? Can the child work well in a group situation? In addition to observing you may want to use a sociometric technique to determine the relationships of the children in the room. Some teachers also like to use incomplete sentences to gather information about the children's social-emotional status. For example, you may want to ask the children to complete these statements: Reading is _____ After school I _____ I think _____ I like to _____ I hate _____ I _____ My friends _____ I like _____ I wish I _____
Interests	An interest inventory is included in the Appendix. You can use this or talk with the children informally to gather information about their interests.
Attitude Toward Reading	Observe the child when you take him to the library. When the child has free time during the class session, does he read? Does the child bring books from home? Does the child seem to pay attention during the instructional groups in reading? Does the child volunteer to read? Does the child relate stories his parents or others might have related to him? Does the child listen attentively when you read stories?
Suitable Content Books	Develop some informal suitability surveys. Complete directions for developing informal suitability surveys can be found in **Teaching Content Area Reading Skills** by Harry W. Forgan and Charles T. Mangrum (Columbus, Ohio: Merrill, 1976).

ROLE 3: THE TEACHER AS ACCOUNTANT—KEEPING RECORDS OF CHILDREN'S NEEDS

After you gather information concerning children's needs, how can you keep records that can be useful and yet not too time consuming? Accurate records of the students' needs in reading are essential to individualized instruction, yet you do not want to get so bogged down in keeping records that time is taken away from working with children. A simple and effective record-keeping device is necessary to (1) identify children who have similar needs and thus could profit from group instruction, and (2) help you select and construct the materials you need to help the children accomplish particular objectives.

APPENDIX ITEM 1

A time-saving device is provided in the Appendix (Item 1) to keep records of children's reading needs. In completing this chart,

1. List the names of your students in the left-hand column.
2. Check no more than five most important skill needs that should be emphasized with each student at this time.
3. Write the highest level of material at which the children can demonstrate the comprehension skills.
4. Write each child's independent level in the category under recreational reading, and use this notation as an indication of what materials children can read during library time or free reading.
5. Use this chart to determine skill groups and learning centers your children need. For example, if you have many children who need help with consonant sounds, you might set up a consonant sounds learning center and form a skill group to emphasize consonant sounds with these children.
6. Add check marks to the chart as the children progress.

This record-keeping device can be very helpful and yet not require hours to complete. Some commercial programs and some teachers use this system but make it more specific. For example, a separate chart might be kept for consonant sounds on which each of the 24 consonant sounds is listed in a separate column. Again, the names of the children would be listed on the left-hand side of the page. The children who need to learn particular consonant sounds would have a check mark by their name and under that sound.

The latter record does provide more specific information about the children; however, it takes longer to complete and keep up to date. I believe the hours spent in keeping records could be better used in working with the children and preparing materials. It seems to me that teachers are capable of remembering which consonant sounds they are teaching. Should they forget, it would take only a few seconds to refresh their memories. In fact, review of some sounds would not hinder the children: review and repetition are valuable because children do forget.

In addition to the class chart, you may want to make individual records to provide prescriptions for the children. A sample prescription sheet which you can use to direct learners to appropriate

APPENDIX ITEM 2

groups and materials is included in the Appendix (Item 2). Again it is suggested that you save time by using the prescription sheet on a weekly rather than a daily basis.

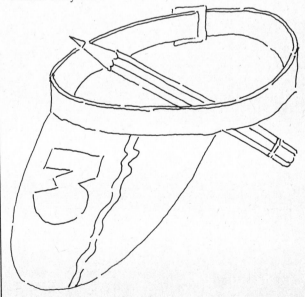

Now that you have identified some of the needs or individual differences of your students, you must plan to meet them. It is not practical to work with each child individually each day. If your instructional day is five hours and you have thirty students, this would only allow ten minutes for each student.

The most efficient technique for providing for individual differences is to group children with similar needs. Grouping is economical in that the teacher does not have to teach the same thing to each student who needs it, but rather she can teach many children at one time and then give individual help as needed. Of course social interaction and opportunities for group members to learn from each other add to the value of grouping.

Traditionally, most teachers grouped children by instructional level. Teachers generally had enough time to meet three groups in one day, thus, three reading groups became the standard even though not all children fit nicely into three groups. Children in a particular group might have similar instructional levels, but differ widely in skill needs. For example, some children at the second grade instructional level might know all the vowel sounds, while others do not. Some children might be able to find the main idea easily, while others cannot.

A recent trend in grouping to provide for individual differences of children is to group children by skill needs. Skill groups are temporary groups consisting of children who have specific skill needs. Skill groups do not meet each day, but rather only when the teacher has time and believes the children are ready for additional instruction.

The major purposes of skill groups are to help children (1) realize why the skill or knowledge is necessary, (2) teach the skill or knowledge, and (3)

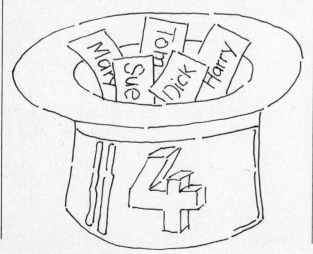

explain the directions for the practice and reinforcement activities. For an example, if the teacher has a skill group on dividing words into syllables, she would help the students understand why they should learn to divide words into syllables. Then she would help the children learn the generalizations for dividing words into syllables. Finally, she would explain the practice and reinforcement activities to be done independently.

The number and nature of the skill groups in a classroom depend on the students' needs and the teacher's time. One teacher might have a skill group for teaching the vowel sounds, one for helping children discriminate sounds, and another one for teaching children to recognize sequence of events. In another classroom the teacher might have a skill group on dividing words into syllables, one for learning alphabetical order, and another one for helping children find the main idea. An upper grade teacher might have a broader skill group on prereading if she only has a few children at the readiness level. Conversely, a kindergarten teacher would have many skill groups concerning particular prereading skills. The most important criterion is the needs of the children. By looking at the charts that have the results of diagnosis, the teacher can see what skills are needed by most of the students and then form skill groups.

A skill group may meet only one or two days a week. Perhaps the group will meet for ten minutes one day, and twenty minutes another day. Scheduling of skill groups is flexible, depending upon the needs and capabilities of the students, and the other demands for the teacher's attention. A skill group continues to meet until most of the children in it have mastered the skill or acquired the knowledge. As the children progress, they may be dropped from the group so more attention can be given to the remaining children. The skill group is dissolved when most of the children have accomplished the objective. The teacher then works on an individual basis with students who need more instruction.

The children in a particular skill group may be of different instructional levels. For an example, if the teacher does have a skill group on dividing words into syllables, she may have some children from the second grade instructional level and others from the third grade instructional level. When conducting the group, she must be careful to use words that all the children can understand.

Skill groups can be used in many different types of reading programs. Teachers who have instructional groups can still have some skill groups to concentrate on particular skills. Teachers who conduct an individualized reading program use skill grouping as their major type of grouping. It is satisfying to see how children progress when specific skills are earmarked as objectives and instruction is directed toward their accomplishment.

This book presents sample teacher-directed instructional ideas for teaching each one of the 32 major reading skills. Generally, one of the ideas suggests a procedure for helping the children understand how the skill or knowledge can help them. The other ideas are suggestions for helping children develop the skill or knowledge. You are encouraged to read the suggestions for skill group activities and then adapt them to your children.

In addition to being grouped according to instructional levels and/or skill needs, children generally enjoy being grouped by interests. Some teachers use interest groups to motivate students to read and to provide opportunities for children to apply newly acquired reading skills. Any interest children share, such as pets, football, dolls, cars, or jets, can be the basis of an interest group. Activities of an interest group include more than reading, but reading is usually required for their completion. Interest groups provide an opportunity for children of different reading levels to be in the same group. Such heterogeneous grouping is possible because reading materials concerning the various interests of children are available at different reading levels. Again it is not necessary for the interest group to meet daily. All interest groups may meet at one time as the teacher moves about the classroom to guide the groups.

ROLE 5: THE TEACHER AS INTERIOR DECORATOR—SETTING UP LEARNING CENTERS

A learning center is a designated storage area in the classroom for materials, supplies, equipment, and suggested activities related to a particular skill or knowledge. For an example, an art learning center would be a place in the classroom at which art media and activities would be located. Because learning centers are simply places in the classroom, they may be located on a table, on top of a bookshelf, in a cardboard box, or even under a table. All learning centers need not be beautifully decorated for visitors; some may be nothing more than functional storage areas for materials used to develop particular skills.

Learning centers are necessary in reading programs to provide (1) independent activities, (2) practice and reinforcement, (3) opportunities for self-instruction, (4) storage of materials and activities, and (5) a stimulating and exciting environment in which children spend over 1,000 hours per year.

A classroom might include many types of learning centers, depending upon the knowledge and skills the children need. Reading learning centers can be organized according to interests, reading levels, or reading skills. When reading centers are organized by reading levels, they generally include books, magazines, and other reading materials at a specified instructional and/or independent reading level. They might also include games and activities to develop the reading skills commonly taught at that particular instructional level. For example, a second grade level reading center might include books, articles, and other second grade reading materials, as well as games and activities to help children develop such skills as learning vowel sounds, using context clues, and using a table of contents. The teacher would use the center to have the children practice and reinforce skills, or to provide opportunities for the children to learn independently.

It is common to see reading centers organized by skills. Many classrooms have a phonics center, comprehension skills center, reference skills center, or visual perception center. The center can be based on a particular broad skill area in reading, such as comprehension, or on some specific skill, such as letter names. Teachers determine the nature of the skill center by considering the needs of the students.

Interest centers are used in some reading programs. Teachers and students establish interest learning centers by collecting materials and activities related to their interests. For an example, in some classrooms you will see a pet center, a sports

center, a game center, and an arts and craft center. Children select the interest centers they want to attend.

It is not possible to say that one type of learning center is better than another. All three types of centers can be used in the same classroom. Again the teacher is the expert on her children and therefore must determine what centers are most appropriate. The learning center activities suggested in this book can be used and organized at any type of learning center.

You will notice most of the learning center activities suggested in this book (1) are in game form, (2) are ready to duplicate or easily made, (3) focus on some particular skills, and (4) are inexpensive to reproduce so that the children can have their own copies to take home. If you desire, you can make the learning center activity sheets found in the Appendix larger by using an opaque projector, or by putting them on a transparency and using an overhead projector to trace them. Perhaps you would like to laminate some of the learning center activity sheets. Regardless of what method of reproduction you use, the cost is low.

After determining which learning centers you want, you must determine the places in the classroom where the different learning centers can be located. Keep in mind that not all learning centers require a table or an entire corner. Some of your learning centers will be cardboard boxes containing supplies, materials, and activities. Other learning centers might be located at the bottom of bookcases, at one of the extra desks in the classroom, on the inside of some closet door, or in some part of the room that is sectioned off by a cardboard divider or shower curtain. Children do not have to remain at the center to do the activities. They can take the materials, supplies, and equipment to other areas in the classroom.

One way of finding more space in a classroom for learning centers is to eliminate some of the desks. The classroom is wall-to-wall furniture if it contains a desk for each child and assorted tables, extra desks, and bookcases. Generally, in a room in which there are both tables and desks, it is not necessary for each child to have a desk: some children can be assigned to sit at certain tables when they come into the room. And each child does *not* have to be sitting at a desk for every activity of the school day. At the same time, it is necessary to provide some place in the classroom, whether it is a cubbyhole or coffee can, for each child to keep his school supplies. Removing some of the desks will enable you to have a more flexible room arrangement and a more flexible program.

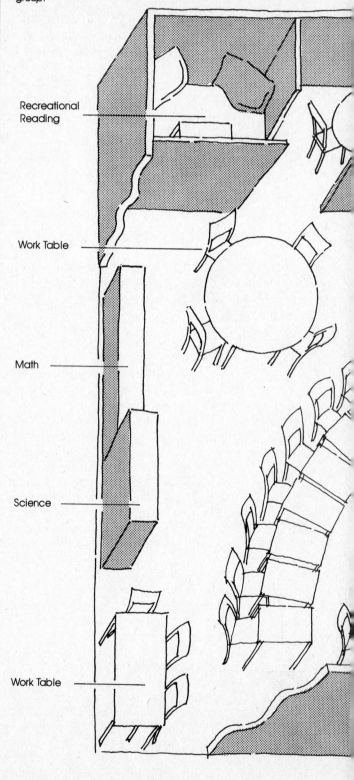

Figure 2. In this self-contained classroom, the teacher is responsible for all instructional areas. The room can easily be prepared for small group work by having some children turn their desks around to face those of other children in the same group.

Recreational Reading

Work Table

Math

Science

Work Table

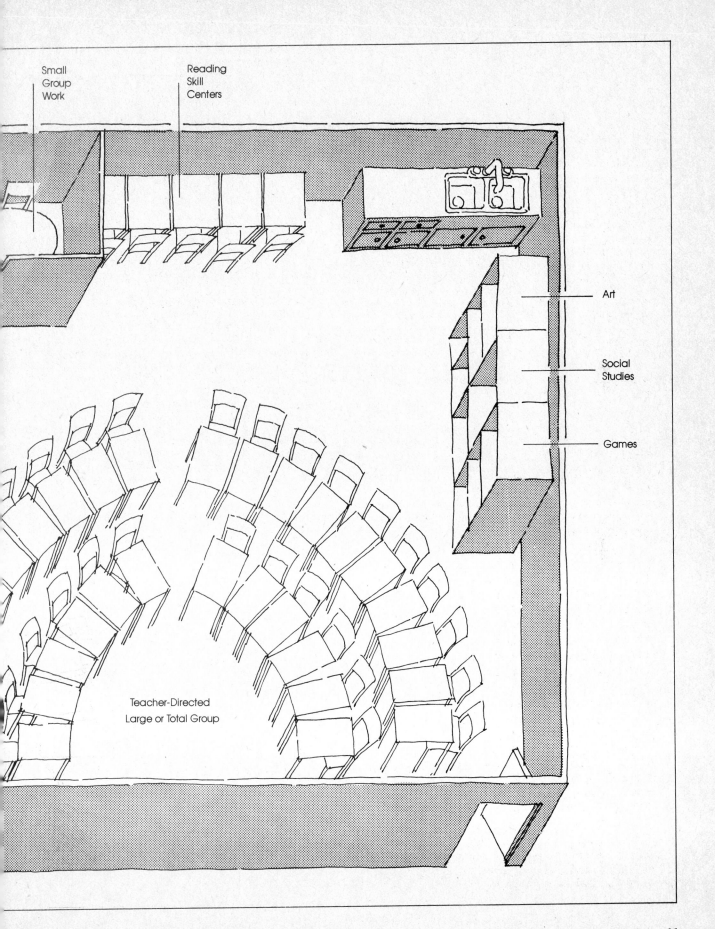

Small
Group
Work

Reading
Skill
Centers

Art

Social
Studies

Games

Teacher-Directed
Large or Total Group

Art Center

Drama

Work Table

Games

Interest
Center

Interest
Center

Listening
Station

Creative
Writing

Language
Skill
Centers

Teacher-Directed
Small Group
Instruction

Figure 3. Departmentalized language arts classroom. For total group activities, the children can move to the semicircle.

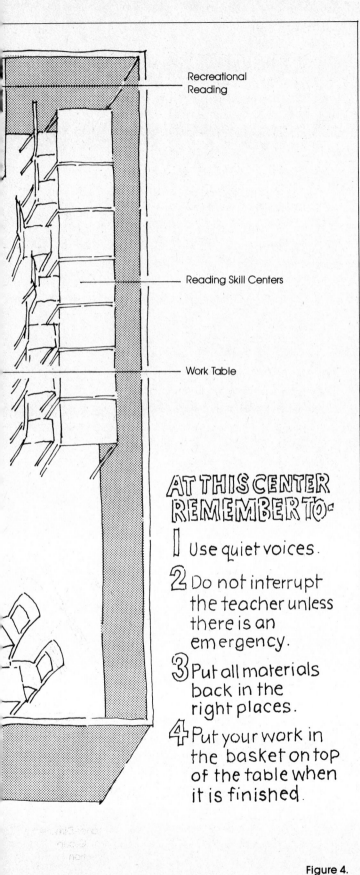

Recreational Reading

Reading Skill Centers

Work Table

AT THIS CENTER
REMEMBER TO:

1 Use quiet voices.

2 Do not interrupt
the teacher unless
there is an
emergency.

3 Put all materials
back in the
right places.

4 Put your work in
the basket on top
of the table when
it is finished.

Figure 4.

When arranging your room, you may want to divide it into a quiet area and a productive noise area. A quiet area is needed for those activities that require concentration. Certainly reading is a good example of such an activity. Other activities require more movement and discussions among the children. Try to locate all the learning centers that require concentration and little or no noise in one part of the classroom and have the learning centers that do require productive noise in the other half of the classroom.

Sample floor plans are given in Figures 2 and 3. After considering these, you can plan your own classroom based on the number of students you have, the students who work well together, and the size of the classroom. Also, remember that different arrangements can be used during the school year as the children develop more self-discipline.

It is necessary to teach the children how to do the activities and use the materials and equipment at a center. This instruction can take place during a skill group or with the entire class if all the children are going to use the center. Generally the instructions must be given *orally* because the children are just learning to read. Some teachers summarize the activities that are possible at the center on a picture chart.

As a part of introducing the children to learning centers, discuss with them what kind of a classroom you desire. Determine the standards and the rules for using the centers and enforce them. You can discuss these with the children and develop a list of guidelines or simply tell them the rules. Help them see that you are trying to make school a stimulating place to be, but that it is essential for them to follow the rules for the *safety* and *success* of each child. You may want to post a sign at each center to remind them of the rules for its use (see Figure 4).

Teachers are encouraged to use the help of aides, parents, or upper grade children in making learning center materials. An afternoon can be set aside when parents are invited to develop materials for learning centers. Perhaps one of the teachers in the building can direct the parents while other teachers work with his or her children.

APPENDIX ITEM 3

A ready-to-duplicate letter soliciting the help of parents is found in the Appendix (Item 3). Instructional aides and upper grade students might participate in a similar workshop.

ROLE 6: THE TEACHER AS RESERVATIONIST—SCHEDULING THE READING PROGRAM

Another major step in planning a more individualized reading program is to schedule time to meet with both groups and individual students. There is never enough time in the day to do everything you would like; therefore, it is important to have a flexible plan.

Teachers have two major concerns as they plan a schedule: (1) with whom are they going to be working during the instructional time, and (2) what are the other children going to be doing independently while they are working with some of the students. The following guidelines can be considered in meeting these two concerns:

1. Not all children need as much time with the teacher. Some children learn best with minimal teacher guidance, while others need much teacher direction.
2. Time must be reserved for the teacher to evaluate the work done independently by students. Children can help by self-checking; however, the teacher needs to evaluate students continually. Likewise, the teacher needs some time to give individual assistance to those children who may encounter difficulty when working independently.
3. Children respond differently on different days. Special events and teachable moments occur. Some children may become so involved in an independent activity that they hate to leave it. Other children cannot work independently for long periods of time. Effective teachers are not bound by a clock.
4. Children like to have some choice concerning the learning centers they attend. Of course, you have particular objectives in mind and thus want them to attend certain centers. Decisions must be made as to which centers are optional and which are required. For example, you might tell the children they may

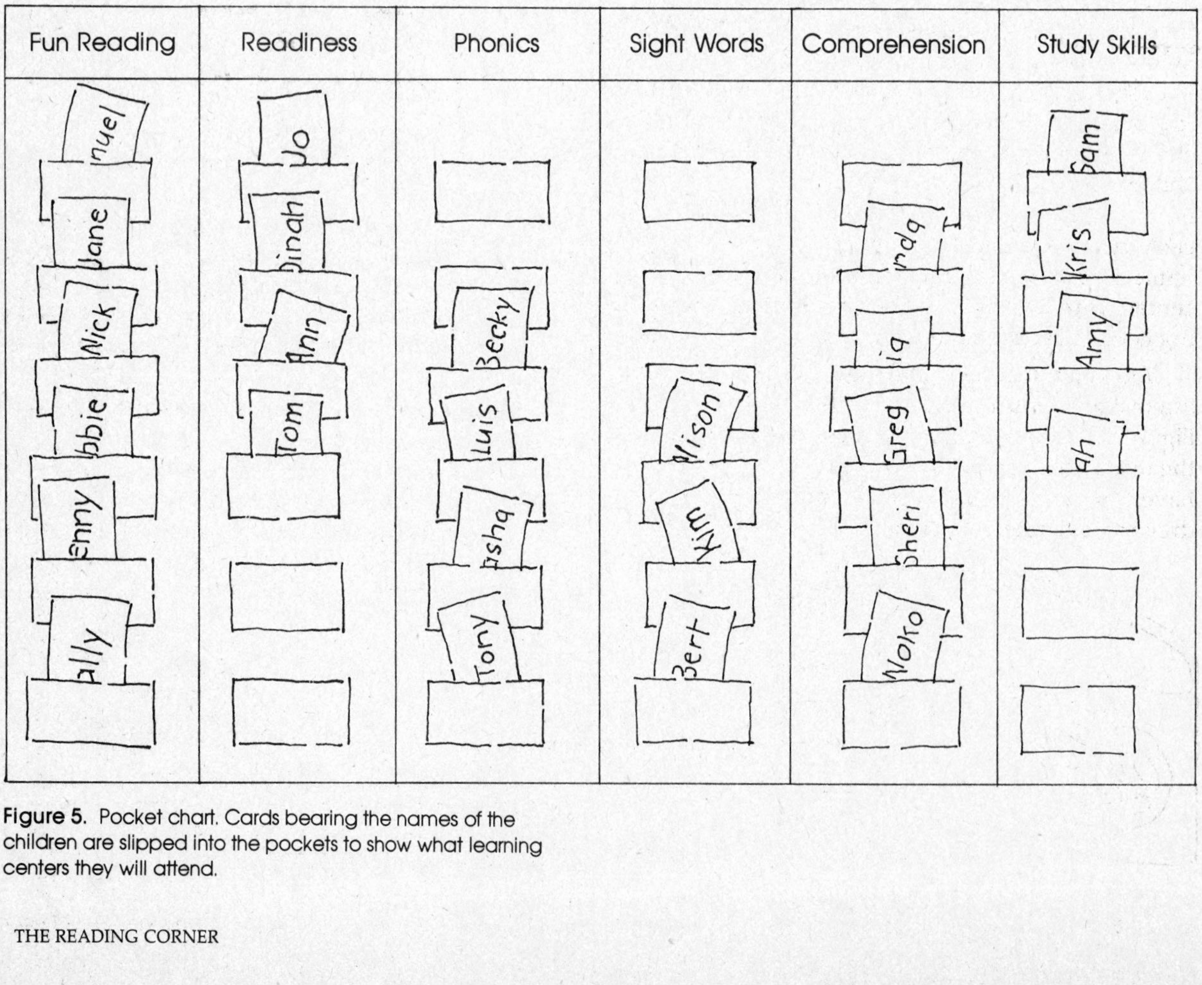

Fun Reading	Readiness	Phonics	Sight Words	Comprehension	Study Skills

Figure 5. Pocket chart. Cards bearing the names of the children are slipped into the pockets to show what learning centers they will attend.

choose whether to attend the art center, the games center, the recreational center, or the industrial arts center, and require certain children in a skill group on consonant sounds to attend the consonant sounds learning center for practice and reinforcement. Learning center requirements and choices can be specified in a prescription.

With all these variables it is understandable why it is common to see many different schedules. Again, you are the expert! Only you know your children's needs and their capabilities for working independently. The schedules presented here should be adapted to the characteristics of your children.

If you have many learning centers in a classroom based on different content areas or skills with activities for all the children to do, it is possible to set up a schedule in which all the children use centers at the same time. In doing so, set aside a period in the day when the children will go to a particular center, depending upon their needs. For an example, you might set aside half an hour during the day and direct the children to follow their prescriptions in choosing what centers they need. During this time you could go around to the different centers and give individual help. If you do not use prescription sheets, you might make a pocket chart (Figure 5) to aid you in keeping track of the children's center choices or assignments. List the names of the centers at the top of the chart. Below each center name glue enough pockets to hold name cards for children who should attend that center. Slip cards into pockets to show what learning centers children are to attend.

You may want to schedule skill groups and interest groups on two days of the week such as in Figure 6. This schedule provides opportunities for the teacher to work with three skill groups and still have time to move about the room and help children in their interest groups.

GROUP	MEMBERS	TUESDAY SCHEDULE	FRIDAY SCHEDULE
A	Maurice Bob Martha Debby Marie	sg 1:45 fu 2:00 rr 2:15 r 2:45 ig 3:00 rts 3:30	ig 1:30 rr 2:15 r 2:45 ru 3:00 sg 3:15 rts 3:30
B	Jerry Lloyd Janet Tom W. Steven	rr 1:45 sg 2:00 fu 2:15 rr 2:30 r 2:45 ig 3:00 rts 3:30	ig 1:30 rr 2:00 r 2:45 sg 3:00 fu 3:15 rts 3:30
C	Brenda Roxann Michael Marilyn Linda	rr 1:45 sg 2:15 fu 2:30 r 2:45 ig 3:00 rts 3:30	ig 1:30 rr 2:00 sg 2:30 r 2:45 ru 3:00 rr 3:15 rts 3:30
D	Mark S. Cathy Debbie Janice Judy	ig 1:45 rr 2:15 sg 2:30 r 2:45 fu 3:00 rr 3:15 rts 3:30	rr 1:30 sg 2:15 fu 2:30 r 2:45 ig 3:00 rts 3:30
E	Mark C. Earl Jimmy Gregg Chuck	ig 1:45 rr 2:15 sg 2:45 r 3:00 fu 3:15 rts 3:30	rr 1:30 sg 1:45 fu 2:15 rr 2:30 r 2:45 ig 3:00 rts 3:30
F	Ron Robert Mary Ann Theresa Tom I.	ig 1:45 rr 2:15 r 2:45 fu 3:00 sg 3:15 rts 3:30	sg 1:30 fu 1:45 rr 2:15 r 2:45 ig 3:00 rts 3:30

Abbreviations:		
	ig	interest group
	rr	recreational reading
	sg	skill group
	fu	follow-up activities (from skill group)
	r	recess
	rts	return to seats

Figure 6. Skill and interest group plan.

Figure 7. Sample structured plan.

Group	Teacher-Directed Instructional Groups or Skill Groups	Learning Centers for Skills (specific or broad areas)	Learning Center Based on Instructional Level	Learning Center Selected by Interests	Recreational Reading
1	8:30-9:00	9:00-9:15	9:15-9:30	9:30-9:45	9:45-10:00
2	9:00-9:30	9:30-9:45	9:45-10:00	8:30-8:45	8:45-9:00
3	9:30-10:00	8:30-8:45	9:00-9:15	8:45-9:00	9:15-9:30

Total Class Activities   10:00-10:30. During this time interest groups meet, children share ideas, the teacher reads to the children, and ⌐so forth.

A more structured scheduling plan is presented in Figure 7. You will notice that the teacher meets with basic instructional groups. The children are then scheduled for particular learning centers for skill development, their instructional level, their interests, and to provide opportunities for recreational reading. Some teachers adapt this plan by having half of the reading program in the morning and the other half in the afternoon. This adaptation is especially good for children who have difficulty working independently for long periods of time.

To provide for individual differences, a plan such as this one must be used in a flexible manner. It is not necessary to meet with each skill group each day, or to spend the same amount of time with each instructional group each day.

Another more flexible schedule which allows the teacher to use the time depending on the students' needs is presented in Figure 8. In this plan the children are divided heterogeneously into five groups of six and then assigned a name or number. The children have a schedule to follow which includes recreational reading, attending an interest center of their choice, working at two skill centers according to their prescriptions, and going to another center such as a listening center. The teacher's time is freed to work with individuals or groups as needed. A makeup time is provided so children can attend centers they missed while working with the teacher. Some teachers use this more flexible schedule only two times a week, while others have it as the major way of scheduling. Likewise, some teachers use this schedule but divide it into a morning and an afternoon session. In other words, one hour is allotted for the reading program in the morning and one hour in the afternoon.

Figure 8. Sample flexible schedule.

Time	Recreational Reading	Interest Centers	Skill Center #1	Skill Center #2	Listening Center
8:30-8:50	1	2	3	4	5
8:50-9:10	2	3	4	5	1
9:10-9:30	3	4	5	1	2
9:30-9:50	4	5	1	2	3
9:50-10:10	5	1	2	3	4
10:10-10:30	Make up / interest groups				

ROLE 7: THE TEACHER AS INSTRUCTOR

The basic foundation has been laid. You now know some of the needs of your children, you have formed instructional groups and/or skill groups, learning centers are set up to provide instructional and practice activities, and a flexible schedule has been developed. The framework needed to meet the needs of the children has been established. It is time to teach!

Ideas for teacher-directed instruction are presented for each of the 32 skills. Regardless of what ideas you select, there are some general guidelines for effective instruction that should be followed when you are working with children. As you teach try to implement this "daily dozen."

1. Make learning meaningful. Help children understand why they are learning certain skills or acquiring specific knowledge. For an example, if children are learning to use guide words, help them realize guide words enable them to locate a word in the dictionary more quickly.

2. Praise children for progress. All children like to be rewarded for what they are learning. A smile, pat on the back, note to parents, and positive comments encourage learning.

3. Have a purpose or an objective rather than simply procedures. For an example, if you are having oral reading with children, make sure you have a reason for asking them to read orally. Perhaps it is for you to diagnose, or to give the children a chance to show others they are learning to read, or to work on the skills of oral reading. Keep the purpose uppermost in your mind.

4. Use a variety of materials, including children's magazines, trading cards, recipes, jokes and riddles, comic books, scout manuals, and songs. Remember the long-range goals of reading instruction are to help children learn to value reading as a source of information and recreation. Do not get so hung up on teaching skills that you never give children an opportunity to read for pleasure or information. Allow time for them to put it all together by actually reading. Children become better readers by reading, reading, and reading.

5. Provide opportunities for children to apply the skills. If you are teaching the vowel sounds, have the children add this as a step to their word recognition strategy. Ask them what they should do when they come to a word they do not know. Looking at the sounds of the vowels may be one clue, but what are some other clues they can use? Application is the goal.

6. When checking comprehension, do not discuss every selection into bits and pieces. Make sure you are asking about significant details that actually influenced what happened in the selection rather than insignificant details that have little or nothing to do with comprehending the story. Children can also show that they comprehend a selection by dramatizing it. Avoid a boring rehash of every story.

7. Maintain eye contact with other children in the classroom while you are working with small groups and individuals. Move around the room after working with each group to see what children are doing.

8. Have faith and "keep on truckin'." Patience is necessary. Practice and repetition are essential to learning. Do not expect children to learn the first time something is introduced.

9. Remember there is more to school and life than reading. Some teachers overemphasize reading to such a point that there is no time to teach social studies, science, and health. The result is a stagnant and dull day. Reading is a skill that can be applied to many interests and content areas. Also, remember a child should not be considered a failure simply because he is not progressing as expected in reading. Help the nonreaders develop positive self-concepts by rewarding the progress they are making in other areas, as well as their small but significant accomplishments in learning to read.

10. Have whole class activities in the reading program in addition to working with small groups and individuals. There are ways of providing for individual differences in large group situations. Large groups are desirable for choral reading, listening to stories, watching dramatizations, and playing academic games.

11. Help children accept themselves and each other as they are. Explain that if they ran a race, all of them would not arrive at the finish line at exactly the same time. It is the same with reading instruction. Each child is different. Just because one student is achieving at a higher grade level in reading does not mean he is a better person than someone else. The important thing is that each person do his best.

12. Be a person. Provide time for yourself to read for pleasure and information. Have friends other than educators. Develop and expand interests and hobbies. Take time to loaf without guilt feelings. Be a learner: keep your curiosity. Forgive yourself for shortcomings. If you are able to lead an exciting life outside the classroom, you will be more exciting in the classroom.

ROLE 8: THE TEACHER AS JUDGE AND INFORMANT—EVALUATING CHILDREN

As you work with children, you are continually evaluating to see if the students are accomplishing the objectives. Evaluation is similar to diagnosis; however, "diagnosis" is the term usually applied to determining the needs of the students *before* instruction; whereas, "evaluation" is used in considering what the students accomplished *during* and *after* instruction. Evaluation is necessary to (1) determine new objectives and (2) inform parents and other interested people of the children's progress.

Children also need to be involved in evaluation. Self-evaluation is important so children know what skills they need to work on or practice. When we ask children to check their own work, we must not pressure them to get everything right; otherwise they will cheat. The teacher who emphasizes and praises children highly for perfect papers will soon find children copying the correct answers from answer sheets or other children, rather than doing their own work, to ensure perfection.

One way to avoid this situation is to praise children who do their best but make mistakes. Spend time reteaching and praise as you reteach. Soon the other children will realize that submitting perfect papers is not the only type of behavior that is rewarded. They will see that students who miss some items do have the advantage of individualized instruction and praise as they learn.

In addition to checking their own work, children may be encouraged to evaluate themselves by filling out a self-evaluation form. On it the child indicates what he did and what he learned. Such a form is included in the Appendix (Item 4). It is suggested that you use this form weekly.

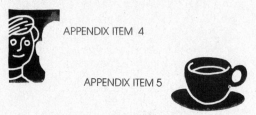

APPENDIX ITEM 4

APPENDIX ITEM 5

Teachers also have the responsibility of informing parents of their child's progress. Traditionally, parents have displayed interest in their child's reading achievement. Reading is a developmental task in a democratic society. Parents want to know how their child is doing!

Many times teachers send papers home with children. This continuous information is valuable, but there is no substitute for face-to-face conferences. The individual record of progress that can be found in the Appendix (Item 5) can be used as a guide for conferring with parents. As you inform parents of needs, be ready to give them some practical ideas about what they can do to help.

If parents are not able to attend conferences, you will be informing them of their child's progress via report cards. You may want to send them a newsletter suggesting ways they can help. Ready-to-duplicate letters are included in the Appendix (Items 6–10). These letters list guidelines for helping children develop prereading, work recognition, comprehension, and functional reading

APPENDIX ITEMS 6-10

skills. One of the letters also suggests general guidelines for working with children.

Remember, parental help is one of your most effective ways of providing for individual differences. You might give parents copies of learning center activity sheets and suggest ways for using them in an informal setting. Many of these sheets are in game form and thus will enable parents and children to enjoy working together as the children practice and reinforce particular skills.

A SUMMARY OF HOW THIS BOOK CAN HELP YOU

The chart below lists the steps that are necessary to provide for individual differences in reading. After each step, there is information on how you can use this book to help you do a more effective job of providing for these differences.

Steps in Providing for Individual Differences	How This Book Can Help You
1. Know the reading skills children should learn.	Read the "What Children Should Learn" section at the beginning of each section concerning that skill. For general information concerning the reading skills, read the introduction for each chapter.
2. Diagnose the needs and interests of children.	Read the section concerning diagnosing needs for each particular skill. You can reproduce or adapt the tests to your children.
3. Keep records of children's needs and progress.	Use the grouping chart found in the Appendix (Item 1).
4. Group the children.	Reread the section in Chapter 1 on how to group children.
5. Set up learning centers.	Reread the section in Chapter 1 about setting up learning centers. Also look in each section of the book to find the learning activities designed for use at learning centers. Reproduce the learning center activity sheets as necessary.
6. Schedule the reading program.	Reread suggestions for scheduling found in Chapter 1.
7. Instruct the children.	Read the suggestions for skill group instruction in each section for each major skill. Review the guidelines presented in this chapter.
8. Evaluate and report the progress of the children.	Reread the section on evaluating in Chapter 1 and use the diagnostic tests presented at the beginning of each section.

THE PREREADING SKILLS

The prereading skills are those skills, knowledge, and attitudes that enable children to learn to read. You will notice the "prereading" skills are broad objectives that are developed throughout life. Learners continually extend concepts, listening and speaking vocabularies, and perceptual skills. The goal of the prereading program is simply to help children develop these skills to a degree that enables them to recognize and get meaning from the words presented during initial reading instruction.

Visual perception skills enable children to see differences in letters and words. Before a child can read many words, he must be able to see the difference between *b* and *d*, *bum* and *bun*, *ran* and *can*, and other words that may appear to be similar. Likewise he must be able to hear the differences in letter sounds. *Auditory perception* is necessary to hear differences in the sounds of *m* and *n*, *p* and *b*, *pine* and *dime*, and so forth.

In addition to seeing and hearing the letters and sounds correctly and noticing the differences among them, children must be able to remember the sequence of letters and sounds. The *visual-auditory sequencing and memory* skills make it possible for children to remember the letters and sounds in a particular order as they appear in words. For example, children must remember the sequence of letters in words such as *was* or *one*. The final perceptual skill, *visual motor perception*, enables children to follow a printed line of symbols without losing their place. Reading is a perceptual process that requires children to respond to the stimuli of letters representing sounds.

As children perceive the letters and sounds in certain combinations, they must be able to integrate these stimuli into their past sensory impressions. Children need adequate *speaking and listening vocabularies* so that, when they see a word, they can relate it to their listening and speaking vocabularies. If a child perceives the word *desk* and relates it to his speaking and listening vocabularies, it makes sense to him only if he has associated the word with a mental image or *concept* of a desk. Reading requires not only recognition of symbols, but also a meaningful reaction to these symbols.

Another prereading skill is *readiness for books*. To help children use books we teach them top and bottom, front and back, left-to-right progression, and how to take proper care of books. Finally, in most prereading programs the *names of the letters* are taught because letters are usually referred to by name when the sound/symbol relationships are introduced.

What Children Should Learn

To read words, children must be able to see differences in letter forms. This task is not as easy as it seems because many letters in our alphabet are similar; thus, many words appear to be similar also, for example,

b/d u/n p/g m/w .n/m p/d p/b o/c
then/them bad/dad went/want pat/bat

While there are only 26 letters in our alphabet, children must learn more than 26 letter discriminations because many uppercase letters differ in form from the corresponding lowercase letters.

Aa Dd Ee Gg Qq Rr

One of the teacher's first tasks is to help children see the differences in letters so later on children can associate particular letters with certain sounds. Children must learn to look carefully at words to see what letters they contain.

Diagnosing Visual Perception Needs

A ready-to-duplicate skill test to determine students' visual perception of letters and words is provided in the Appendix (Item 11). Row 1 contains lowercase letters; row 2, capital letters; row 3, words that differ only at the beginning; row 4, words that differ at the end; and row 5, words that differ in the middle. Analyze each child's responses to determine what kinds of visual stimuli he is able to discriminate.

APPENDIX ITEM 11

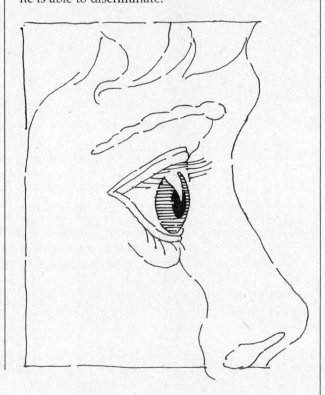

Skill Group Activities for Visual Perception

1 One of the first tasks in working on visual perception is to teach children the concept of *same and different*. If you ask them to point out the letter that is different, they must first understand what you mean by the word *different*. You might teach this concept by using three books and one other object, such as an apple, that is entirely different from the books. Ask the children to show you the one that is different. Then have them say that the apple is different and the books are the same. Draw three circles and one triangle as in Figure 9 and have them again show you the one that is different and those that are alike. As the children develop the concept of "different" and "same," present letters to them.

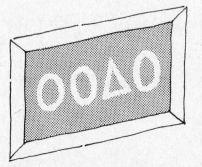

Figure 9. Which one is different?

2 Explain to the children we have many different letters in our alphabet. Ask them to tell you which ones they know. As they name some letters, point them out on alphabet cards. Ask the children why we have letters. You can use the names of the children to show that letters make up words (see Figure 10). Have them notice that all the letters in the word are not the same. Tell them before they can learn lots of words they must see the differences in the letters.

Figure 10. All letters are not the same.

3 Write two letters that have gross differences, such as *t* and *g* (Figure 11), and have the children tell you whether you wrote the same letter twice or wrote two different letters. Do this with other letters, including those that are more difficult to discriminate, such as the *m* and *u*. Ask the children to tell you how the letters differ. The children can trace the letters to notice the differences.

Figure 11. Are these the same?

Figure 12. Which one does not belong?

4 Use a flannel or magnetic board to display letters that are different (Figure 12). Sing the "Sesame Street" version of, "One of These Things Is Not Like the Others." When the children tell you the letter that does not belong, have them point out how it is different. Continue this activity with words.

5 Show the children a letter and direct them to look at it carefully. Then erase it and write only part of the letter on the chalkboard. Ask the children to add the part that is missing (see Figure 13). For an example, if you use the letter *F*, you might leave off one of the horizontal lines. This activity helps children look at the details of each letter.

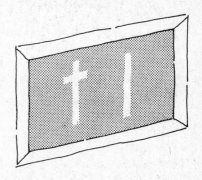

Figure 13. What is missing?

Learning Center Activities for Visual Perception

1 **Haunted House.** Duplicate the worksheet of the Haunted House (Appendix Item 12). Tell the children to look at the ghost outside the house. Tell them he has come to the house to find his five brothers. Direct them to look carefully at each ghost inside the house and find five other ghosts just like him. Then tell the children to color the five brothers so they will always be able to see them.

2 **Hey Look Me Over.** Provide a small box of objects children can trace around. Include cookie cutters, stencils, blocks of different sizes, and plastic alphabet letters. Direct one child to trace around some object or letter and put the paper in a box. Have other children find the object used by matching it to the shape on the paper.

3 **Treasure Word Hunt.** Provide some magazines, newspapers, old books, or worksheets. Ask the children to find a certain letter or word on the pages. For an example, you might have a card that shows the letter **b** or the word **and** . Direct the children to find and circle the letter or word when they see it.

4 **Typewriter.** If an old typewriter is available, you may want to include it in your visual perception center. As the children click at the keys, they will see different letters appearing on the paper. One child can make a worksheet by

hitting one key several times and then putting a letter that is different among letters that are the same. The worksheet can be given to another child who is to find the letter that is not like the others.

5 **Magnetic Board or Flannel Board.** If you have a flannel board with felt letters, or a magnetic board with magnetic alphabet letters, the children can quiz each other on likenesses and differences. Direct one child to put on the board three letters that are alike and one that is different, then ask another child to find the one that is different.

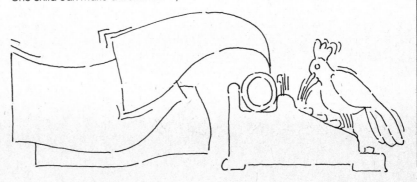

What Children Should Learn

Auditory perception is the ability to hear and differentiate various sounds. This skill is a prerequisite to learning words because children must hear differences in sounds before they can begin to associate symbols with sounds. If a child believes /b/ and /d/ are the same, she cannot be taught to associate a particular sound with its symbol.

Skill in auditory perception is developed by beginning with sounds that are grossly different and continuing until the child can hear differences in sounds that are somewhat similar. The following sequence is suggested:

1. Have children discriminate gross environmental sounds, such as a dog barking and a door slamming.
2. Present gross sounds with different intensities (i.e., louder and softer) and ask the children to discriminate them.
3. Present words and ask the children to tell whether they are the same or different.
4. Ask the children if certain words rhyme.
5. Ask the children to supply a rhyming word for a word you give.
6. Have the children supply words that begin like a word you present.
7. Have the children blend sounds that you say to make a word (i.e., the /b/ and /ad/ to make the word *bad*).

Diagnosing Auditory Perception

The skill test shown in Figure 14 can be used to determine if children can auditorily differentiate

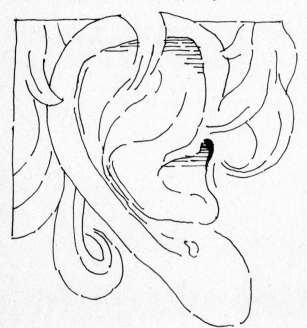

sounds at the beginning, medial, and ending positions of words. To administer the test, pronounce the words in pairs using the same pitch and volume. Ask the children to tell you if you are saying the same word twice or if you are saying two different words. You can make sure the children are not reading your lips by standing to the side of them when saying the words.

If the skill test is being given to one child, agree on a signal (e.g., raising a hand) she can use to indicate when you are saying the same word twice and another to be used when the words are different. If the skill test is to be administered to a group of children, use the auditory perception response sheet found in the Appendix (Item 13). In adminis-

APPENDIX ITEM 13

tering the skill test, direct the children to put an *X* over the smiling face or *Yes* if the words you are saying are the same. Tell the children to put an *X* over the sad face or *No*, if the words you say are not the same. For an example, you would direct the children to look at the umbrella row or row 1 when you present item 1. Say, "bin (pause) fin." Because you are saying two different words, the children should mark the sad face or *No*.

Administer each list of ten items at a different sitting. Analyze the children's responses to determine what sounds they can or cannot discriminate in certain positions.

Skill Test: Auditory Discrimination of Beginning, Medial, and Ending Sounds

Directions:
Pronounce the words in pairs using the same pitch and volume. Ask the children to indicate if you are saying the same word twice or if you are saying two different words. Do not allow the children to look at your lips. In checking the auditory perception response sheet, notice which sounds the children are having difficulty discriminating.

Beginning	Medial	Ending
1. bin–fin	1. big–bag	1. fit–fit
2. pap–pap	2. hit–hat	2. sat–sad
3. go–hoe	3. cat–cat	3. hit–hid
4. make–bake	4. run–rin	4. rope–rope
5. road–road	5. fun–fan	5. cub–cud
6. see–we	6. got–goat	6. hat–had
7. pat–bat	7. boat–boat	7. fair–fair
8. pour–for	8. hid–hide	8. beg–bed
9. bug–bug	9. bowl–bowl	9. fun–fum
10. nice–vice	10. man–men	10. hut–hub

Figure 14. Auditory discrimination skill test.

Skill Group Activities for Auditory Perception

1 Place a group of objects on the table and have the children look at them. Then ask the children to close their eyes as you drop one object at a time. See if the children can identify each object by the sound it makes when it hits the floor.

2 Ask the children to close their eyes while you make two sounds. Direct them to listen to see if the sounds are the same or different. Say two sounds that are grossly different, such as /b/ and /s/. After the children have indicated their recognition of sameness or difference by raising their hands, or simply by saying "same" or "different," ask them to make the sounds with you. Tell them to notice the position of their tongue, teeth, and mouth when they say the different sounds. For example, when beginning to say /b/, the children will notice their lips are together. If they make /s/, they will notice their lips are more open. Repeat these procedures with other sounds.

3 Pronounce three words and ask the children to raise their hands if all of the words begin with the same sound. For an example, you might say words such as *boy, bat,* and *ball.* If the children do miss some of these, again have them think about the relative positions of their lips, teeth, and tongue when producing the sounds. You can vary this game by using words with similar medial or final sounds.

4 Suggest a word in a riddle and ask the children to say a word that rhymes with the word that you give them. Any word may be used, as long as it is within the background of experiences of the children. For an example, you might say, "I'm thinking of a word that rhymes with red. You can sleep in it. It's called a _____." Another example would be, "I'm thinking of a word that rhymes with mouse. We live in it. It's called a _____." These little clues will help children initially. Later you should be able to say a word such as *fat* and have the children provide words that rhyme.

Learning Center Activities for Auditory Perception

1 On the Way Home. Duplicate the game board in the Appendix (Item 14) for this activity. Direct the children to roll a die or spin a spinner to see how many spaces they may move. When they get to the space, they must say a word that begins like the one pictured. If they do so, they may stay there. If not, they must go back until they can say a word beginning like the pictured word. When they get to the house, they must say a word that begins with /h/. You can adapt this game by having the children give rhyming words.

2 Load the Train. The object of this activity is to have children load the train cars with pictures of words beginning with the sound written or pictured on the engine (see Figure 15). Have the children cut and paste or draw pictures on train cars.

3 My Name Starts Like. Children find pictures of words that begin like their own names and assemble them into miniature posters of four or five pictures. For an example, if a child's name is Susie, she might find pictures of soap, a saw, a seal, and a sewing machine. Posters can be displayed to help other children learn to identify sounds.

4 Sound Cans. Coffee cans and many pictures or objects that begin with particular sounds are needed for this activity. Label each coffee can with a certain sound, such as /b/, and tape a picture of an object beginning with that sound, such as a ball, to the front of the coffee can (Figure 16). Children can help you collect pictures and/or small objects for the cans. Once you have developed many sound cans, the children can empty the contents of the different cans, mix them, and then sort them according to beginning or ending sound, depending on your instructions.

Figure 16. Sound cans.

5 Sound Puzzles. Provide 4" x 6" cards or 5" x 8" index cards for this next activity. Tell the children to paste pictures of two objects whose names rhyme side by side on a card. After the pictures have been pasted on the cards, cut the cards between the two pictures using a zig-zag cut. When the children have developed many of these, mix them together and then ask them to separate them by rhyming words. The children will know if they are right or wrong by whether or not the puzzle fits together. Some easily pictured words are:

bed–red	hand–band	pan–man
top–mop	rug–bug	coat–boat
ink–sink	clock–lock	tree–bee

6 Silly Sentences. Have the children think of sentences in which several beginning sounds are repeated such as "Harry has heavy hogs." They will enjoy sharing their sentences with each other. These alliterative sentences will help the children think of sounds that are similar.

Figure 15. Take the "B" train.

VISUAL–AUDITORY SEQUENCING AND MEMORY

What Children Should Learn

Children soon learn that the words in our language have a particular sequence of letters. The neophyte who is learning letters often says a few letters and asks, "What does d–z–y spell?" If you respond by saying those letters do not make a word, the child begins to realize that not all letter combinations produce words: there are certain sequences.

Our objective, then, is to help children realize there is a sequence of letters in particular words, and furthermore to improve their ability to memorize the symbols and sounds in our alphabet. This is not saying that we are teaching children to memorize words rather than using word identification skills. Before children can apply any word identification skills, they must have adequate visual and auditory memories so they can remember the sequences of symbols and sounds in words.

Diagnosing Visual-Auditory Sequencing and Memory

A diagnostic test is provided in the Appendix to help you identify children who need more help with visual-auditory sequencing and memory. This test can also be used to determine informally whether a child's visual or auditory modality for

APPENDIX ITEM 15

learning is better developed. Doing so will give you some idea of what modalities to strengthen as you work with him.

To administer the visual sequencing skill test, cut out the Master Cards found in the Appendix (Item 15). Reproduce the Response Sheet (Item 16) using a thermofax copier and ditto machine and give one to each child. Tell the children to turn their response sheets face down. Explain that you are going to show (or say) some letters and that, when you say "Go," they are to turn their sheets over and put an X on the box with the letters in exactly the same order as the ones you showed (or said). Flash each card to a small group (4 to 6 children) for 10 seconds. If you give this test to a larger group, use an opaque projector to display the Master Cards, or make transparencies and use an overhead projector. Analyze the responses to determine how many letters a child can remember in sequence (3, 4, 5, 6, or 7).

The same testing materials can be adapted for use as an auditory sequencing test. Provide the children with Response Sheets and then read the letters at the rate of one per second. Begin by reading the three-letter sequence and then progress to the seven-letter sequence. After you read each Master Card sequence, have the children turn their response sheets over and mark the one you read. Remember, this test presupposes that children know the names of the letters. If the children do not know the letter names for *e, f, g, h, i, l, o, p, q, r, s, t, u, v, w,* and *y,* this test should not be administered.

Skill Group Activities for Visual-Auditory Sequencing and Memory

1 Write a child's name on the board or make his name with plastic alphabet letters on a magnetic board. Ask the children whose name it is. Rearrange the letters and ask the person if it is still his name. Direct the child whose name is on the board to rearrange the letters so they spell his name once again. Repeat these steps using other children's names. Help the children realize that letters must be in certain positions to make words.

2 A "memory run" helps increase auditory memory. Begin this activity by having a child name an object in the room. For an example, she might say, "Chalkboard." The next child repeats the name of the first object and adds a new one. This is continued to see how many objects the children can say and remember.

3 You can begin to teach some sight words while working on visual and auditory sequencing and memory. Remember, the purpose of this skill is to enable children to remember visual and auditory stimuli—in this instance, words and sounds—so they will be able to read.

Choose a word such as *one,* and discuss the meaning by illustrating one boy, one girl, one apple, and so forth. Point out the letters in *one,* then rearrange them. Have the children put them back in order.

4 Have each child make a booklet of things he should remember, for example, his name, his telephone number, his address, and his birthday. You will be making visual-auditory sequencing and memory meaningful by emphasizing important words and numbers.

Learning Center Activities for Visual-Auditory Sequencing and Memory

1 **Letter Concentration.** Print individual letters on cards cut from heavy paper or tagboard, or print letters in 2" x 3" spaces on a large piece of tagboard, laminate the board, and then cut it into cards. Remember to indicate the bottom (perhaps by underlining) of such letters as lowercase **d** and **p** or **m** and **w** so there will be no confusion if the cards are turned around. Be sure there are two cards bearing each letter you decide to use. Give a deck of these cards to a small group of children (2 to 4 players). Have the children spread the cards face down on the floor or table. In turn, each child turns over two cards. If the letters on the cards are the same, he keeps that pair of cards and takes another turn. If they are not the same, he turns the cards back over in place, and the next player takes his turn. The winner is the player with the most pairs of cards.

2 **I Can Read My Name.** Direct children to cut out the letters on the bottom half of the activity sheet provided in the Appendix (Item 17). After cutting them apart, children should arrange them to read, "I can read. My name is _____." The letters can then be pasted in the correct boxes and the child's name printed in the space provided on the sheet. Children will be thrilled by the fact they can "read," and these positive attitudes are so important in beginning reading.

3 **I Love a Parade!** Set out a little box containing a variety of objects and letters. You might include some small plastic animals (dinosaurs, horses, elephants), small cars or motorcycles, and plastic alphabet letters. Direct one child to arrange a pattern or a "parade." For example, he might line up two horses, a car, and the letter a. He would tell the other children to look at the objects carefully. Then the children would be instructed to close their eyes while the first child rearranged the sequence of the objects. When the children opened their eyes, they would be asked to tell which objects had been moved.

4 **Envelopes.** For this activity, you will need envelopes and 3" x 5" cards. Print a word on the front of each envelope. Make a separate letter card for each letter in the word by rewriting the word on a 3" x 5" card and then cutting the card between the letters. Put these letters in the corresponding envelope. Tell the children to take an envelope and look carefully at the word on the front. They should then turn the envelope face down, take out the letters, and see if they can reproduce the same word from memory. They can check their work by comparing their word with the one on the envelope. Of course, they are not expected to read the words, but rather simply to reproduce the same sequence of letters.

5 **Store or Restaurant.** As a part of the visual-auditory sequencing and memory center, you might want to set up a miniature store or restaurant. You can do this simply by asking the children to bring empty food boxes and/or cans from home. The children can enjoy playing store or restaurant by going to the storekeeper and asking him for several items. Instead of giving his customer each item as she asks for it, the storekeeper should try to remember the entire shopping list or order and fill it for the "customer." This activity develops visual as well as auditory memory in that the children begin to associate the names of products with the labels on their containers.

6 **Can You Remember?** Make available some pictures. Direct one child to hold up a picture while the others look at it carefully. Once the picture has been put away, they should name all the things they can remember about it. When they have exhausted their memories, they may refer to the picture to see what they did not notice. The children can help you select pictures for this activity by looking in magazines and cutting out pictures at home. Introduce this activity in a skill group so the children will be able to do it independently at a learning center.

ARCADIA
LMC

VISUAL-MOTOR PERCEPTION

What Children Should Learn

Reading requires eye movements from left to right and then from right to left as the reader makes the return sweep. Children's eyes must work together to follow the printed lines of symbols without losing their place. Adequate visual-motor perception is also necessary to write letters. Because writing is often used to reinforce letters or words children are learning, coordination of hand and eye movements becomes an important objective of the pre-reading program.

Diagnosing Visual-Motor Perception Needs

A skill test is provided in the Appendix (Item 18) to aid you in identifying children who may need instruction and practice to develop their visual-motor perceptual skills. Duplicate and hand out the test. Direct the children to look at the shape in each box and to draw one exactly like it. When evaluating the children's responses, notice the following:

1. Is the circle essentially round and closed?
2. Does the square have even sides and corners?
3. Does the triangle have corners and a base line?
4. Is the stick of the d on the right side of the circle?
5. Do the lines of the N touch each other? Are the lines straight?
6. Are all lines included and do they cross at the center?

APPENDIX ITEM 18

Skill Group Activities for Visual-Motor Perception

1 Write a series of sentences on the board using the names of some members of the class (Figure 17). Read the list to the children and use a pointer to indicate your eye movements. Ask the children to describe what would happen if your eyes skipped down too far. Lead them to realize that their eyes must work together so they will not miss what they are reading. Tell the children you know some ways to help their eyes work together, and you will be helping them develop this skill.

2 Draw a series of dots on the board and have children connect them by beginning at the left and going to the right. Ask the children to make their lines as straight as they can. On another chalkboard draw a circle, then have children trace over this circle as many times as they can without enlarging the circle. Designate a part of the chalkboard on which they can practice independently.

3 A balance beam is an excellent activity for visual-motor perception. You can use the balance beam in the skill group by directing the children to walk forward while they keep their eyes on a particular spot on the chalkboard. As they walk forward, they should be placing heel in front of toe. After the children are skillful in walking forward, have them walk backward, this time touching toe to heel. Balance beam activities can be varied by using the Indian walk, which requires the children to spread their arms out and move them up and down slowly while walking along the beam. You can reverse the directions while the children are walking on the balance beam. When they reach a certain point, you might say, "Okay, go backward."

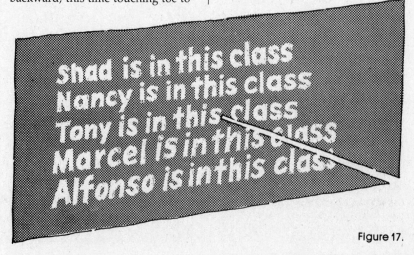

Shad is in this class
Nancy is in this class
Tony is in this class
Marcel is in this class
Alfonso is in this class

Figure 17.

Learning Center Activities for Visual-Motor Perception

1 **Bicycle Obstacle Course.** Provide copies of the activity sheet included in the Appendix (Item 19). Direct each player to put his pencil on the bicycle. When someone says "Go," the players draw a line from the bicycle around the obstacles, in order, to the finish line. They must not touch an obstacle or they will fall down. The player who goes over the course in the shortest amount of time without falling down is the winner.

2 **Clothespins.** The old-fashioned game of dropping clothespins into a milk bottle is great for eye-hand coordination. Cut a plastic milk container, put the clothespins into it, and have this available at the learning center. Children can play the game with each other and see how many pins they can get into the milk carton.

3 **Lacing.** You can make your own sewing or lacing cards. Get a simple picture, glue it on tagboard or chipboard, laminate it if you wish, and punch holes around the outer edges or along distinctive lines within the picture. Tie a shoestring to one of the holes and ask the children to reproduce the design on the card by going in and out the holes with the string.

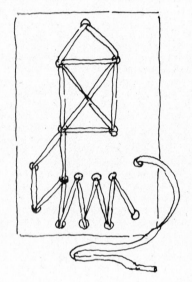

4 **Beanbags.** Make beanbags for children by filling and stitching old washcloths. Have children throw the beanbags into a wastebasket placed at a certain distance. Each child can see how many of the beanbags he can throw into the basket. You can increase the distance between the children and the basket as they become more proficient.

5 **Stringing Beads.** Provide some beads or macaroni for the children to put on shoestrings. If desired, provide a timer so the children can compete to see who can string the most beads in the least time.

6 **Dot to Dot.** Dot-to-dot activities are great for visual motor coordination. You can make many worksheets where the children follow dots without numerals or letters. For example, you may have a child draw a line from the dog to his dish, from the letter to the mailbox, and so forth. A simple worksheet can be made by drawing lots of dots and having children connect them in any order to make straight lines.

LISTENING AND SPEAKING VOCABULARIES

What Children Should Learn

Children develop four different vocabularies. The first vocabulary that is developed is the *listening vocabulary*. Infants learn to listen before they can talk. As the listening vocabulary is being developed, children grow physically and mentally so they can say some words and then sentences, their *speaking vocabulary*. A third vocabulary that is learned is the *reading vocabulary*. Finally, or perhaps as children are learning to read, they develop a *writing vocabulary*.

Before learning to read, children must have adequate listening and speaking vocabularies because these vocabularies help them understand words and sentence structure. Also, if a child is able to "sound out" a word but has never heard the word, he will not be able to make any sense from the sounds. For an example, if you saw the word *bammer*, you would be able to sound it out since it is like *hammer*, but you would not be able to associate it with anything because *bammer* is not a part of your listening vocabulary: it is a nonsense word. If a child comes across the word *cat* and is

able to sound it out but does not know the word *cat* as a part of his speaking or listening vocabulary, he is in the same predicament. It is essential to help children develop adequate speaking and listening vocabularies as a basis for the reading vocabulary.

Diagnosing Speaking and Listening Vocabularies

It is not practical to use paper-and-pencil tests to determine the students' speaking and listening vocabularies; therefore, Figure 18 is a checklist to guide your observations of children.

_____ 1. Is the child attentive when asked to listen?

_____ 2. Is he able to listen to stories and remember some of the important facts?

_____ 3. Does he seem to understand the concepts in the stories you read and tell?

_____ 4. Is he able to listen and follow directions?

_____ 5. Is he able to name common objects?

_____ 6. Does he have problems with any of the speech sounds? Remember, it is typical for children to have difficulty with sounds of **l**, **sh**, voiced **th**, **v**, **s**, **z**, **j**, and **r** until the age of 7.

_____ 7. Is he able to describe places he has been by expressing his thoughts in sentences?

_____ 8. Does he often use new words?

_____ 9. Can he use detailed and descriptive words?

_____ 10. Can he tell about a personal experience or picture in a manner that is intelligible to the listener?

Figure 18. Listening and speaking vocabularies checklist.

Skill Group Activities for Developing Listening and Speaking Vocabularies

1 Perhaps the most important skill group activity you can have for children who are trying to improve their listening and speaking vocabularies is to read and tell stories to them. Doing so helps the children develop listening comprehension while expanding concepts and providing hours of enjoyment. Stop as you read and ask questions about the characters and events in the stories. You might have the children dramatize part of the story to help them develop adequate speaking vocabularies. After reading the book or story, put it at the learning center so the children can look at the pictures again and retell the story.

2 Describe some object with which the children are familiar. Have them guess what you are describing with as few clues as possible. This game teaches children to listen and helps them develop better concepts. For example, when describing an apple, you might say, "I am round. I am red or green. I have seeds. I am used to make cider." By introducing new knowledge along with familiar facts, you can expand the child's world.

3 Sharing is also an important skill group activity for listening and speaking skills. Ask three or four children in the skill group to bring something or tell about some situation. The children will be working on both listening and speaking vocabularies as they take turns talking and then listening to others. You can have the children use puppets when sharing information, too.

4 A round robin activity can also be used in this skill group. Begin a story by saying one sentence. For example, you might say, "Once there was a monkey monster." In turn, each child adds another sentence. Continue until you have a complete story.

Learning Center Activities for Developing Listening and Speaking Vocabularies

1 Puppet Cutouts. Duplicate the activity sheet (Appendix Item 20) and provide small paper bags for children to use in making their own puppets. Tell the children to color the pieces on the worksheet, then cut them out and paste them on a paper bag to make a puppet.

As each child finishes his puppet, have him make up a story about the puppet. Provide opportunities for the children to tell their stories during small skill group sessions.

2 Words I Can Say. Provide paper and old magazines, newspapers, or catalogs for this activity. Direct the children to cut out and paste on the paper small pictures of words they can say. Ask the children to bring their papers to the skill group to share with others.

3 Working Together Center. This center could include blocks, toys, games, dollhouses, and a sandbox. Rather than having one "working together" center, you may want to have a separate game center, block center, housekeeping center, or store. Children develop their speaking and listening vocabularies by communicating with other children. Provide opportunities for informal talks so children can learn from each other.

4 Discovery Center. As a part of the learning center for speaking and listening skills, you might include objects children are to examine and explore. If you place new objects at the center each morning, give the children an opportunity to examine them and be ready to describe them to you and the other children. Some of the things you might have at this center are rocks, shells, flowers, and things children bring to school.

5 Telephones. Many times telephones encourage children to talk. If you have play telephones located at the listening and speaking skills learning center, children can use these as they

listen and talk to each other. Of course, children can make their own telephones with cans and string. Shy children will usually speak more freely when talking into a telephone than when looking at someone.

6 What Is Going to Happen? Provide colorful action pictures in which something seems about to happen. Tell the children to look at the pictures and tell you what they think is going to happen next. Discuss the children's responses in the skill group.

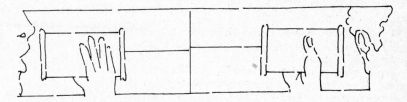

CONCEPT DEVELOPMENT

What Children Should Learn

Reading is the process of getting meaning from printed symbols. One of the steps in this process is associating mental images with visual stimuli. For example, when a child sees the word *horse*, he should associate it with his mental image of a horse. Getting meaning is impossible unless the child has formed some mental images of the concepts included in the selection.

One of the most important tasks of every teacher, regardless of grade level, is that of concept development. Concepts are not taught in any one lesson or skill group, or at any particular learning center, but rather they are developed throughout the school years. Yet, it may be helpful to have a skill group for those children who do have inadequate concepts. Likewise, a learning center or

many learning centers at which the children can develop many common concepts should be included for those children whose experiences have been limited. When the children have had some experiences with the content of the selections, their ability to understand increases.

Diagnosing Children's Concepts for Initial Reading Experiences

An observational checklist (Figure 19) is useful to determine if children have developed some of the concepts that are important to success in initial reading. You can use the following checklist to guide your observations. Asking questions in informal situations will help you determine what concepts different children have developed.

_____ 1. Does she know the names of common objects found in the classroom, home, and neighborhood? Can she describe some objects without looking at them?

_____ 2. Does she know the names of the colors? Can she associate objects with numbers from 1 to 10?

_____ 3. Has she had a wide variety of experiences? What places has she visited? Can she recall personal experiences related to the story you are reading to her?

_____ 4. Can she classify things, such as animals, food, clothing, and toys?

_____ 5. Does she know the meanings of common words, such as **under**, **over**, **before**, **after**, **up**, and **down**?

_____ 6. Can she recognize the main idea of a picture? Can she arrange pictures in a story sequence?

_____ 7. Can she infer the feelings and mood of characters in a story you read to her?

_____ 8. Can she associate events in a sequence and see the cause-and-effect relationships?

_____ 9. Can she point to and name different parts of her body: arm, ankle, feet, fingers, legs, ears, head, neck, waist, and so forth?

_____ 10. Can she name five things that can be found in the kitchen, bedroom, living room, and garage?

_____ 11. Can she name five types of transportation? Occupations? Weather?

_____ 12. Can she name the days of the week? Months? Holidays?

Figure 19. Concept development checklist.

Skill Group Activities for Concept Development

1 Filmstrips and picture books should be used along with actual objects to help develop and extend concepts. When showing children pictures or objects, discuss the characteristics and function. You might ask questions such as:

1. What do you see?
2. How can this help us?
3. How is this like _____?
4. What color is this?
5. Where would you find this?
6. How does it feel?
7. What sound does it make?
8. How many _____ do you see?

2 Many times children confuse the meanings of small words, such as *over*, *up*, *on*, *under*, *beside*, *in*, *down*, and *around*; yet, these words are commonly found in primary grade reading materials. You can help children clarify their understanding of these sight words by using an object such as a block and giving the children these directions?

1. Put the block *under* the table.
2. Put the block *on* the table.
3. Put the block *in* my hand.
4. Make the block go *around* the table.
5. Make the block go *up*.
6. Make the block go *down*.
7. Put the block *beside* the table.

3 Classification activities aid children in organizing knowledge. Show the children three different objects that are related and one that is completely different. For example, you may want to show them a pencil, a crayon, a paintbrush, and paper. Ask them to tell you which one is not like the other ones and why it is different.

4 You can help children see relationships between concepts by giving them incomplete sentences to finish. For an example, you might say, "Chairs are to sit in, beds are to _____." Another example would be, "Books are to read, pencils are to _____." The children also might make up some of their own incomplete sentences to say to each other.

Riddles can be used to help children develop concepts in that many characteristics of objects are usually mentioned in a riddle. You might say to the children, "I have a rug, a light, and walls. What am I?"

Learning Center Activities for Concept Development

1 **The Weirdies!** Duplicate the activity sheet (Appendix Item 21) and direct the children to find 15 things in the picture that are weird or wrong. Perhaps some of the children will enjoy drawing "weird" pictures and letting others determine what is wrong.

2 **Find and Tell.** Duplicate Appendix Item 22. Tell your children that an apple, a banana, a swan, a cup, a butterfly, a fish, a squirrel, a turtle, a spoon, a school, and a pear are hidden in the picture. Let them look for these items and outline or color the ones they find, then tell them exactly where each object is hidden. In discussing the picture with children, try to develop their understanding of such words as **under**, **behind**, **beside**, **on**, and **in**.

Your children will enjoy finding objects hidden in pictures. Laminate the hidden object pictures featured in **Highlights** or **Playmate** so they can be used many times.

3 **Feel Me.** Put objects with different textures in manila envelopes or shoe boxes. Ask the children to reach in and describe what they feel without looking. They might say the object is soft, smooth, hard, or prickly. Some of the items you may want to use are cotton balls, sandpaper, waxed paper, burlap, and leather.

4 **Making Scrapbooks.** Old catalogs with pictures will be needed for this learning center activity. Begin several scrapbooks of different things children can classify by category. For an example, you may want to have a scrapbook of toys, one of people, one for things that belong in the kitchen, and one for things to eat. When the scrapbooks are finished, you will have picture books about particular topics which you might be able to use for other teaching activities.

5 **How Big Am I?** Provide pictures of objects for the children to arrange by size. During the skill group you can show them pictures of objects, such as a frying pan, a house, a horse, a car, a cup, and a chair, and tell them to put the things in order from the smallest to the largest.

6 **How Was I Made?** Put some objects or finished products at the learning center and ask the children to guess how they were made. For example, you may want to have a small box containing a book, pencil, paper clip, doll, toy car, piece of carpet, and a tennis ball. What is it made of? How many parts are there? What was put on first? The children can manipulate and talk about the objects at the learning center and then tell you their ideas when the skill group meets. At this time you can clarify and extend meetings.

7 **We Work.** Children can develop concepts of what people do by using tools and materials. Perhaps you will want to set up a separate learning center that includes the tools or materials of different workers. You could provide combs, brushes, and wigs for a beauty shop. Some teachers provide hammers, big nails, screws, and screwdrivers at a woodworking center. Use resource people to help gather discarded tools and materials common in the community.

READINESS FOR BOOKS

What Children Should Learn

There are certain skills, knowledge, and attitudes that children must have before they can read books. For example, children must learn that books have a front and back, that the words are arranged from top to bottom and from left to right, that words represent talk written down, and that the pages are numbered in a particular sequence. Of course, children must also learn to care for books properly.

In addition to developing these readiness skills for using books, children need to develop the skills of working together with others in a group. Children must learn to sit by others without disturbing them, to pay attention to the teacher, to cooperate, and to take their turns. These behaviors are prerequisites to learning to read because reading instruction generally takes place in group situations.

Diagnosing Readiness for Books

An observational checklist is the most appropriate diagnostic device for determining students' readiness for books. You can use the checklist in Figure 20 to guide your observations of children.

_____ 1. Does the child seem to enjoy looking at pictures in books?

_____ 2. Does the child know the difference between the top and bottom of a book? The front and back?

_____ 3. Does he seem to be careful when using books?

_____ 4. Can he follow along as you read picture books?

_____ 5. Has he developed left-to-right directional sense?

_____ 6. Does he show interest in printed symbols? In other words, does he ask you what certain words are?

_____ 7. Is he able to cooperate and take his turn with other children?

_____ 8. Is he able to work independently to finish a reasonable task?

Figure 20. Readiness for books checklist.

Skill Group Activities for Developing Readiness for Books

1 One of the most beneficial activities for developing readiness for books is to have children make their own booklets, for example, "All About Me" books. Prepare booklets by making ditto masters of series of such incomplete statements as "My name is _____," "There are _____ people in my family," I am _____ years old," "I weigh _____ pounds," "I like to play _____," "I like to watch _____," "I like to read _____," "I don't like _____," "I am afraid of _____," "On Saturday I like to _____," and "My favorite color is _____." If you choose a 5½" x 4¼" format for the booklet, you can get two pages on each master. Run off the masters, fold the resulting two-page spreads down the center, assemble and staple them in construction paper covers. During skill group, help the children fill in the blanks and illustrate their booklets. Provide old magazines as a source of pictures, but also encourage children to draw illustrations or bring snapshots from home. Of course, the children will not be able to read all the words in

their booklets; however, they will realize that reading is talk written down, that words go from left to right, that pages are numbered in sequence, and so forth. At the same time, you will be gathering valuable information from them.

2 Conduct a discussion on how to hold and care for books. This might result naturally if you ask children to share their books with others.

Explain to the children that most of the books at school are used by many children. If pages are torn or marked, children cannot enjoy them. You might want to share the fact that their parents and neighbors bought the books for them so they could learn lots of things. The points you and the children make in the discussion will need to be reinforced frequently as you help children extend these values.

3 Picture books can be used to help children develop left-to-right progression. If you have duplicate copies of some of the picture books, you can have the children follow along as you tell the story.

4 Another activity to teach children left-to-right progression is to make a calendar with them. They will notice you begin at the left and go to the right. Rather than having them write the numerals, make the numeral shape in dots for the children to trace over or connect.

1 **Read to Me.** Children learn to value reading and books by finding out what books contain; therefore, reading to children is most important. Because your time is limited, you may want to use a listening station where children may listen to tape recorded stories while they follow the pictures in their books. Another good practice is to ask upper grade children to read to your children at this learning center.

2 **Surround Them With Books.** Many kinds of reading materials should be located at this learning center to help children develop interest in reading. You may want to include Cub Scout and Brownie books, bubble gum trading cards, children's magazines, cereal boxes with attractive offers, simple comic books, and pamphlets with pictures of interesting places. The children will enjoy looking at the pictures, and may develop a stronger desire to learn to read.

3 **Can You Find Me?** Label many of the objects in your classroom, such as your desk, a window, the chalkboard, the television set, the learning centers, and so forth. Prepare duplicate cards with these words and place them in an envelope at the learning center. Direct the children to take a card from the envelope and find the same word on an object in the room. This activity develops visual discrimination and an interest in words.

4 **How High Is It?** Building blocks should be provided at this center or some center in the classroom. Ask the children to divide into teams of two and see which team can build the highest tower by taking turns adding blocks. Team members will soon learn the importance of cooperation as they try to build the highest tower. Follow up this activity with a discussion when the skill group meets. Relate this example to the importance of cooperation in the skill group. Talk about what a good group member does.

5 **Follow the Line.** Old workbooks, children's magazines, or newspapers will be needed for this activity. Direct the children to draw a line under each sentence beginning at the left and going to the right. When they get to the end of the line, they should lift the pencil from the paper and go back to the next line on the left-hand side. This activity is good for visual-motor coordination, as well as left-to-right progression.

NAMES OF LETTERS

What Children Should Learn

Children are expected to learn the names of letters as part of the prereading period so teachers can refer to them later on when teaching sounds. For example, when teaching children to associate *b* with /b/, it is convenient to refer to the sound by its letter name. Knowing the names of letters is more important when learning to spell words than when learning to read them, but there seems to be a trend to teach children to spell the words they are learning to read; thus, the names of letters are generally taught during the prereading program.

Children need learn the names of only 26 letters; however, they must be able to recognize more than 26 because many differ in lower and upper-case form. The printed letters *a, b, d, e, g, h, i, l, m, n, q,* and *r* have different upper and lowercase forms. Conversely, upper and lowercase *c, f, j, k, o, p, s, t, u, v, w, x, y,* and *z* are very similar except for size.

A particular sequence need not be followed in introducing letters. Many teachers follow alphabetical order, even though knowing alphabetical order is not a prerequisite for beginning reading. Others teach the letters frequently found in their students' names. Perhaps the most important con-

cern is to not introduce a second letter that is similar to the first until the first has been mastered. For example, generally it would be unwise to teach the letter *b* one day, and the letter *d* the next day.

Diagnosing Children's Knowledge of Letters

A skill test is provided in the Appendix (Item 23) for testing children's knowledge of letter names. For each item, read the name of the letter as shown

APPENDIX ITEM 23

in List 1 and ask the children to put an X over it. You can make another form for this test using uppercase letters if desired. When checking the papers, notice which letters the children do not know.

List 1. Letters for Letter Names Skill Test

1. e	2. t	3. b	4. g	5. n
6. r	7. s	8. q	9. c	10. f
11. m	12. h	13. i	14. l	15. o
16. j	17. d	18. y	19. u	20. a
21. p	22. v	23. k	24. z	25. w

Skill Group Activities for Teaching Children the Letters

1 Begin by teaching the names of the letters that are most meaningful to the children. You might want to teach the names of the letters in the children's names, the school's name, your name, or perhaps in familiar words such as *mommy* and *daddy*. Write a word on the chalkboard and tell the children that each letter in the word has a name. Write the first letter of the word below the word and say its name. Now ask the children to say the name of this letter. Provide clay for the children to make the shape of the letter. You can also have them make pipe cleaner letters and then glue these to a piece of tagboard. Go on to other letters as the children appear ready.

2 Explain to the children that each letter has a lowercase form and an uppercase form. Show the children alphabet cards that include both forms of each letter. Provide stories and ask them to find words with uppercase letters. Help them realize that the uppercase form of some letters is simply larger, while that of other letters, such as *g*, is a different shape.

Prepare ditto masters that include both the lowercase and uppercase forms of the letters side by side. Have the children trace both forms of the letters as they say the letter names. Some easily pictured words you may want to draw on the masters appear in List 2.

3 After the children have learned the names of several letters, play "cross the river." Simply draw a river on the chalkboard and put many letters on the left side of it. Tell the children that if they can say the name of a letter, that letter will be able to cross the river. If they say the name correctly, erase the letter from the left-hand side and write it on the right-hand side of the river. Remind them there are alligators in the river so they should make sure the letters do not fall in and get eaten. If the children come to a letter that is difficult, have them draw it in the air or on the chalkboard as they say it. Tracing letters you have outlined with dots is a good reinforcement activity, too. Have the children say the name of the letter as they trace it.

List 2. Easily Pictured Words

a – apple	n – nest
b – boat	o – orange
c – cat	p – paint
d – duck	q – queen
e – egg	r – rake
f – fish	s – sun
g – ghost	t – table
h – house	u – umbrella
i – ice cream	v – vase
j – jar	w – wagon
k – kite	x – xylophone
l – lamp	y – yo-yo
m – milk	z – zebra

Learning Center Activities for Teaching Children Names of Letters

1 **Letter Land.** Duplicate the game board (Appendix Item 24) for this activity and demonstrate how the game is played. Have children put one, two, or three paper clips under each of three paper cups. In turn, each player picks up a cup, after they have been shuffled, moves the same number of spaces as there are paper clips, and reads the letter on the space where he lands. If he cannot read the letter, he stays there but loses his next turn. The first person to reach the Letter Factory is the winner.

2 **Load the Truck.** Direct the children to see how many plastic or paper alphabet letters they can load into a truck, box, or some other container. Have them name each letter as they put it in. Other children at the learning center can unload the truck by naming the letters. The object of the activity is to see who can name the most letters.

3 **Scratch My Back.** Ask a child to use her index finger to trace a letter on someone's back. If that person can guess which letter is being traced on his back, he gets a turn to trace a letter on the next person's back.

4 **Up and Down the Tower.** Blocks with letters on them are needed for this activity. Have children stack the blocks — with letter sides showing — as high as they can, then "climb up the tower" by starting at the bottom and reading the name of the letter on one side of each block. To get down the tower, children start at the top and must read the names of the letters on another side of each block. Children can compete to see who can build and climb up and down the highest tower.

5 **Toss a Letter.** Take a 3' x 3' sheet of paper (butcher paper will do) and divide it into nine equal sections as are used in playing tic-tac-toe. Write a letter the children are learning to make in each space. Or, if you desire, use tagboard rather than paper. Mark off nine equal squares and laminate the board. You can then use grease pencil to write a letter in each square and will be able to erase the letters and replace them with others as they are mastered.

Once the board has been made, make eight 1' x 1' cards. Print X's on four of these and O's on the others. These cards can also be laminated if you wish.

Divide the children into two teams and give one team the X cards and the other, the O cards. Direct a child to toss a beanbag onto the tic-tac-toe board while standing five feet from it. If the child can name the letter on which the beanbag lands, he may cover it with his X or O card. A player from the other team then takes his turn. The first team to make a straight line three spaces long wins.

6 **Which Hand?** Plastic alphabet letters are needed for this activity. One child takes a letter from the box and holds it in one hand while holding both hands behind his back. The other children take turns guessing which hand contains the letter. If the guesser points to the correct hand **and** can name the letter, he gets a turn to hide another letter in one of his hands. A variation on this activity would be to make the children point to and name the hand (right or left), as well as the letter it contains.

WORD RECOGNITION SKILLS

The word recognition skills are those skills and that knowledge which enable children to determine the pronunciation and meanings of words. When recognizing a word, children might (1) recognize it by sight, (2) use phonics to sound it out, (3) use context clues, (4) notice the structure of the word, and/or (5) use a dictionary to determine the pronunciation and meanings of the word. Generally children must use a combination of these word recognition techniques. Our task is to help children develop a useful strategy to pronounce and understand words.

The first section of this chapter deals with *sight words*. There are some words in our language that appear so frequently that children should recognize them immediately. Knowing words by sight improves the rate of comprehension and makes reading an enjoyable activity rather than a burdensome task. A large sight vocabulary also enables beginning readers to feel successful.

The next four sections of this chapter deal with one of the most important word recognition techniques: *phonics*. We teach children to sound out words by noticing the positions of the consonants and vowels in them. Even though the English language does not have a perfect correlation between the sounds and the symbols that represent the sounds, there is a high correlation. It has been said that approximately 80 percent of the words in the English language are consistent with the principles of phonics.

To sound out words or apply phonics, children must know the 44 sounds in the English language and the symbols that represent them. Because there are only 26 letters in the alphabet, we also teach children generalizations that help them realize what sound a particular symbol represents in a certain position. The second section of this chapter deals with the *consonant sounds* and generalizations concerning consonants. A separate section is devoted to *sound patterns* because we try to teach the children to look for sound patterns in words rather than looking at each separate sound. *Vowel sounds* and vowel generalizations are presented in the fourth section of this chapter. Finally, a section concerning *syllabication and accent* is included because children must divide multisyllabic words before sounding them out. Also, in pronouncing multisyllabic words, children must accent the correct syllables.

Phonics is a useful word recognition technique for determining how to pronounce words; however, "sounding a word out" does not help the reader determine its meaning unless the word is in his listening vocabulary. For example, if the reader

sounds out the word *verify* but has never heard the word, he cannot get meaning from the printed symbols. Word recognition techniques in addition to phonics are necessary to help children understand words that may not be in their listening vocabularies.

One word recognition technique that is particularly helpful in understanding the meaning of a word that appears unfamiliar is the use of *context clues*. Many times the context in which the unfamiliar word is used provides some insight into its meaning and/or pronunciation. A separate section of this chapter presents ideas for helping children use context clues.

The *structure of a word* may also be used to determine its pronunciation and meaning. We teach children to look for prefixes, suffixes, inflectional endings, separate parts of compound words, and contracted forms of words which might help them identify words. A section of this chapter deals with structural analysis.

The final section of this chapter is devoted to teaching children how to use the dictionary to discover the pronunciation and meanings of a word. Generally, elementary school children avoid using the dictionary because it is so time-consuming. Our task is to teach children the many skills involved in using the dictionary so they will be able to locate words easily.

Even though the word recognition techniques are separated for emphasis in this chapter, you should keep in mind the importance of helping children develop a plan of action when they come to a word that seems unfamiliar. For example, you might teach them to apply the 3SD strategy. The symbols in this mnemonic device stand for: **s**ound out the word, analyze the **s**tructure, **s**kip the word and read the remainder of the sentence, and use the **d**ictionary to find the meaning or pronunciation. Our goal is to help children synthesize the many different aspects of word recognition into a meaningful strategy for pronouncing words.

SIGHT WORDS

What Children Should Learn

There are many reasons for teaching children some words by sight. One reason is that some words appear so frequently children should be able to recognize them within 3 seconds. If children must try to sound out every word they encounter, or figure it out by using the context, the structure, or a dictionary, reading becomes a laborious task.

Another reason for learning sight words is so children can begin to learn particular sound/sym-

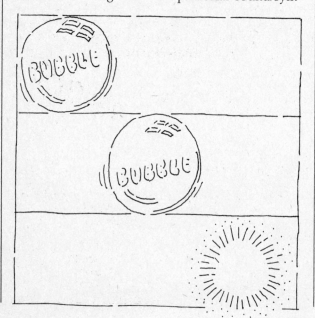

bol relationships. Some reading specialists believe children should learn 50 to 100 words by sight before instruction in phonics is attempted. In other words, if children learn some words by sight, the different sounds of the words can be isolated and taught. For example, if a child knows the words *went*, *were*, and *was* by sight, he can be asked how these words sound at the beginning, and thus learn /w/.

Finally we teach children to memorize some words by sight because not all words follow the principles of phonics. For example, the words *one* and *have* do not.

Forgan's 100 Initial Sight Words (List 3), are words that (1) are important and meaningful to the children, (2) appear frequently, and (3) contain each of the 44 sounds in the English language. These 100 words can be used to make many interesting and personalized sentences and stories.

In teaching sight words, you should remember not to make children memorize a list of words. You should work on only a few words at a time in meaningful context. Notice that many of the sight words are prepositions and conjunctions; thus, these words will have to be used in sentences. Keep in mind that the typical child needs several repetitions before he masters a word at the automatic response level, thus, practice and reinforcement activities are necessary after introducing the words.

Nouns and Pronouns	Adjectives and Adverbs	Verbs	Prepositions and Conjunctions
mommy	this	is	to
daddy	the	like	in
sister (or sister's name)	a	can	for
brother (or brother's name)	your	am	at
pet (or pet's name)	one	are	with
child's name	good	have	or
friend (or friend's name)	my	see	on
name of favorite toy	when	will	out
name of favorite food	our	be	of
name of favorite place	his	has	from
home	her	been	by
you	new	go	if
we	all	was	and
it	which	come	but
I	their	get	about
he	soon	think	so
she	that	look	up
they	as	run	
boy	some	would	
girl	then	do	
me	(child's favorite color)	make	
there	very	work	
them	not	play	
		were	
		take	
		eat	
		give	
		saw	
		came	
		could	
		said	
		went	
		did	
		jump	
		bring	
		use	
		had	

These words are arranged according to the part of speech in which they are normally used, so sentences can be formed easily. Keep in mind that some of the words can be used as more than one part of speech. For example **there** can function as an adverb, pronoun, or noun.

Diagnosing Children's Knowledge of Sight Words

You can use the skill test in the Appendix (Item 25) to determine if children in your class know the basic sight words. Reproduce and hand out the test sheets, then tell the children that they are to circle in each box the one word that you read. The test items (List 4) are arranged according to frequency of use (i.e., the first word is written more frequently than is the second, and so forth). Allow only 3 to 5 seconds for each word, then go on to the next one. When analyzing the test results, you should be able to determine if children know the words that are used frequently.

APPENDIX ITEM 25

List 4. Basic Sight Words Arranged According to Frequency of Use

1. and	8. are	15. so	22. was	29. give
2. we	9. of	16. my	23. our	30. look
3. in	10. this	17. very	24. make	31. run
4. not	11. have	18. been	25. his	32. think
5. at	12. good	19. there	26. she	33. friend
6. on	13. about	20. from	27. said	34. play
7. can	14. when	21. go	28. work	35. went

Skill Group Activities for Teaching Sight Words

1 Have children make a picture book of some words they know by cutting out advertisements or drawing pictures. Ask them to dictate a sentence about the picture. In doing so, they will include some of the most frequently used sight words, such as *of, a, in, is, it, at,* and *an,* in their sentences. Write their sentence below the picture on one page and then on the back of that page so they can begin to learn the words without picture clues.

2 In teaching sight words you should remember to have children use as many of the five senses as practical. Children have three modalities that can be used to learn to associate symbols and the concepts they represent. They can *see* the word, *hear* the word, and *feel* the word. As you introduce a new sight word to the children, make sure they are looking at it. Point out the different letters and the configuration or shape of the word. At the same time, say the word and then give them a chance to say the word. You may find it helpful for some children to trace the word at the chalkboard. If children trace a word, they should say the word rather than each individual letter. Remember to use the words in context so the children understand them.

3 Children like to note their own progress. Make a word card for each word a child is learning. He can take them home and have his parents review the words with him. Or, the word cards can be used in such whole class activities as a game of word recognition baseball. In this game each child has his own word cards, and when it is his turn to bat, these words are "pitched" to him. This game allows for individual differences within the classroom because each child has a chance to pronounce the words he is learning.

Learning Center Activities for Sight Words

1 **Touchdown!** The football field on the game board (Appendix Item 26) and some flash cards with sight words are needed for this activity. Direct the children to place two paper footballs on the 0-yard line and the word cards face down on the game board. The children form two equal teams. A player from one team turns over a word and has 3 seconds to read it. If he reads it correctly, he moves the ball 10 yards toward his team's goal. If the word is missed, the ball is not moved. A player from the other team then takes a turn. Play continues in this manner until one player crosses the goal line to score a touchdown for his team.

2 **Auto Racing.** Use the racetrack game board (Appendix Item 27) and provide two racing cars. Divide the children into two teams and direct them to alternately turn up a card and read it within 3 seconds. If the child pronounces the word correctly, he moves his team's racing car one section closer to the finish line. A child from the other team then takes a turn. If a child cannot say the word within 3 seconds, he cannot move the car. See which team can go around the racetrack first. Tell the children to put aside words they are having trouble pronouncing and bring them to the skill group for instruction.

3 **Sad Face.** A deck of 25 cards with basic sight words is needed for this activity. You will need to make 5 additional cards with a sad face drawn on each. Direct the children to shuffle the cards and place them face down on the table. Each child in turn is to pick up a card and pronounce the word. The child keeps it if he says the word correctly. Each child continues his turn until he misses a word or draws a sad face. The object is to pronounce correctly as many words as possible before drawing a sad face or missing a word.

4 **Spin and Win.** Sight word cards are needed for this activity. Direct the children to place cards face down on a table and spin a spinner or roll a die to see how many cards to pick up. One child picks up the cards and then reads the words to the others at the center. One point is given for each word read correctly. Unknown words are placed under the pile. The idea is to see which child can get the most words right on each turn.

5 **Help a Friend.** Make it possible for children to help each other at this learning center by having children who know some of the basic sight words flash the cards to students who are learning. If a child says the word correctly, he keeps the card. If he misses the word, the card is given to the person who is helping him. Direct the student who is helping to have the child look at the word as he says it and to trace the word while saying it, so the child actually does learn during the practice session.

6 **Word Hunt.** This activity requires that printed materials, such as magazines, newspapers, baseball cards, or some old books, be available at the learning center. Ask the children to circle those words they know. You can also write a Word Hunt Activity on the chalkboard. For example, tell the children to find 16 words in this line:

daddyouplayourunothemakeathisaididoutbathem

CONSONANT SOUNDS

What Children Should Learn

Consonants are all those letters of the alphabet except *a, e, i, o, u,* and sometimes *y*. The consonant sounds are generally taught before the vowel sounds because consonants usually are the first sound in a word, are more consistent in their sounds, and are more important to word identification than are vowels. Concerning the latter reason, notice that abbreviations are made up of consonants rather than vowels.

The 24 commonly accepted consonant sounds in the English language, along with a key word for each, appear as List 5. Notice that 18 of the consonants are represented by a single letter, whereas 6 are combinations of letters. *Ch, sh, th,* (voiceless), *th,* (voiced), *ng,* and *wh* are called consonant digraphs because two letters make up one new speech sound. Also, notice that *c, q,* and *x* do not have distinct sounds of their own.

List 5. The 24 Commonly Accepted Consonant Sounds in the English Language

b as in baby	ch as in chin	d as in did
f as in fit	g as in go	h as in hat
j as in job	k as in kind	l as in little
m as in mom	n as in not	p as in paper
r as in rat	s as in see	sh as in shell
t as in tie	th as in thin (voiceless)	th as in then (voiced)
v as in vase	w as in wax	wh as in whale
y as in yard	z as in zoo	ng as in ring

In addition to learning the sounds of the consonants, children learn the sounds of the consonant blends. Consonant blends are sounds represented by two or more consonants which are blended together to make one speech sound. Consonant blends differ from consonant digraphs in that the consonant sounds of the letters are blended together and do not form a new speech sound. Some common blends are *sc, st, bl, pl, tr, fr, fl, cl, gl, sp, sl, sm, sw, tw, sk, sn, dr, br, cr, gr,* and *pr*. Common three-letter consonant blends are *str, sch, thr, scr, spr,* and *spl*.

In addition to the consonant sounds, children should learn some generalizations concerning consonant sounds. The most frequently used rules for consonant sounds are:

1. When two alike consonants appear together, the first one is sounded and the second one is silent (e.g., *sitting, happy*).
2. Only the second consonant is heard in words like *gnat, write, palm, half,* *knee,* and *walk*. Sometimes a consonant is silent.
3. The first consonant is heard in words like *lamb, scent, sword, often,* and *ghost*. Again some consonants do not make a sound in the word.
4. The letter *s* represents different sounds: /s/ as in *sell,* /z/ as in *his,* and /sh/ as in *sugar*.
5. *Qu* has the /kw/ sound as in queen, or the /k/ sound as in *conquer*.
6. The consonants *c* and *g* have two sounds:
   - Usually *c* is /k/ in words like *care, coke, cube,* and other words where *c* is followed by *a, o,* and *u*.
   - Usually *c* is /s/ in *city, cent, cycle,* and other words where *c* is followed by *e, i,* and *y*.
   - Usually *g* is /j/ in *gem, giant, gypsy,* and other words where *g* is followed by *e, i,* and *y*.
   - Usually *g* is /g/ in *go, game, gum,* and other words where *g* is followed by *a, o,* and *u*.
7. The letter *x* represents three different sounds: /z/ as in *xylem* and *Xerox,* /ks/ as in *six* or *box,* and /gz/ as in *example* and *exit*.

Diagnosing Children's Knowledge of Consonant Sounds

The tests in Figures 21 and 22 can be used to determine students' knowledge of consonant sounds. In administering these tests, use the response sheet in the Appendix (Item 28) and direct

APPENDIX ITEM 28

the children to write the missing letters of the word you read. Notice that there are two tests. The first measures children's knowledge of each one of the consonant sounds. The second is designed to measure children's knowledge of common consonant blends.

When evaluating the children's responses, determine which specific sounds they need to learn. Also, informally determine whether or not the children know some of the generalizations or rules concerning consonants. For example, when you are working on /n/, you may be using some words such as *knead, know, knot,* and *knife*. If so, see if the children realize words beginning with *kn* have /n/ at the beginning because the *k* is silent.

The response sheet provided in the Appendix can be used for either test. Before administering either skill test, tell the children you have received two dozen pet rocks that need names. Part of each rock's name is written on the rock but part is missing. Read each name aloud and have the children write the letter or letters for the missing sound in the blank. Note that the missing sound occurs in the initial position in all items except the last /ng/ and /st/.

1. beg	13. cheg	7. veg	19. neg
2. heg	14. theg	8. reg	20. zeg
3. jeg	15. sheg	9. deg	21. feg
4. leg	16. seg	10. geg	22. keg
5. meg	17. yeg	11. theg	23. peg
6. teg	18. weg	12. wheg	24. ding

Figure 21. Consonant sounds test.

1. sk, sceg	13. smeg	7. treg	19. spleg
2. sneg	14. cleg	8. speg	20. streg
3. sweg	15. pleg	9. bleg	21. screg
4. fleg	16. creg	10. gleg	22. threg
5. sleg	17. greg	11. breg	23. preg
6. dreg	18. spreg	12. freg	24. dist

Figure 22. Consonant blends test.

Skill Group Activities for Teaching Consonant Sounds

1 When introducing sounds to children, tell them most letters in our alphabet make a sound in addition to having a name. You can use the letter *b* as an example. Write the letter *b* on the chalkboard and ask the children to tell you the *name* of the letter. Write some words the children know that begin with the letter *b*, such as *ball, bat, boy,* and *bed*. Tell them, "Now we are going to learn what the *sound* of the letter *b* is." Ask them to say the words with you or listen as you read the words to notice the first sound. As you read the words, say the /b/ very distinctly so the children can hear it. After you are through ask them what sound the letter *b* has. See if the children can think of more words that begin with /b/.

After the children can identify /b/, tell them you are going to say some words. If a word begins with /b/, they should raise their hands. If a word does not begin with /b/, they should

not raise their hands. Conclude the lesson by writing the letter *b* on the board and asking the children to name it and also tell you what sound that it makes. This can be done for all of the other symbols, but make sure you are not introducing more than one sound at a time. Key words you can use as examples in teaching the 24 consonant sounds appear in List 6.

2 Some children will remember the consonant sounds if you teach them to associate the sounds with common sounds in their environment. For example, when teaching /h/, you can refer to it as the sighing sound. Have the children sigh and then say some words that begin with /h/ to notice the similarities. The associations in List 7 are usually suggested.

List 6. Sample Words For Use in Teaching the 24 Consonant Sounds

b	ch	d	f	g	h	j	k
baby	chair	dog	fat	got	happy	job	cook
ball	chore	door	for	goat	how	giraffe	key
banana	cherries	day	feed	get	hot	jacks	cat
bath	chill	dinner	fit	give	help	jet	kid
belt	child	dish	five	gave	hold	joke	kitchen
bike	cheese	dollar	fast	gas	hand	jump	kitten
book	chocolate	down	fall	gold	had	just	come
bomb	chief	dad	few	go	hit	joy	call
boat	chat	did	foot	goose	hat	jingle	carry
by	chart	duck	fair	gun	hard	gentle	color

l	m	n	ng	p	r	s	sh
little	man	no	sing	pay	rat	see	shell
like	make	never	finger	paper	race	saw	shake
lie	mother	name	rang	paint	run	seven	shoot
lay	meet	not	thing	pack	rake	save	shoe
lady	made	need	hung	pet	red	sorry	shirt
less	money	new	bang	peach	rest	some	she
land	my	night	ping-pong	pepper	row	said	shut
library	move	note	hang	pie	rose	say	ship
line	meal	nut	sang	pig	rag	sat	sharp
listen	monster	now	ding-dong	poor	rub	sit	sheep

t	th	th (voiced)	v	w	wh	y	z
take	thin	then	vase	wash	what	yard	zap
tie	third	there	violin	waste	wheel	yellow	zebra
took	thing	they	vision	wait	when	year	zero
time	thumb	that	vein	water	where	yell	zig-zag
ten	thaw	this	velvet	we	which	yes	zip
table	thick	the	vent	went	why	yet	zipper
tea	thought	than	very	want	white	young	zone
tear	thousand	their	vest	way	whistle	your	zoo
touch	thermometer	them	vine	week	whisper	yo-yo	zoom
today	thank	though	visitor	well	while	yoke	zinc

List 7. Suggested Consonant Sound / Common Sound Associations

b— bubbling sound	v— motorboat sound
p— pipe sound	sh— quiet sound
m— humming sound	l— singing sound
w— windy sound	th— airplane sound
h— sighing sound	th— soft wind blowing sound
t— tickling sound	s— snake sound
n— motor sound	z— bee sound
k— coughing sound	r— growling sound
f— angry cat sound	j— loud train sound
d— knocking sound	g— gurgling sound
ng— ringing sound	ch— train sound

3 When teaching the consonant blends, the most important point to make to children is that sometimes two letters combine together to make only one sound. If children know this, they will not try to make a separate sound for each of the letters. Use the analogy that the letters that make up a consonant blend are the best of friends and, when they are together, they both speak at the same time. Instead of hearing two distinct sounds when they talk, only one sound is heard. This sound is a blend made up of a little bit of each sound. Again the technique of listing words or saying words that begin with a particular consonant blend is appropriate for teaching the sounds of the consonant blends. Sample words for common consonant blends appear in List 8.

4 In teaching children some of the rules concerning consonant sounds, make a list of words on the board in which the rule is followed. For example, if you are teaching the children that *k* is silent in *kn* combinations at the beginning of words, you might want to list words such as *knapsack, kneel, knee, knife, knight, knit, knob, knot, knock,* and *know* on the board. Tell the children to listen to the words as you read them. Then ask them what sound these words begin with. Help them notice that the *k* is not heard at the beginning.

The same teaching procedure can be used to teach children the different sounds of *c* and *g*. List words beginning with *c* and then ask the children to listen to the beginning sounds as you read the words. Help them notice that some of the words begin with /k/ while others begin with /s/. Tell them the second letter usually gives the clue as to whether the sound is that of /k/ or /s/. Help them draw their own generalization about when the *c* makes the /s/ sound and when it makes the /k/ sound. Make some nonsense syllables such as *cim, cet,* and *cus* so the children must apply the generalization. Finally, have the children find in their reading materials words that follow the generalization.

List 8. Sample Words for Use in Teaching Common Consonant Blends

bridge	cross	dress	friends	green	pretty
bread	creek	drink	fruit	grandma	present
brush	crowd	drum	frog	grass	proud
broom	crumbs	drugs	frozen	gray	product
brown	crying	driving	frightening	graph	president
trees	black	class	flower	plants	sleeping
train	blue	clothes	flies	planes	sleds
trick	blanket	club	flour	plates	slowly
trail	blocks	clock	flags	playing	slippers
treats	blinds	clown	floor	place	slick

spot	store	smile	snow	skates	swimming	straight	screen
sports	story	smoke	snakes	sky	sweater	string	screw
spoons	stop	small	snail	ski	sweeper	straw	scrubby
space	states	smooth	snap	skirt	swings	strap	scratch
spear	steps	smell	snicker	skunk	switch	stream	scribble

Learning Center Activities for Teaching Consonant Sounds

1 **Silly Pops.** This activity is bound to bring laughter as the children have fun creating words! Duplicate the worksheet (Appendix Item 29) and direct the children to make the popsicles look like their names. After doing so they can think of another name that begins with the same consonant blend.

2 **Surprise Box.** Get a small box and put some pictures of different objects in it. For example, you might have pictures of a shell, marble, lady, radio, TV, and toy. Direct the children to reach into the box and take out one of the pictures, name the object, and say another word that begins with the same sound. The children continue the activity until all the objects are out of the box. Encourage the children to find more pictures to put into the box.

3 **Toss the Block.** Regular alphabet blocks or small building blocks that have letters on them can be used for this activity. Direct the children to toss or roll a block, notice what letter comes up on top, and then say a word that begins with that letter. Two children or two teams can compete to see who can think of the most words.

4 **Bicycle Riding.** On a large piece of cardboard draw a bicycle path, bringing the path together so there is a start and a finish. Divide the path into blocks and print a symbol representing a different sound in each box. Direct the children to roll the die or spin a spinner to see how many squares they can move. As they move, they must read each sound along the way and give a word beginning with that sound. If a child

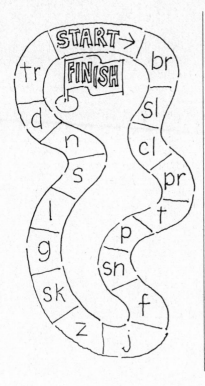

comes to a sound he does not know, he goes back to the space before it and listens to one of the other children say the sound. The game continues until someone reaches the finish line.

5 Soft and Hard Football. Use the **Touchdown!** game board (Appendix Item 26). Make 30 index cards with words beginning with the letter **c**, fifteen having the hard sound /k/ of **c**, and fifteen having the soft sound /s/ of **c**. The children divide into two teams, one called "soft" and the other called "hard." To begin the activity, the cards are shuffled and placed face down on the table. Direct the teams to take turns drawing a card from the pile and reading it. If the word has the soft sound of **c**, the football is moved 10 yards toward the goal of the soft team. If the word has the hard sound of **c**, the ball is moved 10 yards toward the goal of the

hard team. The first team to score a touchdown is the winner. Sample **c** words appear in Lists 9 and 10.

List 9. Sample Words for the Hard Sound /K/ of C

can	cold
cap	come
car	cob
cat	cup
came	cut
cow	cub
cot	curl
	cute

List 10. Sample Words for Soft Sound /S/ of C

cent	cigar
celebrate	circle
cement	city
center	cycle
cereal	cyclone
cider	cymbal
circus	cylinder
	cypress

SOUND PATTERNS

What Children Should Learn

Some sounds in the English language appear together frequently and produce a sound unit. For example, *all* is found in *ball, call, fall, gall, hall, mall, small, tall,* and *wall*. Some other common sound units are *it, at, et, en, in, an, ill, ell, un, ot, or, ake, ight,* and *ick*. Sound patterns are generally taught early in the reading program so children can learn many words quickly. If children know the consonant sounds and the sounds of these sound patterns, they can make hundreds of words.

Teaching sound patterns is different from teaching children to look for small words in big words. The latter practice is generally frowned upon because it is not reliable. In the word *father*, for example, a child can find the words *fat, the, he,* and *her*; yet these words are not likely to help the child figure out the pronunciation of *father*. Remember, a sound pattern is not a word in most instances, but letters that appear together so frequently that children should know them as a *sound unit* rather than trying to sound out each separate letter and then blend them together. If the child is trying to sound out the word *cat*, he must sound and blend three different sounds if he looks at each sound separately. Conversely, if the child is aware of the /at/ pattern, he will have to see and blend only two separate sound units, /k/ and /at/.

Diagnosing Children's Knowledge of Common Sound Patterns

A skill test is provided (Appendix Item 30) to determine what sound patterns different children know. Duplicate the test and tell the children that

APPENDIX ITEM 30

the pool balls are sad because they do not have numbers. Tell the children to look at the sound patterns written on the balls. Explain that you will say a sound pattern and tell them what number to write on the ball that has that sound pattern. They are supposed to find the sound pattern and write the number on the ball. Read the sound patterns and numbers found in List 11 by saying, "*Un* as in *sun* should be number 1. Mark it number 1."

List 11. Sound Patterns

un = 1	ill = 4	et = 7	in = 10	at = 13
an = 2	it = 5	all = 8	ot = 11	ell = 14
ick = 3	ake = 6	en = 9	ight = 12	or = 15

Skill Group Activities to Teach Sound Patterns

1 Explain to the children that some letters appear together so often they are called families. Give them examples of *a* and *t*. *A* and *t* make the word *at*, but they are also found in many other words such as *cat*, *that*, *sat*, *mat*, *gnat*, *fat*, *bat*, *hat*, *pat*, *rat*, and *that*. Tell them you are going to teach them what letters are families so when they see them they will be able to call them by their family name.

When teaching a sound pattern, ask the children if they can think of any words that rhyme with it. For example, if you are teaching the sound pattern /an/, they might mention *tan*, *Dan*, *than*, *man*, *pan*, *sand*, *can*, *fan*, *land*, *ran*, and *hand*. As the children mention the words, write them on the board. Then have a child come up and circle the sound pattern in each one of the words. Next, make some nonsense syllables with the sound pattern and

consonant sounds the children know. For example, you might make *wan*, *gan*, *tran*, and *jan*. In each instance, write these on the board and have the children blend the beginning sound and the sound pattern to form a nonsense word. Summarize this activity by having the children make a silly sentence using the sound pattern as many times as possible.

2 Write the name of one sound family on the chalkboard or a piece of paper. Say to the children, "I'm thinking of a word that belongs to this family" and then point to the sound pattern. "I'm going to tell the word to one of you, then all the others will have one turn each to guess what it is." Tell one child the word and then direct each other child to come up and write an initial

consonant sound in front of the sound pattern and say the word he has made. For example, if the sound pattern is *ell* and the child puts a *b* in front of it, he should say the word *bell*. If he guesses your "secret word," he gets a turn to write a sound pattern and tell someone else what his secret word is while the others try to guess it.

3 The idea of this activity is to have one child say a consonant sound and another child say a sound pattern, and then both children blend the two sounds together to make the word. For example, one child might say /b/ and the other child might say /at/, and then simultaneously they would say *bat*. This activity will teach children new consonant sound patterns and give them practice in blending as well.

Learning Center Activities for Sound Patterns

1 **New Words.** Reproduce and hand out Appendix Item 31. Direct the children to cut out the small squares containing letters and staple these to the left side of the larger rectangle, covering the letter **c**. Direct the children to turn back each letter square and read the new word that is made by combining each different initial consonant with the **at** sound pattern.

2 **Bowling.** Use Appendix Item 32 for this activity. Provide five chips for the children to flick at the bowling pins from behind the line. Each child flicks all five chips and then says a word containing the sound pattern on the bowling pins his

chips touch or rest on. He receives one point for each correct word. Chips not touching a pin or off the sheet do not count. The score can be kept in the grid provided on the activity sheet, and the person with the highest score wins.

3 **Word Wheel.** To make word wheels, direct the children to cut out two circles and fasten them together through the

center so they can rotate freely. One circle should be at least one inch larger in diameter than the other. The centers might be fastened with a brass brad. Write consonants on the larger circle and sound patterns on the smaller one. By rotating the circles, initial consonants can be combined with sound patterns to make words. After the children have experimented with their word wheels, direct them to make a list of the many words they can form.

4 Lucky Ducky. Two decks of 3" x 5" index cards are needed for this activity. On one deck of cards write consonants and consonant blends. The other deck should include cards that have sound patterns. Direct the children to place both decks side by side and to turn up one card in each deck. If the consonant sound and sound pattern make a word the player can read, he keeps those cards and takes another turn. If a word is not made, the cards are discarded in a separate pile and the next player takes her turn. The play continues until both decks are exhausted. The children should count the number of cards they have. The player with the most pairs wins.

5 Spill and Read. Some blocks with different letters of the alphabet on them are needed for this activity. You will also need a container, such as a large plastic milk carton or a clean bleach bottle, to hold the blocks. Direct the children to spill the blocks from the container and, without turning any blocks over, make as many words as they can with the letters showing on top. Count two points for two-letter words, three points for three-letter words, and so forth. As an additional challenge, use a timer to limit the word-making time. The child who gets the most points within a designated number of turns is declared the winner. Have the children keep a list of the words they are able to make for each turn so you can go over the words with them and point out some of the sound patterns they have made.

VOWEL SOUNDS

What Children Should Learn

Our English language has 44 sounds but only 26 letters in the alphabet; thus, some symbols must represent more than one sound. In general, it is the vowels *a, e, i, o,* and *u,* that represent more than one sound. The vowel sounds appear in List 12.

List 12. Vowel Sounds

Long Vowel Sounds	Short Vowel Sounds
a as in ate	a as in apple
e as in eat	e as in egg
i as in bite	i as in ink
o as in go	o as in octopus
u as in use	u as in us

Vowels Affected by R	Special Vowel Sounds
a as in are	oo as in tool
a as in care	oo as in book
er, ir, ur as in her, first, burn	oi and oy as in oil, boy
er, ir, as in here, irrigate	ou, ow, as in out, cow
or as in horn	schwa as in ago a go

Notice that, in addition to the long and short sounds, new vowel sounds are formed when the vowels precede the letter *r* as in *care, car, here, her,* and *horn.* Children learn that, when a vowel precedes *r,* it does not have a long or short sound, but rather it has a new vowel sound.

Two of the vowel sounds are called vowel diphthongs: the sound of *oi* as in *oil* and the sound of *ou* as in *out.* Here again the vowels are neither long nor short but rather the sounds *glide* together to produce a new vowel sound. We teach children that, when they see these letter combinations, they should not try to say the separate sound of each letter, but rather realize the two letters represent one sound.

The schwa sound is the vowel sound that is often heard in the unaccented syllable of a word. Each of the five vowels make the schwa sound in unaccented syllables as in dis*a*ppear, tel*e*gram, happ*i*ness, c*o*mply, and foc*u*s.

The only other vowel sounds then are the sounds of the double *oo.* The /oo/ makes the sound in *tool, zoo, too, choose, spoon, pool, soon,* and *room.* The short *oo* sound is /oo/ as in *book, took, stood, roof, cook, foot,* and *brook.*

Because there are so many vowel sounds, children must learn the generalizations or rules that help them know what sound the vowels have in different words. The following vowel rules are the ones most frequently applied.

1. When a word or syllable ends in a vowel (open syllable), the vowel sound is usually long, as in *he, go, be, fly, table, open,* and *vacation*.
2. When a word or syllable ends in a consonant (closed syllable), the vowel sound is usually short, as in *bad, hid, pat, fan, rit, sing, on, bet,* and *fat*.
3. When two vowel letters appear together in a one-syllable word or in an accented syllable, the first vowel often represents its long sound and the second is silent. This holds true most often of *ai, oa, ee,* and *ay* combinations as in *rain, boat, feet,* and *day*.
4. When a one-syllable word or accented syllable contains two vowels, one of which is a final *e,* the first vowel usually represents its long sound and the final *e* is silent as in *rake, bike, bone, ate, ride, use, place, parade,* and *name*.
5. The letter *y* functions as a vowel when it concludes a word having no other vowel (*try*), concludes words of more than one syllable (*daddy*), or follows another vowel (*day*).
6. If the only vowel in a word or syllable is an *a* followed by *w, ll,* or *u,* the sound of the *a* is usually /o/ as in *tall, law,* and *haul*. (Some dictionaries include *aw, all,* and *au* as another sound, thus indicating 45 sounds in the English language. Follow your school's list of sounds.)

7. When *i* is followed by *gh, nd,* or *ld,* as in *light, find,* and *child,* the *i* usually represents its long sound. The vowel *o* followed by *ld* usually has a long sound, as in *old, cold, told, bold, fold, gold, hold,* and *sold*.

Diagnosing Children's Knowledge of Vowel Sounds

The skill test in the Appendix (Item 33) can be used to determine if children know when vowels have their long or short sounds, or a different sound

APPENDIX ITEM 33

rather than long or short. The test contains words that represent each one of the 20 vowel sounds except the schwa sound. Tell the children that the Three Blind Mice have found some pieces of cheese and that they are to see which mouse can pick up the most cheese by writing the words with a long vowel sound on the Long Tail, the words with a short vowel sound on the Short Tail, and the words with neither a long nor a short vowel sound on the No Tail. Tell them to make a smiling face on the winner. In evaluating the children's responses, notice which sounds they are confusing and the vowel rules or generalizations they do not know.

Skill Group Activities for Teaching the Vowel Sounds

1 Begin working with a vowel sounds skill group by telling the children we have 44 sounds in our language. Ask them how many letters we have in our alphabet. Help them understand that some letters must have more than one sound. Tell them the vowels *a, e, i, o,* and *u* usually have more than one sound. Tell the children some of the vowel sounds are called short vowel sounds. You can explain that each vowel has a short vowel sound by saying the short sound of each vowel and a word containing that vowel sound. A good sentence to illustrate each short vowel sound is, "Fat Ed is not up."

Give the children an example of each sound using the letters *b-g* and saying each of the five short vowel

sounds. For example, you would say, *bag, beg, big, bog,* and *bug*. Have the children see how the word changes when a new vowel is used. Tell the children that, even though the sounds are called the "short vowel sounds," the word *short* has nothing to do with the duration of the sound. Some children erroneously believe when you say the short vowel sounds you say them very quickly, and when you say the long vowel sounds you drag them out.

After this introduction begin working on one vowel sound such as the short *a*. Tell the children to listen as you say many words having a short *a*. Some words you may want to use are: *bag, bat, bad, at, flag, dad, had, cab, brag, apple,* and *bad*. As you

say these words, blend the sounds slowly and audibly and then say the word naturally. Have the children say each word after you so they can produce as well as hear the short sound of *a*. Finally, ask the child what the sound is. A similar procedure such as that described above can be used to teach the sounds of the other vowels. Remember, it is not possible to teach all the vowel sounds in one easy lesson. Sample words you can use in teaching the short vowel sounds appear in List 13.

2 When introducing the long vowel sounds, tell the children the long sounds of vowels say their letter name. For example, we have /a/ as in *ate*, /e/ as in *eat*, /i/ as in *iron*, /o/ as in *old*, and /u/ as in *use*. Have the children listen to compare the short *a* to the long *a*, the sound of the short *e* to the long *e*, and so forth so they can realize the sounds are different.

Play a game such as "Thumbs Up" to see if the children can hear the long vowel sounds. Say many different words with long vowel sounds and have the children put their thumbs up if you say a word with a long vowel sound and put their thumbs down if you say a word without a long vowel sound. After pronouncing many words, tell the children to think of some words that have long vowel sounds. You can use the sample words in List 14. A sample sentence containing all the long vowels is, "Apes eat ices over Utah."

3 When teaching the sounds of vowels controlled by *r*, begin by telling the children the letter *r* is very bossy. This letter tells the vowel sounds to say a new sound that is neither long nor short. When a vowel stands in front of *r*, the *r* will not let it say the short vowel sound or the long vowel sound, but instead the bossy *r* tells the vowel to say a different sound. Give the children examples of the bossy *r* by listing the following words on the chalkboard and pronouncing them for the children: *far, for, her, fur, first, share.* Have the children tell the name the bossy *r* told each vowel to say. After the children realize the *r* is really a bossy letter, isolate one sound to teach them.

You may begin with the sound of *or*. Have the children listen to /or/ in each of the words you pronounce and suggest new words having this sound. When the children have mastered one of the sounds influenced by *r*, concentrate on another one. Sample words for each of the bossy *r* sounds appear in List 15.

List 13. Sample Words for Use in Teaching Short Vowel Sounds

short a	short e	short i	short o	short u
fat	bed	Indian	stop	up
mad	beg	fit	hot	us
add	egg	kid	pop	sun
fast	wet	pick	not	cut
black	west	is	on	rug
glad	end	in	off	bud
apple	step	his	October	much
back	chest	it	ox	tub
last	peg	sit	pot	pup
tan	set	mix	pod	but

List 14. Sample Words for Use in Teaching Long Vowel Sounds

long a	long e	long i	long o	long u
say	eat	like	open	cute
pay	feed	I	over	use
may	bee	bike	boat	bugle
rain	tree	by	soap	cue
ape	mean	mice	snow	blue
ate	east	die	row	rude
way	team	ride	coat	unit
pain	see	pipe	home	cube
take	seat	nice	rope	duke
day	beads	pie	goat	uniform

List 15. Sample Words for Each of the Bossy R Sounds

a as in car	a as in air
bar	air
car	fair
are	bear
hard	carry
farm	hair
tar	fare
scar	marry
far	tear
guard	barrel
heart	pair

e as in hear, irrigate	e as in her, first, burn	or as in horn
dear	earth	orange
fear	heard	for
gear	dirt	war
irrigate	fir	organ
irresponsible	her	more
near	burn	poor
deer	sir	sore
peer	jury	score
queer	skirt	tore
year	hurt	door

4 When teaching the diphthongs, tell the children sometimes when two vowels are together they like to sing a sound together. When they do so, they lose their original sounds and make a new sound. Tell them that *oi* and *oy* do this in such words as *oil, boil, toil, toy, soil, boy, joy,* and *voice*. Write these words on the board so the children can see the letters *oi* or *oy* represent this sound. Have them say /oi/ and think of other words with it.

When the children have learned /oi/, you can teach them the other diphthong that also consists of two letters: either /ou/ or /ow/ as in *cow* or *ouch*. Again say some sample words, such as *couch, cow, now, how, mouth, pound, house,* and *pouch*. Help the children realize that, when they see the letter combinations of *oi, oy, ow,* and *ou*, they should not try to say the short or long sound, but rather

realize the two letters represent a new sound.

5 When teaching a vowel rule, it is necessary to list many words to which the generalization applies. For example, if you are teaching children when two vowels appear together in a word or a syllable, the first one is usually long and the other one is usually silent, you might list the following words: *meat, bead, boat, soak, clean, sleep, day, cream, rain, team*. Ask the children to look at the words and listen for the vowel sounds as you pronounce the words. Tell them to look at the words to see how they are alike. If they do not notice the fact there are two vowels together, tell them or ask them what they notice about the position of the vowels in the words.

Say the words again and direct the children to say the words or listen to them to notice what vowel sound is heard. Exaggerate the long sound so they are sure to hear it. Help them notice that the first vowel is long and the other vowel is not

heard at all. Have a child come to the board and cross out the silent vowel and put the long mark over the first vowel. Ask the children to suggest some other words to which this generalization or rule applies. When you believe the children know the rule, write some nonsense syllables, such as *dain, maet,* and *seot,* on the board and see if they can say them applying the generalization.

Make an analogy to help the children remember the pattern. For example, you might say if two children came to your desk, the one who got there first would talk, and the other one would be silent. This is the same way when two vowels are together. The first one says its name, and the other one is quiet.

This teaching procedure can be applied to the other generalizations that were presented. The important steps are to (1) list many words to which the generalization applies, (2) give the children an opportunity to listen and look to find out what the pattern is, and (3) have them apply it by using some nonsense words or other words that are not familiar.

Learning Center Activities for Teaching Vowel Sounds

1 **Scat or Skate.** Duplicate the game board (Appendix Item 34) for this activity. Direct the children to throw a die to see how many spaces to skate. They must move as many spaces as indicated and then read the word on the space on which they land. If they cannot read the word, they scat back until they come to a word they can read. If a child lands on SCAT, he must move back as directed by the arrow. When a child lands on SKATE, he may move his token ahead as indicated by the arrow. In both instances, the child must read the word on the space or continue backward until he comes to a word he can read. The first one to land on the word WIN is the winner.

2 **Follow That Sound.** Duplicate the game board in the Appendix (Item 35). Direct the children to drop a button on the circle. If the button lands on LONG, the player moves his token to the first word that has a long vowel sound. If he lands on SHORT, he moves his token to the first word that has a short vowel sound. Likewise, if the child lands on DIPHTHONG, he moves his token to the first word with a diphthong. Finally, if a child lands on BOSSY R, he moves his token to the first word that has a vowel sound influenced by **R**. A player cannot cross the finish line unless his button lands on SHORT. You can make this game self-checking by providing a master list of words for each of the four categories.

3 **Go Fish.** Make a pack of 20 cards which includes 2 words for each of the short and long vowel sounds. For example you may want to use the following pairs:

    long a — play and say
    long e — cream and keep
    long i — like and pie
    long o — boat and go
    long u — cute and use

    short a — mat and tan
    short e — bed and red
    short i — bit and did
    short o — hot and top
    short u — bug and truck

This game is played exactly like the game of "Go Fish" except books are made of two cards with the same vowel sound. Direct the children to deal four cards, one at a time, to each player. The extra cards are spread out face down on the table. Each player then removes from his hand all the pairs (i.e., two cards on which the words have the same vowel sound). In doing so, she must state the vowel sound of each pair and read the words. To begin play, the dealer allows the player at his left to ask by sound for any card from any player. If the player who is asked has a word containing the sound, he must give it to the asker. If the player does not have the card, she tells the asker to "go fish" (i.e., take one card from the ones spread out on the table). Each player continues his turn if he can make a pair. The player with the most pairs is the winner.

4 Cross Out. Ask the children to take an article from a magazine, newspaper, or old book and cross out the vowels that are not heard in each word. For example, in words such as **speak**, **say**, and **chain**, the children would cross out

the second vowel. Ask them to bring their "cross outs" to the skill group and state the generalization or rule that applies.

5 The Magical E. Index cards (3" x 5") are needed for this activity. On the left half of the front of each card write a word that can be changed by adding an **e** at the end (see Figure 23). For example, words such as **hid, rid, rat, cut, past**, and

plan can be changed by adding a final **e**, thus making the vowel sound long rather than short. Fold over an inch wide vertical flap. On the folded flap (back of each card), write the letter **e**. Unfold the card. Direct the children to first read the word without folding the card, then fold the card so the **e** appears and read the new word. The children can make other word cards with words that follow the magical **e** rule.

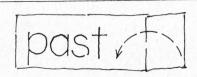

Figure 23. Magical **e** word card.

SYLLABICATION AND ACCENT

What Children Should Learn

When children attempt to sound out multisyllabic words that appear unfamiliar, they first must divide the words into syllables. If the "unfamiliar" word is in the child's speaking and listening vocabulary, she might be able to sound it out matter-of-factly without applying the rules for accent. If not, she must apply the generalizations for accent and later check her response by noting the pronunciation in the dictionary or by asking someone. The most common rules for *dividing words into syllables* are:

1. When a word contains two consonants between two vowels (vccv), the syllables are divided between these two consonants as in *yellow, donkey, runner, signal, ladder, tonsil, puppy, pencil, pretty*, and *lumber*.
2. When a single consonant is between two vowels (vcv), the consonant usually begins the following syllable as in *begun, motor, stupid, final, cement, label, human, music, unit*, and *silent*.

3. When a word contains prefixes such as *ex-* or *im-* or suffixes such as *-ly* or *-ness*, the prefix or suffix usually forms a separate syllable as in *exit, recite, unhappy, prepare, unkind, happiness, beautiful, useful, helpless*, and *foolish*.
4. When a word ends in *le*, the consonant immediately preceding the *le* usually begins the last syllable as in *purple, handle, paddle, jungle, table, apple, simple, candle*, and *bottle*.
5. Compound words are usually divided between their word parts or elsewhere if the word part has two syllables or more, as in *basketball, horseshoe, mailman, playhouse, butterfly, rainbow, tiptoe, earphone, football*, and *pancake*.
6. Consonant digraphs and consonant blends are considered as single consonants and are not divided, as in the words *machine, reply, children, enclose, anchor*, and *orchard*.

The most common rules children learn for *accenting words* are:

1. In a two-syllable word containing a double consonant, the accent usually falls on the first syllable, as in *happy* or *carrot*.
2. The accent usually falls on or within the root word of a word containing a prefix or a suffix, as in *return* or *useful*.
3. The accent usually falls on or within the first word of a compound word, as in *horseback* and *football*.

4. A final syllable containing a long vowel sound is usually accented, as in *parade* and *entertain*.

5. In a multisyllabic word ending in *-tion*, the primary accent falls on the syllable preceding the *-tion*, as in *vacation* and *satisfaction*.

6. When there is no other clue to accenting a two-syllable word, the accent most often falls on the first syllable as in *lumber* and *pencil*.

Diagnosing Students' Ability to Divide Words Into Syllables and Accent Syllables

The test provided in the Appendix (Item 36) can be used to determine if children can divide words into

syllables and mark the accented syllables. Direct the children to draw arrows to divide the words into syllables and use a bullet (dot) to indicate which syllable receives the primary accent. Notice that some of the words on this test are nonsense words. Nonsense words are used to see if children can apply the rules to words that are unfamiliar to them. In evaluating the papers, notice which generalizations the children can and cannot apply.

Skill Group Activities for Teaching Syllabication and Accent

1 The first step in teaching syllabication is to have the children hear how many syllables are in a multisyllabic word. Direct the children to clap their hands for each syllable they hear in words you pronounce. After they are able to do this successfully, see if they are able to tell how many syllables there are without clapping. When they can hear the syllables, tell them you are going to teach them how to divide words into syllables. Before going any further, ask the children why it is necessary to divide words into syllables. See if they realize that, before they sound out a word, they must divide it into the separate syllables. Also, if they do not have enough space to write all of a word on one line, they should break the word between syllables.

2 When working on some particular generalization for dividing words into syllables or identifying the accented syllables, begin by listing words that follow one principle. For example, if you are teaching children to divide the words between two consonants that come between two vowels (vccv), you can list the following words: *public, rescue, goblin, permit, winner, rabbit, dentist, picnic, summer, muffin, perhaps, lesson, after,* and *sudden.* Read the words to the children and ask them to notice how many syllables they hear in each one. Then say each word again and direct the children to pay attention to the last

sound of the first syllable. Ask the children to make slashes to indicate where the words are divided. Tell them to look at the words to see if they can make a rule or generalization concerning the vccv pattern. See if they can give you other words that follow the principle. Summarize the activity by teaching them the abbreviations of vccv and having them come to the board and mark the vowel, consonant, consonant, and vowel for each of the words. The vccv can serve as a mnemonic device to help them remember this generalization.

3 When introducing accented syllables, explain that, after words are divided into syllables, we need to find out which syllable we say louder or loudest. Say some words and ask the children to listen to see if they hear which syllable is louder. You might say: *always, welcome, sudden, happen, famous, eager, hotel, student, title, bundle, bugle, remember, vacation, necktie, suddenly, smiling,* and *slippery.* Help the children realize they already know something about accent because when they talk, they accent some of the syllables.

Discuss why it is necessary to learn more about accent marks. Help them realize that, when they come to a word they have never heard, they need to know which syllable is accented so they can pronounce it correctly. Provide examples with some words the children may not have in their speaking vocabularies,

such as *insinuation, skirmish, zenith, simultaneous,* and *torrential.* If the children locate these words in the dictionary, they will notice the accent mark; however, they will not have to rely on a dictionary as much if they are able to apply the generalizations.

4 When you are teaching children to divide words into syllables, review some of the vowel principles, such as those concerning open and closed syllables. This activity will help children develop a strategy of what they should do when they come to a word they do not know. You might want to make a checklist with them so that, when they are reading independently and come to an unfamiliar word, they can refer to the list to review the steps. The following steps might be listed:

1. Divide the word into syllables.
2. Notice the sound patterns as you try to say the sounds of each syllable.
3. Determine which syllable is accented.
4. Pronounce the word to yourself to see if it sounds familiar.
5. Skip the word and read the rest of the sentence to see if you can tell its meaning from the context.
6. Look for prefixes and suffixes that may help you understand the word.
7. Locate the word in the dictionary to determine its pronunciation and meaning.

Learning Center Activities for Dividing Words Into Syllables and Accenting

1 Syllabication Walk. Duplicate the game board in the Appendix (Item 37) and provide a deck of cards with words on them. Make a master list of the words indicating how many syllables each has and which ones are accented. Children play this game by shuffling the cards, placing them face down, and then, in turn, drawing a card from the pile. Each child moves his token as many spaces as there are syllables in the word on the card he has drawn. If the child is able to say which syllable has the primary accent, he moves an extra space. The object is to get to the finish line first.

2 Syllable Baseball. Draw a diagram of a baseball field and provide tokens to keep track of the runners. Make 60 word cards by writing the following one-, two-, three-, or four-syllable words on them. Also make 6 cards saying, "You are out." Direct the children to (1) shuffle the cards, (2) place them face down in a pile, (3) divide into two equal teams for the baseball game, and (4) follow the regular rules of baseball. The object of the game is to see which team can get the most runs by naming the number of syllables in the words. If a child turns up a card with a word of one syllable and correctly identifies it as such, he goes to first base. If the word has two syllables, he

goes to second base. Three-syllable words indicate a triple, and a four-syllable word is a homerun. If the child makes an error in saying how many syllables are in a word or draws a "You are out" card, he makes an out. After three outs the other team is up. Words that could be used for Syllable Baseball appear in List 16.

3 Mathematical Syllables. Make a list of five words and then draw a line below the five words as if they formed an addition problem. Direct the children to find out how many syllables are in each word and then add up the number of syllables in all five words. Have several lists of five or more words and see if the children can figure out which list has the highest syllable sum. Ask them to make some of their own problems by using their spelling words, glossaries in social studies or science books, or dictionary. You might start with

every	basketball
forever	school
nicely	wanted
returning	calendar
+ someone	+ coffee

especially	boy
many	is
for	daddy
gasoline	summer
+ sudden	+ little

4 War. Make word cards for this activity by writing a word the children are learning on each card. Direct the children to shuffle the cards and deal an equal number face down to each player. (This game is most successful if played by only 2 to 4 players. If more are to play, provide additional decks of cards.) This game is played as "war" in that each child turns up a card and compares it to another person's word to see how many syllables are in the word. The child whose word contains the most syllables takes the other players' cards. Make a master list of the words, indicating the number of syllables in each, so that the children can refer to it if necessary.

5 Haiku. During one of the skill group sessions, introduce children to the **haiku** by explaining it is a Japanese poem having three lines. The first line always has 5 syllables, the second line has 7 syllables, and the third line has 5 syllables. Read a **haiku** to the children such as:

Reading can be fun.
You learn so many new things.
You take lots of trips.

Direct the children to create their own poems and bring them to the skill group to read to the others. The children can listen to see if the number of syllables in each line is correct.

6 Quiz Show. The children can play a quiz game at the learning center if you make cards with the following questions concerning the number of syllables in words:

1. Who in our class has the most syllables in his name?
2. What game can you think of that has the most syllables in its title?
3. What city can you think of that has the most syllables in its name?
4. What kind of car can you name that has the most syllables?
5. What month has the most syllables?
6. What day of the week has the most syllables?
7. What number between 1 and 10 has the most syllables?
8. What color has the most syllables?
9. What food can you think of that has the most syllables?

Ask the children to bring their answers to the skill group. Tell them to make up some of their own questions for the quiz, also.

List 16. Words for Syllable Baseball

One Syllable	Two Syllable	Three Syllable	Four Syllable
is	very	another	impossible
will	about	evermore	considering
your	any	anything	nationally
when	little	yesterday	increasingly
from	before	misconduct	beautifully
which	other	government	ideally
give	again	different	
could	after	remember	
school	many	together	
think	upon	family	
say	into	company	
where	away	several	
bring	pretty	settlement	
why	never	afternoon	
thing	present	idea	
call	over	tomorrow	
warm	open	already	
start	study	important	

What Children Should Learn

Context clues provide readers with suggestions as to the meaning of a word that appears unfamiliar. This meaning is gained from the relationship of the unfamiliar word to the other words in the sentence or paragraph. Of course, it may also be necessary to apply phonics to make sure the word is correct. For example, if a child is reading the sentence, "Tell me _____ you did it," he may substitute *why* or *how* for the blank or unfamiliar word. When the child looks at the word and sees the /h/*ow*, he knows the word is *how* rather than *why*. Context clues, then, are used along with other techniques for word recognition to help children determine the pronunciation and/or meaning of words that appear unfamiliar.

There are different types of context clues: definition clue, synonym clue, familiar expression clue, contrast clue, and the mood or situation clue. The following descriptions illustrate each type.

Definition Clue. In some sentences the word that seems unfamiliar is defined later on in the sentence. For example, you might have the following: (1) The President *dictated* a letter by recording it on the tape recorder. (2) The *rationale* stated four reasons for doing it.

Synonym Clue. The unfamiliar word may be used along with a synonym that is familiar. The following sentences are examples: (1) The girl was joyful and *buoyant* with the victory. (2) The boy was *weary* and tired after walking so far.

Familiar Expression Clue. The unfamiliar word may be illustrated by using some familiar expression. For example: (1) It was *lucid* and clear as a bell. (2) He was *nimble* and as fast as lightning.

Comparison or Contrast Clue. The unfamiliar word is compared or contrasted with another familiar word as in the following sentences: (1) She was *loquacious*, but he was very quiet. (2) Her father was *pliable*, but Susan's father would not yield.

Mood or Situation Clue. The mood of the context can give the reader an idea of the meaning of some unfamiliar word: (1) The new father showed *anxiety* by pacing back and forth. (2) She showed her *animosity* by not speaking to the girl.

As you can see from these examples, context clues enable the reader to understand words that may be unfamiliar. At the same time, phonics must be applied to make sure the guess is appropriate. The importance of stressing a combination of word recognition techniques is clear.

Diagnosing Children's Skill in Using Context Clues

You can make paper-and-pencil tests to determine the students' use of context clues by selecting some material at the children's instructional levels and crossing out every fifth or seventh word. Ask the children to read the selections and then fill in the words they believe belong in the blanks. If the words they supply to complete the sentences are in line with the meaning of the selections, they are able to use context clues.

The following example is written at the third grade level according to Fry's Graph for Estimating Readability. Children who have a third grade instructional reading level would be directed to read the paragraphs and fill in the blanks with the words they believe belong. When evaluating the responses, give credit for words that are in line with the meaning of the missing words.

Jimmy and Jennifer live (with) their mother and daddy. (They) both wake up early (on) Saturday mornings. Each one (calls), "Mommy, daddy, time to (get) up." Then they wait (to) see if their parents (are) awake. Finally, their parents (get) up.

One morning Jimmy (and) Jennifer decided not to (call). They got up and (fixed) their own breakfast. They (ate) suckers, pretzels, and cake. (Then) they had pop to (drink). They ate some potato (chips) while watching cartoons.

Two (hours) later they cleaned the (kitchen) and then hopped back (into) bed. Both began calling (their) parents. Their parents finally (woke) up and said it (was) nice of the children (to) sleep late. Then they (asked) the children what they (wanted) for breakfast. Jimmy and (Jennifer) just laughed!

You can also learn much about children's use of context clues by not introducing all the new words in a story you are preparing the children to read. After the children have read the story or selection silently, go back to words in particular sentences and have them read the sentences orally and then tell the meanings of new words.

Skill Group Activities for Teaching Children to Use Context Clues

1 Give the children examples of how context clues can help them figure out words that might be unfamiliar. The example sentences for different types of context clues presented above can be used; however, it is not necessary to have children memorize the types of clues. Ask them why it is helpful to skip a word that seems unfamiliar and read the rest of the sentence or paragraph to get the meaning of the word. Also show them that phonics can help them know whether or not the word they selected is correct if they carefully notice beginning and ending sounds. Talk with them about the importance of using both context clues and phonics when trying to figure out words that seem unfamiliar. The following sentences can be used to illustrate the application of "mood" clues and phonics.

1. Tina fell down. She was ____t.
2. Chrissy lost a tooth. She was h____ because the tooth fairy might come.
3. Karen made a treat for her friends. They were gl____.
4. Jimmy saw a big snake. He was ____d.
5. Sally lost her ball and started to ____y.
6. Greg hit a homerun. He was ex____.
7. Jeff's bike was stolen. He was ____d at the person who took it.

2 Read a story to the children and every once in awhile leave out a word for them to fill in. In some instances, the word might be at the end of the sentence; in others, in the middle of the sentence. Read the rest of the sentence, and ask the children what the word should be. The children may want to take turns reading to each other in the same manner at the learning center if they enjoy the activity.

3 You can have the children make a booklet of familiar expressions entitled "People Say the Funniest Things." This activity will help them understand the meaning of some expressions that may be unfamiliar to them. It will also help the children use familiar expressions as context clues. Direct the children to write sentences using the following expressions as you discuss the meanings in the skill group. The children can have fun creating their own expressions, too!

as clever as a magician
as stiff as a starched collar
as rough as sandpaper
as sharp as a tack
as wrinkled as a prune
as graceful as a deer
as precious as your last dollar
as cool as a cucumber
as fast as a deer
as dry as a bone
as pretty as a picture
as fast as lightning
as quiet as a mouse
as sly as a fox
as black as the ace of spades
as white as snow

Learning Center Activities for Context Clues

1 **My "Guess What" Book.** The children might enjoy making their own mini-riddle booklets for others to read. Direct them to divide a sheet of paper into quarters and write one riddle on each quarter of the page. For example, they might write, "I am red. I have wheels. I carry hoses. I carry ladders. I am a ____." Ask the children to bring their booklets to the skill group to read to others. Discuss how the context provides the clues necessary to determine the word and relate this to using context clues when reading other materials.

2 **Lift Up.** A piece of tagboard or a file folder is needed for this activity. Write a paragraph leaving out every fifth word. In place of every fifth word, paste a piece of construction paper folded horizontally, with the missing word written inside. Direct the children to read the selection and try to supply the missing words. This activity is self-correcting in that the

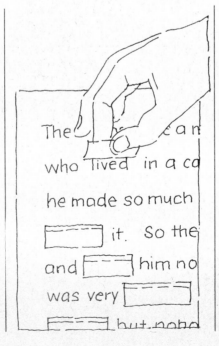

children can lift up the little piece of construction paper to see if they were right or wrong. The children will enjoy making "lift-ups" and will learn more about context clues as they prepare selections for others to read.

3 **What's the Word?** Take a magazine article or **Weekly Reader** article and black out the beginning or final letters of some of the words. Make a master list of the words that have been blackened. Direct the children to fill in the right words by using both context clues and phonics.

4 **Happy, Sad, or Straight.** Provide some old readers on which the children can write. Tell the children to read a story, select a paragraph in it, and then draw a happy face, sad face, or straight face by the paragraph indicating the mood. This activity will help children learn to detect the mood of the story which will in turn help them use mood or situation context clues. Tell them to be ready to read their favorite paragraph to other members of the skill group who will listen to determine the mood.

5 **Read On.** Provide reading materials at the children's instructional reading levels and ask the children to read using context clues when they come to a word that is unfamiliar. Ask them to write the words that appeared unfamiliar and remember the clues they used to determine the pronunciation and meaning of the words. Discuss their procedures and give suggestions when the skill group meets. Perhaps you will want to provide some specific sentences using the words that children are learning. The following are examples:

1. She got on her bike and went to _____.
2. Dogs like to _____.
3. They lived in the same _____.
4. The cat ate all the _____.
5. We like to _____.
6. It is fun to play in a _____ box.
7. Did you see the _____ at the zoo?
8. He was _____ when she called his name.
9. It is a _____ day.
10. Go in the _____ to get there quickly.
11. It is time to _____.
12. We heard it on the _____.
13. They like to talk into a _____.
14. We looked and looked and then gave up the _____.
15. Mother did not say _____.
16. Did you see it on _____?

school	furious	anything	swim
cardboard	rise and shine	beautiful	search
elevator	food	neighborhood	radio
bark	giraffe	microphone	television

STRUCTURAL ANALYSIS

What Children Should Learn

In addition to using phonics and context clues for word recognition, sometimes children can figure out words that seem unfamiliar by noticing their structure. For example, a compound word may seem unfamiliar to the child because of its longer and different shape; however, if the child analyzes the words that make up a compound word, he may be able to say and understand it. Our task, then, is to teach children to look at the "unfamiliar" word to see if it consists of two words they already know.

Contractions and possessives are also a part of structural analysis because the structures of words are changed with the added apostrophe or omitted letters as in contractions. As simple as this may seem to adults, the child who does not recognize "they're" as a contraction, but rather tries to blend it together, may encounter difficulty. Children should learn that some letters have been omitted from contractions so it is not possible to sound them out. Likewise, children must learn that not all words with apostrophes are contractions. Apostrophes are also used to show possession and thus aid comprehension if the reader recognizes them as clues.

Prefixes, suffixes, and inflectional endings also change the structure and meaning of words and therefore may make them seem unfamiliar. Children should learn to look for these and should know how they change the meaning of the root word so that they can recognize words that initially appear unfamiliar. Some of the most frequently used prefixes, suffixes, and inflectional endings appear in List 17.

Diagnosing Children's Knowledge of Structural Clues

A skill test is provided in the Appendix (Item 38) to determine if the children are aware of the different structural clues. The children are directed to look

APPENDIX ITEM 38

at the cars and the four garages and then decide which cars should go to which garages. They then write the words that belong on each garage. Evaluate the different parts of the test separately. You may find some children are aware of contractions, but need further help on compound words and affixes. Keep this in mind as you meet with the skill group on structural analysis.

Prefixes	Meaning	Sample Word	Suffixes	Meaning	Sample Word
ab-	from, away	absent	-able	that can be	portable
ad-	to	adjoin	-ance	act of	disturbance
be-	by	beside	-ant	one who	assistant
com-	with	compile	-ence	state of being	indifference
de-	from	depart	-ent	one who	president
dis-	apart, not	disbelief	-ful	capable of being	hopeful
en-	in, into	encircle	-less	without	painless
ex-	out of, from	exit	-ment	state or condition	amazement
in-	into, not	insecure	-ness	state of quality of being	kindness
pre-	before	preview	-ship	office status or rank of	assistantship
pro-	in front of, toward	project	-tion	act, state or condition	action
re-	back	rebound	-ward	tending or leading to	homeward
sub-	under	submarine			
un-	not	unhappy			

Common Inflectional Endings	Sample Word
-s	works
-ing	working
-ed	worked
-er	worker
-est	latest

Skill Group Activities for Structural Analysis

1 Ask the children if they know some "pencil saver words" in our language. Lead them to realize contractions are "pencil saver words" because in writing contractions some letters are left out and an apostrophe is added to make one word that means the same as two words. Write on the board the contractions the children can name or use in their oral language. For example, you might write *we're, she's I'll*, and *you're*. Ask the children if they can find the missing letters and name the two words included in the contractions. Have them use the contractions in sentences to make sure they understand the meanings. Summarize the lesson by asking the children how they can recognize contractions when reading and why this is important to them.

2 Ask the children if when reading they see some long words they do not know. Tell them one way to figure out the long words is to look at them and see if they are made up of two words. Again, give the children some examples of words that you are sure are part of their speaking vocabulary, such as *airplane, outside, summertime, everywhere, basketball, policeman, popcorn, grandmother, raincoat, horseback*, and *doorway*. Write the words on the chalkboard, read them, and then have the children circle each part of the compound word. Ask the children if they can think of other words that are compound words.

Make a set of flash cards with compound words and divide them by cutting zig-zags between the two words. Shuffle the cards and give one piece to each child. Direct each child to find the person whose card fits with his to make a compound word. Have the children say the words and use them in sentences. Summarize the lesson by asking the children what they should do when they see a long word that seems unfamiliar.

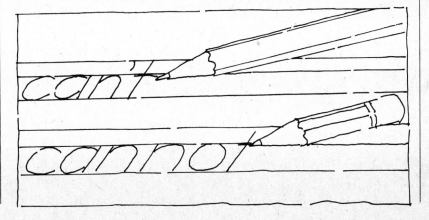

3 Tell the children some words in our language are made by adding a syllable at the beginning of another word. This syllable changes the meaning of the other word. Again use some of the words from the children's speaking vocabularies, such as *return, unhappy, unfair, unload, disobey, untrue, uneven, reread, rewrite, redo, defrost, dishonest,* and *disappear.* Use each one of the words in a sentence and discuss the meaning of the prefixes and root words. Lead the children to understand how the prefixes change the meaning of the words. Ask the children to suggest other words with prefixes. Summarize the lesson by asking them what can be done when they come to a word they do not know. Help them realize they should look to see if there is a syllable at the beginning that makes the word look unfamiliar at first glance. They may be able to recognize the prefix and root word and thus be able to pronounce and understand the word.

4 Tell the children sometimes there are syllables at the ends of words, rather than at the beginning, which may make the words look different or unusual. List some examples on the board, such as *working, sadness, beautiful, sleepless, cupful, fearless, careless, useless, harmless, careful, kindness, slowly,* and *eater.* Have the children use the words in sentences to make sure they understand the

meanings. After doing so, direct the children to circle the syllables at the end of the words which change the meaning of the words. Introduce some other suffixes to the children with sample words. Summarize the lesson by helping the children see the purpose of looking at the endings of words to see if this gives them a clue to the word.

5 Write on the board some sentences that contain possessives, such as *boy's, cat's,* and *teacher's.* See if the children can tell you why there are apostrophes in these words. If they cannot discover that the apostrophe shows ownership or possession, tell them so. Then go back to each sentence and see if they can tell you what each person owns. Have the children make other sentences with possessives. Also, have them circle the apostrophes so they can be looking for this when they meet words that seem unfamiliar in their reading.

Learning Center Activities for Structural Analysis Clues

1 Movin' On. This game can be played by two to four players and requires the game board in the Appendix (Item 39). Each child uses four tokens of the same color and occupies a certain corner. The object of the game is to move each token around the board and return it to the home position. Direct the children to spin the spinner and move one token as many spaces as indicated. If the player lands on a word, she must pronounce it and use it in a sentence. If she cannot do so, she returns to start. The first player to move all of her tokens home is the winner.

2 Circle the Endings. Provide some newspapers, magazines, or other printed material for this activity. Direct the children to circle the endings of words, such as **-ed**, **-ing**, or other inflectional endings and suffixes they are learning. The children can bring their words to the skill group to show how the added ending has altered the meaning of the

word in addition to changing its structure.

You can adapt this activity by having the children make a mini-book entitled "The Ends." They can devote a page to different endings, i.e., the children might have an **-ing** page where they write in those words that end with **-ing**. Have them find words from their reading to write in their booklets.

3 Draw, Man, Draw. A deck of 40 cards on which are written the words from List 18 is needed for this activity. The object of the game is to make books by getting all four cards that have the same inflectional ending or suffix.

Direct the children to shuffle the cards, deal four to each player, and place the remainder of the deck face down on the table. Each player in turn asks any other player for words with a particular inflectional ending or suffix he is already holding. For example, a child may ask another player for his **-ing** words if the asker has at least one **-ing** word in his own hand. If the player does not hold a card with a word having the inflectional ending or suffix requested, he must give it to the asker. If not, he tells the asker to "draw, man, draw." The asker then draws a card from the top of the deck.

Players continue their turn until they do not get or draw the card they are seeking. When a player has four cards with the same inflectional ending or suffix, he puts them down in front of him in book form. The winner is the person who has the most books at the end of the game.

4 What's My Name? Write the following definitions and direct the

---

List 18. Sample Words for Draw, Man, Draw

-ing	-es	-ed
looking	dashes	asked
staying	peaches	rained
fishing	churches	painted
sleeping	glasses	played

-er	-s	-est
longer	drops	funniest
later	apples	happiest
funnier	stars	biggest
thicker	hats	saddest

-ful	-ly	-less
painful	quietly	careless
hopeful	gladly	harmless
careful	nearly	boneless
playful	softly	sleepless

-ness
sickness
neatness
darkness
goodness

---

children to make up compound words that could replace each one.

1. A box for mail
2. A bag filled with beans
3. What we wear under our clothes
4. A ball that goes through the basket
5. A ball that you kick with your foot
6. A board that you can put cups on
7. A man made out of snow
8. A case to hold books
9. A man who fights fires
10. A hole for a key
11. A board you can write on with chalk
12. A room for storing goods
13. A boat used as a house
14. A plane that goes into the air
15. A tie that goes around someone's neck

5 Transformed. Have each child draw a picture illustrating a root word and then draw another picture illustrating the same word with a prefix. For example, one child might draw a picture of a happy person and then make another picture showing an unhappy person. After doing so, have them write the key word below the picture. Post the pictures on a bulletin board to show how a prefix can change the meaning of the word.

DICTIONARY SKILLS

What Children Should Learn

If all other methods of word recognition fail, children need to realize they can use the dictionary to find the pronunciation and/or meanings of a word that is unfamiliar. Most elementary school children do not frequently use this technique for word recognition because it interrupts the reading process for a longer period of time. The child has to locate the glossary or a dictionary, and then employ many skills to find the word and determine pronunciation and meaning.

Children need to know alphabetical order, what quarter of the dictionary the word will most likely be in (first quarter, *a-d* words; second, *e-l*; third, *m-r*; and fourth, *s-z* words), how to use guide words, how to use the pronunciation key, and how to select the appropriate meaning. Using the dictionary, then, consists of many skills rather than simply one skill. Our task is to help children develop these skills so using the dictionary to find

the meaning or pronunciation of a word is not a laborious task.

Diagnosing Skill Needs in Using a Dictionary

A four-part skill test (Appendix Item 40) is included for this assessment because there are many skills involved in using the dictionary. Separate

APPENDIX ITEM 40

parts are presented for (1) knowing the quarter of the dictionary, (2) using guide words, (3) interpreting diacritical marks, and (4) alphabetizing words. Directions for administering each part are presented at the beginning of the test. Consider the results of each test separately when evaluating the papers so you will know what dictionary skills to emphasize.

Skill Group Activities for Teaching Children to Use the Dictionary

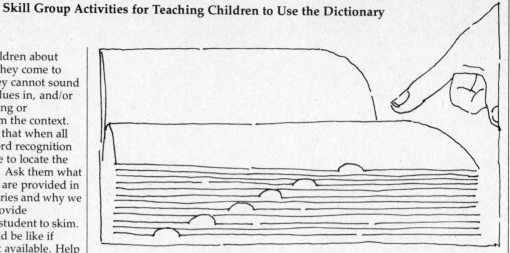

1 Talk with the children about what they can do if they come to unfamiliar words they cannot sound out, find structural clues in, and/or determine the meaning or pronunciation of from the context. Lead them to realize that when all these methods of word recognition fail, they may be able to locate the word in a dictionary. Ask them what kinds of information are provided in dictionaries or glossaries and why we have dictionaries. Provide dictionaries for each student to skim. Discuss what it would be like if dictionaries were not available. Help them realize they would have to be very dependent upon other people if dictionaries did not exist. Tell them you know some good tips for locating words quickly which you will share in the group.

2 Teach the children why words are arranged in alphabetical order and why guide words and pronunciation keys are used by distributing dictionaries and then asking the children to find a particular word. Ask them how they could ever find a word if the words were not arranged in alphabetical order. Have them notice that guide words are at the top of the page to make it easier to locate the desired word rather than having to look at the first and last word on each page. Ask them to check a few pages to see if the guide words really indicate the first and last words on particular pages. List words to locate by using the guide words.

Have the children notice the pronunciation key and the fact that key words are given so they will know what sounds to say for the different diacritical markings. Use the pronunciation key to check the pronunciation of some word that is already in the students' speaking vocabulary. Have them notice how the word is divided into syllables, the way the accented syllable is marked, and the way the different sounds are marked. Ask them why a pronunciation key is included on every other page of the dictionary and why the words are marked according to their sounds. It is only when children realize these are dictionary *aids* that they will begin to use them.

Learning Center Activities to Help Children Learn Dictionary Skills

1 **The Champion Is _____?** Duplicate Appendix Item 41. The children will find out who the champion is by seeing which player (Before, On, or After) gets the most words. In doing so, they must decide what words would be before, on, or after a page in the dictionary which has the guide words **pear** and **rest**. The children may enjoy changing the guide words to see if another character can win.

2 **The Winner Is _____.** Provide dictionaries and a set of word cards for this game. Shuffle the word cards and place them face down on the table. Have each child choose a number from which to start. Turn one word card up. Each player tries to find the word on the card as quickly as possible in the dictionary. The player who finds the word first puts an **X** on his first square. The first player who gets 6 **X**'s is the winner.

3 **Fool Me.** Provide some letters and ask the children to put them in alphabetical sequence. While the other children close their eyes, have one child rearrange a letter. Tell the other children to open their eyes and try to determine which letter was rearranged and is out of sequence.

4 **Private Eye.** Provide newspapers or old magazines and ask the children to find the first **a** they see in print. After doing so, they should look for the first **b** that follows the **a** and circle it. They continue until they have circled every letter of the alphabet in sequence. You may want to make a ditto master for this activity.

5 **First, Second, Third or Fourth?** Prepare four index cards by writing A-D on one, E-L on another. M-R on a third, and S-Z on the last one. Turn the cards over and write **1st**, **2nd**, **3rd**, and **4th**, respectively. Provide cards with words and ask the children to determine what quarter of the dictionary they would open to locate each word. The children can indicate their responses by placing the words under the numbered index card indicating the quarter of the dictionary: first, second, third, or fourth. Direct them to check their answers by turning the numbered index cards over and comparing the beginning letters of their words with the letter sequences suggested on the cards.

6 **Would You?** Provide practice in having the children use the dictionary to look up new vocabulary words by making sentences that include new words. The children will be motivated to find the meaning of the word if you put each new word in a sentence with "would you." The following sentences might be used:

1. Would you like to be an imbecile?
2. Would you like to have an oculist check your hearing?
3. Would you vote for a shyster?
4. Would you like a tapir for a pet?
5. Does ice cream tantalize your taste buds?
6. Would you like to be a drover?
7. Would you like for your teacher to boggle you?
8. Would you like an aster?
9. Would you put balm on a cut?

7 **It Sounds Like?** Write a list of words down the left-hand column of a piece of tagboard or a file folder. Write the respelling of the words as they would be found in the dictionary in a different sequence down the right-hand column. Write the answers on the back of the folder if you want the children to correct their own work. Laminate the tagboard or folder and provide a grease pencil. Direct the children to use the grease pencil to draw lines from the words in the left-hand column to their respellings in the right-hand column.

It Sounds Like?

Directions: Match the words and their respellings. Use the grease pencil. Check your answers with those on the back.

Words	Respellings
drastic	drēm
drain	drūp
drama	drĕd
dream	drän
dribble	'dram ə
drupe	'dras tik
dread	'drib əl

COMPREHENSION SKILLS

Just as there are many word recognition skills, there are numerous comprehension skills. The first section in this chapter concerns *main idea*. Children will be better able to understand what they read if they can organize their thoughts into some frame of reference. Of course noting the main idea also aids when outlining or briefly telling others about what has been read.

The next section deals with helping children identify *significant details*. Notice the adjective "significant" because children encounter many details as they read; however, not all details are equally relevant to their understanding of the selection. The fact a boy was wearing a red shirt may be significant in a story in which a boy meets a bull and insignificant in some other story. If children can develop skill in noting and remembering the most important details, comprehension will improve.

Sequence of events is the comprehension skill presented in the third section of this chapter. Being aware of the order in which events occurred is very important when comprehending selections concerning history, adventure, science, and directions for completing a task.

The fourth section of this chapter concerns *drawing conclusions*. Comprehension is better when the reader is able to organize facts and realize why certain events are taking place. Reading is a thinking process that requires the reader to look for cause-and-effect relationships. Children must be able to find reasons for particular actions as they read.

Another goal of the elementary school reading program is to teach children not to believe every-thing they read, but rather to *evaluate critically*. Children must learn to separate fact from fiction, evaluate the authenticity of facts, recognize propaganda techniques, and be aware of the author's motives. A child who literally accepts everything he reads is comprehending at a very low level. Higher level comprehension skills involving judgment are desirable.

A special section of this chapter is devoted to *vocabulary* because vocabulary is the most important factor in comprehension. It has been said that 60% of comprehension is accounted for by vocabu-

lary or word meaning. In order to get meaning, the child must learn to associate words and the concepts they represent. If one's vocabulary is meager, comprehension is certain to be a problem.

The seventh section of this chapter deals with *rate of comprehension*. With so many reading materials available today, there is pressure to help children improve their reading rates. The emphasis in this section, however, is not on helping children develop a fast rate of reading, but rather on enabling them to be flexible in adjusting their rate to the nature of the material. If children learn to employ a flexible rate, their comprehension will be improved.

The final section of this chapter concerns *oral reading* so others can *comprehend*. Oral reading skills are included in this chapter about comprehension because, when children or adults read orally, their main responsibility is to read the selection so the audience gets meaning from it or comprehends it. Also, oral reading sometimes aids the reader's comprehension. For example, consider the situation when you are trying to follow complicated directions. You may read the directions silently first, but if you do not understand them you may read them again aloud. Hearing the directions may help you comprehend. At the same time we should remember that reading orally may also hinder comprehension if the reader is overly concerned with ''sounding good'' rather than getting meaning.

Diagnosing students' comprehension skills is not as clear-cut as assessing word recognition techniques because children continue to work on the same aspects of comprehension as they read different levels of material. For example, both a first grader and a sixth grader are concerned with getting the main idea of the selection they are reading. If a first grader is able to state the main idea of a first grade reading selection, there is no guarantee that he will retain this skill as he moves to higher level reading material.

It is important then to know the reading level of the material being used to determine the students' comprehension skills. A Comprehension Skills Test is provided in the Appendix which includes selections from the first through sixth grade levels (Items 43-48), along with questions to measure particular comprehension skills. In addition, lists of sample questions designed to assess students' accomplishment of certain comprehension skills are presented in each section in this chapter. Teachers are encouraged to select materials at particular reading levels and then adapt the key questions to the selections in addition to using the Comprehension Skills Test.

When evaluating students' comprehension skills, try to determine what particular aspects of comprehension are hindering the students. You will find some children are fantastic at identifying significant details, but cannot state the main idea and thus may have a difficult time organizing the information they glean. Other children will be able to state the main idea, but will not be able to relate the sequence of events. Notice these specific weaknesses in comprehension as you continually evaluate each child's responses to questions. Do not rely exclusively on a test having only one question for each skill, as does the Comprehension Skills Test.

You will notice the directions for keeping records of students' comprehension skills on Appendix Item 1 are a little different from those for other parts of the record-keeping chart. You are to indicate the highest reading level at which the student was able to use each skill satisfactorily by writing the grade level by the child's name and under the skill. For example, if a student was able to recognize main ideas when reading third grade level materials, but not while reading fourth grade materials, write a 3 in the ''main idea'' category. By looking at the chart, you will be able to see the particular strengths and weaknesses in comprehension according to reading levels.

In determining skill groups, you can consider both skill needs and reading levels. Some teachers successfully work with many children, regardless of reading level, who need help with a particular comprehension skill, such as identifying the main idea. Of course, these teachers use different levels of materials as they work with the skill groups and make many levels of materials available at the learning center. Other teachers prefer to emphasize the particular comprehension skills needed by students who are reading at the same instructional level. Likewise, some teachers prefer to have one learning center for comprehension rather than several separate ones based on the different comprehension skills. If this is your desire, simply read the suggestions for learning activities for the various comprehension skills, and combine those you like and your children need at a reading comprehension center.

APPENDIX ITEMS 43-48

Using the Comprehension Skills Test

The Comprehension Skills Test (Appendix Items 43-48) consists of six graded selections, one from each grade level from first through sixth according to Fry's Graph for Estimating Readability. All of the selections concern dogs because nearly all children have had many experiences with dogs. Each selection is followed by six comprehension questions, one for each of the major comprehension skills. *The first question is designed to see if students can determine the main idea; the second, significant details; the third, sequence of events; the fourth question is to see if they can draw conclusions; the fifth is for vocabulary, and the sixth, for evaluating critically.* The purpose of the Comprehension Skills Test is to provide the teacher with sample selections that can be used to gather information concerning the comprehension skills. The test is not designed to be used in isolation, but rather only as one means of gathering information concerning the comprehension skills children possess.

The Comprehension Skills Test can be administered individually or in a group situation. To administer it as an *individual* test, follow these directions:

1. Make sure you can spend 15 minutes with the student in a quiet place.
2. Tell the student you want to determine how well he can understand what he reads. To do so, you are going to ask him to read some stories about dogs, and then you will ask him some questions.
3. Begin by reading the motivation statement to the child. Then have him silently read the selection two years below his present grade level.
4. When the student has completed the silent reading, ask the six comprehension questions orally.
5. If you want to determine skill in word recognition, you can ask the student to read the selection orally. Notice if the child recognizes at least 95% of the words (he should miss no more than 1 in 20 consecutive words). Make a check mark over any words the child misses, does not know, or omits, and where the child inserts words. As the child is reading, observe his reading habits using the oral reading skills checklist (Figure 27 on page 82).
6. Continue having the child read the different selections until he misses two questions on any one selection. If the child misses two questions on the first selection you ask him to read, drop back to an easier selection.
7. Analyze the child's responses to determine the highest level at which he is able to answer the different types of questions. Combine this information with the other observations you have and then record the highest levels at which the child is typically able to answer different types of comprehension questions. For example, if the child is able to answer questions for significant detail at the second, third, and fourth grade levels, but generally cannot answer such questions with fifth or sixth grade materials, record a 4. You would then select material at the fourth and fifth grade levels to work with him on that particular comprehension skill.

To administer the Comprehension Skills Test to a *group*, follow these directions:

1. Have two 30-minute periods available for the test. In addition, suggest activities for children who finish earlier.
2. Explain to the students that you want to determine how well they understand what they read. Tell them you are going to give

them some stories about dogs and then will ask them to answer some questions concerning these stories.

3. Distribute the test sheets to the students. Administer the first three graded selections at the first sitting. Read the motivation statements for each selection, and direct the children to read the selections and write answers for the questions.
4. Observe the students to notice their silent reading habits and attitudes toward the task.
5. Administer the second part of the test (levels 4 through 6) only to those children who do not miss more than two

comprehension questions on the third grade selection. Of course this part of the test would be administered at a separate sitting.

6. Check the papers to find out what questions the children missed on the different levels. Record the highest level at which the students were able to answer correctly the different types of questions. Again combine this information with your other observations. Keep in mind that this test is only a sample of behavior, and that it will be necessary to evaluate the children's comprehension skills continually by using the sample questions provided in each section of this chapter.

MAIN IDEA

What Children Should Learn

Many times children read to get the gist or main idea of a selection. Main ideas are especially important when developing a purpose for reading and when summarizing information after reading. If the reader only notices details, he has a difficult time organizing his newly acquired knowledge or information into some usable form. The task of the teacher, then, is to help children identify the central or main idea of their reading selections.

Diagnosing Children's Skill in Identifying the Main Idea

After selecting paragraphs at the children's instructional levels, you can ask some or all of the following questions to determine if the students can find the main idea of a reading selection:

1. Can you summarize the story with one word?
2. What would be a good title for this story?
3. What kind of story was this?
4. Have you read any other selections that were similar to this one? How were they similar?
5. What is the most important sentence (in a particular paragraph)?

If a child seems to respond only with significant details rather than with the main idea, you will realize the need to provide special instruction on determining main ideas.

Skill Group Activities for Teaching Children to Identify Main Idea

1 You might begin this skill group by telling the children that sometimes when we read, we just want to get the major idea of the paragraph or selection. We do not want to notice every fact, but rather simply to find out what the story or selection is about. Other times, when the facts are important, we still need to know the main idea so we can briefly tell others what we have read. For example, if you wanted to quickly tell someone the story about the "Gingerbread Boy," you would not want to tell where he ran and who chased him, but rather the major thought of the story. Help the children understand what main idea means by showing them a picture and asking them to tell you in one word what the picture is about. Compare their ability to identify the main idea and to note significant details by then having them notice the details in the picture. Tell the children this group will be working to determine the major ideas of different paragraphs and stories.

2 Direct the children to discover that many times authors state the main idea of a paragraph when they write. Explain that usually the first sentence of the paragraph tells what the selection is about. The other sentences then provide facts or details about the first sentence. Have the children look at *Weekly Readers* or some other written materials to see how often this is true. They might diagram this method of writing by writing the topic sentence in a long box and then putting the supporting details in smaller boxes beneath it (see Figure 24).

3 Direct the children to notice that topic sentences can also be found in the last sentence in the paragraph. Again you can have them look at sample selections to see where the topic sentence is located if indeed there is one. Have the children diagram the two different types of paragraphs by using triangles. If the topic sentence is the first sentence of the paragraph, they can illustrate this with a triangle in which the base line is at the top ▽. The base line stands for the topic sentence. The narrowing of the triangle indicates the supporting details. Conversely, if the topic sentence is the last sentence of the paragraph, the base line of the triangle is located at the bottom of the traingle △. In this case the author begins with some significant facts that lead to the main idea of the paragraph. Have the children find the two different types of paragraphs in their reading materials. Extend this knowledge by having the children write paragraphs together. Write one paragraph using a topic sentence at the beginning and then giving details. Write another paragraph by beginning with details and concluding with a summary.

4 The children might enjoy reading or writing a selection together and then making a movie or mural showing the major events in the story. This activity provides practice in finding main ideas because the children must identify the major events of the story. A "television set" can be made to show the movie by using a cardboard box, shelf paper, and dowel rods.

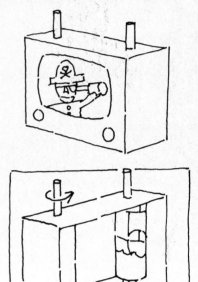

Figure 24

The children in Miss Thompson's class do many different things during the week. Sometimes they have fun doing science experiments. On Wednesdays they have a special art teacher. The children can go to many learning centers to read, play games, and make things during the week. On Friday they get to play bingo.

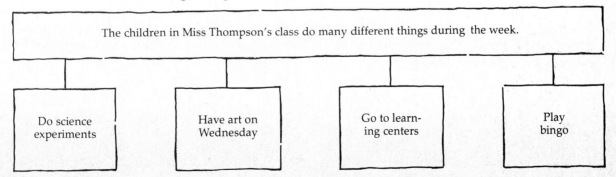

The children in Miss Thompson's class do many different things during the week.

| Do science experiments | Have art on Wednesday | Go to learning centers | Play bingo |

Learning Center Activities to Help Children Identify Main Ideas

1 **Category Tic-Tac-Toe.** Duplicate Appendix Item 49. Direct the children to play this game the same as regular tic-tac-toe, but before they can put an **X** or **O** on a space, they must be able to name the categories (school supplies, furniture, food, sports, TV programs, living things, toys, buildings, and fruit) and name one more item that belongs in that category.

2 **On My Hand.** You can provide more practice in identifying the main idea by asking children to read certain selections, draw around one of their hands, and then write the main idea on the palm and a supporting detail on each finger. The children can bring these to the skill group to share with others.

3 **Give Me a Name.** Provide some pictures and titles for the pictures at the learning center. Direct the children to match each picture with the correct title. If you write the same number on the back of a picture and on its title, the activity will be self-correcting. Encourage the children to look in magazines for other pictures and then write titles for them.

4 **Newspaper Headlines.** Have the children cut out some articles from their **Weekly Reader** or the regular newspaper and cut off the titles or headlines. Direct them to give the articles to others in the group to match with the headlines. This activity can be self-correcting if the children cut the headlines from the articles using different zig-zags and cutting patterns.

5 **Writing Telegrams.** After the children have read a story, ask them to write a telegram describing the selection. Of course in doing so, they will need to use as few words as possible and thus include only the major ideas. Read the telegrams when the skill group meets. Perhaps other children in the group will develop an interest in reading the same story.

6 **Underline the Key Words.** Old textbooks or other materials on which the children can write are needed for this activity. Direct the children to underline the most important word in each sentence. After doing so, they should look back to see if these words provide the major idea of the selection.

You could also direct them to underline the most important sentence in a paragraph. This provides practice in locating the topic sentence. The children should bring their responses to the skill group so you can check them and use them for instructing.

7 **Triangles and Squares.** Provide practice for noticing whether the topic sentence occurs at the beginning or end of a paragraph by asking the children to make a triangle beside each paragraph. The triangle should be drawn with the base line at the top ▽ if the topic sentence is the first sentence. If the topic sentence is the last sentence in the paragraph, direct the children to draw the triangle with the base line at the bottom △ . If a topic sentence is not included at the beginning or end of the paragraph, the children should make a square. You will need to provide old textbooks or children's magazines for this activity.

8 **Find the M.I.** Index cards on which you list many specific details and one main idea are needed for this activity. Direct the children to read all the sentences on the card and then indicate which one is the main idea. If you number the sentences and write the number of the sentence with the main idea on the back of the card, the activity will be self-correcting. An example is:

1. Jimmy and Jennifer got up early.
2. Jennifer played with her new dolls.
3. It was Christmas Day.
4. Jimmy rode his new bike all day.
5. They had lots of presents.
6. Grandma and Grandpa came to visit.

SIGNIFICANT DETAILS

What Children Should Learn
Details are essential to help children form vivid mental images while reading. The descriptions of characters or events make the reader feel as if he is actually there. Significant details are also necessary to draw conclusions. Likewise, details are very important when reading recipes, factual stories, directions for putting something together, and mathematical or scientific problems. Children should realize the value of details and develop skill in selecting and remembering the most significant ones.

Diagnosing Children's Skill in Selecting Significant Details
The following questions can be adapted to deter-

mine if children can identify significant details in reading materials at their instructional levels:

1. Who were the characters in the story?
2. What were they like?
3. When did the story take place?

4. Where did the story take place?
5. How did something happen?

Select appropriate passages, and then have the children read the selections and answer these questions.

Skill Group Activities for Teaching Children to Identify Significant Details

1 Ask the children what they want to look for when they read. Lead them to point out we usually want to know the who, what, when, where, and how of the story. Tell them these four W's and the *how* help us understand what we read because we can picture what is taking place. Give them an example by reading a story to them and seeing if they can point out the four W's and the *how*.

Ask them what it would be like if certain facts were not told in the story. Lead them to realize facts are really important in following recipes, reading directions to games, doing science experiments, and so forth. For example, discuss what would happen if someone did not notice the important details in a recipe. Conclude by telling the children you will help them notice the four W's and *how* when they read.

2 Children need to learn that some facts are more important than others. Read a story and ask them to point out the facts that really make a difference in the story. For example, if you read a story about a girl, perhaps the color of the clothing she is wearing, her age, where she lives, and so forth make a major difference in the story. As you discuss the selection with the children, have them list the facts that made a difference in the story and those that were included to give the reader background information, but did not affect the events in the selection.

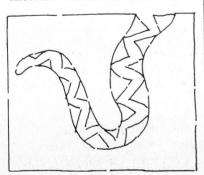

Lead the children to realize that, when they read, they cannot remember all the facts in the selection, so they should be looking for the ones that are the most important.

3 One way to help children recognize details is to guide them in circling or underlining the descriptive words in a selection. For this activity, write a brief selection on the board or use an opaque or overhead projector to show the selection on a screen. Read it to the children and ask them which words describe something in the story. In answering your question, they will be pointing out the adjectives and adverbs. Cross out the adjectives and adverbs and lead the children to see that, without the descriptive words, the selection is rather general and unexciting. The following example will help children realize the value of details.

(a) Selection with details

During the first week of their summer vacation, the Hartong children had nothing to do. Mrs. Hartong suggested having an end-of-the-school-year party. They liked the idea and decided to call the party, "We're Flying High—It's Vacation Time." Lynette made invitations in the shape of rockets. Beth used some of her old school papers to make paper airplanes for decorations. Bobby made favors by constructing parachutes with candy bars tied to the strings. The children had fun preparing for the party.

(b) Selection without details

The children had nothing to do. Their mother suggested a party. They liked that idea. They had fun making invitations, decorations, and favors.

4 Another way to help children become more aware of details is to have them write their own stories. When the child is acting as an author, he realizes the importance of including details to explain what he means. Do not accept the first copies of stories the children have written, but rather, take one or two of the stories as examples and put them on the chalkboard or use an opaque or overhead projector to show them on a screen. Have the children as a group rewrite the story, adding more details that explain who, what, where, when, and how. Compare the two selections, and discuss the addition of the details.

Perhaps you can reinforce this activity by having the skill group build sentences with significant details. Begin with a four-word sentence that has only the subject and predicate, such as, "The horse was eating." Ask the children to expand this sentence by adding details. When the children have finished, they may have a sentence such as, "The big black horse was eating the grass very slowly." Summarize by discussing how the details add to the meaning of the sentence and give the reader a better description of what is taking place.

1 Follow the Directions.

1 **Follow the Directions.** Duplicate Appendix Item 50, which has directions for two projects. You can also provide recipes, directions for art projects, games, and science experiments, and other types of materials in which details are essential. Children will be motivated to note the details as they do these activities.

2 **The Four W's and How.** Ask the children to read a selection and then outline it by noting the who, what, where, when, and how of the selection. They might simply write a sentence or some of the important facts for each one of the questions. Direct the children to bring their responses to the skill group to share with others.

(Title of the Story)

1. **Who** was in the story?
2. **Where** did the story take place?
3. **When** did the story take place?
4. **What** happened?
5. **How** did that happen?

---

3 **Facts in Math.** Details are especially important in mathematical problems. Provide old math books or have the children read the present math book to notice the most important details. If old books are available, you might have the children underline or circle the key details in the problem. Otherwise, have the children mark on plastic overlays.

Extend this activity by having the children write their own math problems. Ask them to include some insignificant facts in addition to the important facts. For example, they may make up a problem such as:

Mrs. Roth went to the store to buy some groceries. She bought two half gallons of milk at 90¢ each. She also got three loaves of bread for 48¢ each. It took her 15 minutes to check out because the store was so busy. She gave the clerk a $10 bill. How much change did she get back?

The children can exchange problems, cross out the facts that are not significant, and circle the facts that are very important.

4 **Mobiles of Stories.** One technique to help children identify significant details of a story is to provide materials to have them make mobiles. The children can use a large shape or design for the main idea of the story and then use smaller shapes or designs to include the important facts or details in the selection. By looking at the mobile the children will be able to see how details support the main idea. Have the children share their mobiles in the skill group.

5 **Let's Write a Play.** Children who have read a common story may want to work together to make it into play form. This requires the children to outline the characters, describe them, note the time the story took place, the scene or background of the story, and other significant facts. You can structure this activity by providing the following outline:

Writing a Play

1. What characters are needed?
2. When is the play taking place?
3. Where is the play taking place?
4. What are the major things that are going to happen?
5. How are these things going to happen?
6. What props are needed for presenting the play?

---

6 **Believe It or Not.** Prepare index cards with facts from an almanac, **Ripley's Believe It or Not**, Joseph Kane's **Famous First Facts**, or the **Guinness Book of World Records.** Elementary school children generally enjoy facts and will be motivated to notice the significant details. Fold 3" x 5" index cards in half so the 3-inch sides meet. On the front write, "Do you know _____?" Write the question on the inside of the card and the answer on the back. Children learn to read by reading with a purpose.

The answers to the following questions can be found in the **Guinness Book of World Records:**

1. How tall is the tallest living man?
2. How short is the shortest adult?
3. How much did the heaviest medically weighed man weigh?
4. What is the longest record for hiccoughs?
5. What word is used most often when people talk?
6. What word appears most often in writing?
7. What is the tallest animal on record?
8. What animal lives the longest?
9. What kind of dog is the most popular in the United States?
10. What letter is most frequently used?

7 **Jokes for Jokers.** Jokes generally include some significant details that are essential to make them funny. For example, if you are telling the old joke that asks why the moron tiptoed past the medicine cabinet and you forgot to include the word "medicine," the punch line (because he did not want to wake up the sleeping pills) is meaningless. Cut jokes from children's magazines or newspapers and paste them on index cards. The children will enjoy reading them and at the same time will have practice in noting significant details.

SEQUENCE OF EVENTS

What Children Should Learn

Some written materials include a series of events which children must recognize in order to comprehend. The sequence often enables the reader to draw conclusions and to see relationships since the events are usually in a logical order. The sequence of events is also very important in reading materials that require the reader to follow directions in a specified order. Children in elementary school need to be able to note the sequence of events when reading and realize why this skill is important.

Determining Skill in Noting the Sequence of Events

The following questions can be asked after the children have read a selection that has a sequence of events or directions. Again, not all of the questions need be asked; however, several are included to add more variety in checking this skill.

1. What happened first in the story? Second? Third?
2. Tell me what happened in the story?
3. Did the story end the way you thought it would?
4. If the story were a play, what would be the major events in each scene?
5. Can you number the events in the order in which they happened? (Provide the children with a list of the events in the story.)

Skill Group Activities for Teaching Children to Notice the Sequence of Events

1 Explain to the children that, in many of the stories and selections they read, several different events happen and sometimes one event leads to another. Relate this to their daily lives by saying the first thing they do in the morning is to get up, then they eat breakfast, go to school, and then go home. Help them realize that events must occur in a certain order (i.e., they cannot go to school before they get up). Explain to them this is also true in stories, so when reading they should try to notice what events are taking place and in what order. Read a story to the children and have them note the events. Discuss why the events occurred in that particular order. Also read some directions such as might be found in a science experiment, recipe, or rules to play a game. Again help the children discover the importance of noticing the events in a particular order by discussing what would happen if the order were changed.

2 Begin an action story with a general statement, such as "Once there was a boy who got lost," and then see if the children can add events to make it really exciting. When the children have dictated the story, have them copy it on paper using a separate line for each sentence. Direct the children to cut the sentences apart, mix them, and

then see if they can put them back together again in the sequence in which they took place. Have them read the story using a different sequence to illustrate the changes in meaning. Again help them see that certain events usually lead to other events, and that it is important to recognize their sequence. Doing so will help children comprehend as they read because they will be thinking and perhaps predicting what is likely to happen next.

3 Read to the children a story that has many different events, such as the "Old Lady and the Pig." In this story, one event does lead to another. Have each child make a train car and write or draw a particular event on it. When the children have completed their cars, ask them to put the cars in order. Help them see how each event leads to another. You might display the train in the classroom so other children can see it or read it.

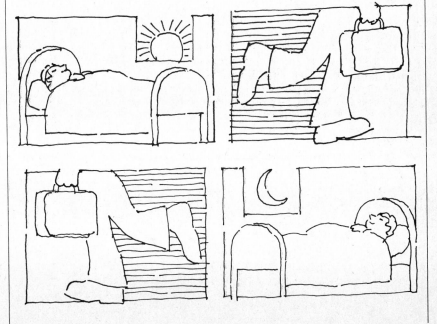

1 **Old Black Magic.** Duplicate Appendix Item 51. Also, get a few books on magic and make them available. Magic tricks usually have a series of steps that must be followed **exactly** to obtain the desired outcome. Children enjoy magic, and performing tricks will provide meaningful practice in noting the sequence of events.

2 **Comics.** Comic books or cartoon strips from the newspaper are exciting materials for helping children organize events according to sequence. Ask the children to bring in some of their favorite comic books or the cartoons from the Sunday newspaper. Direct the children to cut the picture squares apart, number them on the back according to sequence, and then have others try to put them together without looking at the numbers.

3 **Story Puzzles.** Obtain a children's magazine or old reader and select stories the children will like and can read at their independent levels. Cut the stories apart between paragraphs to get no more than ten separate pieces. Write a letter-number code on the back of each piece to indicate the story (letter) it came from and its place (number) in the story sequence. Put each story in a separate envelope and direct the children to put them together in the correct order.

4 **Time Lines.** Direct the children to bring their social studies book to this learning center. Have them read selected pages of the social studies book on which a sequence of events is presented. After the students read the selection, have them make a time line of the events. You can structure this activity by including either the events or the times on a ditto master and having the children complete it to include both times and events. The children can bring their time lines to the skill group to be discussed.

The emphasis of the discussion should be on how one event leads to another event.

5 **Who Did It?** Mystery stories usually rely on a sequence of events to create suspense. Tape record some mystery stories for the children to hear. When they come to the skill group, discuss the stories with them. You might also place at the center some books with mystery stories written on their independent reading levels.

6 **First Aid.** When one administers first aid, the sequence of actions may save a life. Provide a first aid book and ask the children to copy each step in a common first aid procedure on a separate index card. Put all the cards for one procedure in an envelope and label the envelope. Direct the children to read certain pages in the first aid book and then to take an envelope and arrange the steps it contains in correct sequence. For example, after reading the section about fainting, the children should be able to arrange the following steps in order:

_____ Lower his head to his knees.
_____ If he becomes unconscious lay him down with head turned to the side.
_____ Loosen clothing and open window.
_____ Keep him quiet for at least 15 minutes after he recovers.
_____ If a person feels faint, seat him and fan his face.

1500   1600   1700   1800   1900

DRAWING CONCLUSIONS

What Children Should Learn

Drawing conclusions is a process of relating the main idea, supporting details, and sequence of events. Conclusions deal with the *why* of events; whereas, sequence concerns *when*, and significant details concern *how, what, where,* and *who.*

To draw conclusions, the reader must see the relationships among the facts. Elementary school children must learn how to draw conclusions both by considering all the facts when they are available, and by making inferences when only a few of the facts are available. Drawing conclusions by inferring rather than seeing the relationships among all the facts is necessary for children to predict

outcomes. For example, many times teachers help students develop a purpose for reading by asking them to predict what is going to happen. To make a prediction, a reader must draw conclusions based on the facts that have been presented and then make some inferences. Our task, then, is to help children draw conclusions and at the same time realize that some of their conclusions may be based on inferences.

Diagnosing Students' Skill in Drawing Conclusions

The following questions can be asked after children have had an opportunity to read some material at their instructional level. These questions will help the teacher see if further instruction is needed in helping students draw conclusions.

1. Why do you think that happened in the story?
2. How did the characters feel?
3. What do you think will happen next?
4. What was the main character like?
5. Why did he do that?
6. What conclusion can you draw?
7. How do you know that?

Skill Group Activities for Teaching Children to Draw Conclusions

1 Read to the children a story that requires them to draw some conclusions. Fables are particularly good for this activity because they are brief and do have a conclusion or moral. Do not read the moral or conclusion to the children; however, ask them what they think it is. After they have told you, ask them how they arrived at this conclusion. What facts are presented in the story? What other information did they use to arrive at this conclusion? Explain to the children that this group has been formed to help them learn how to gather facts by reading and then use this information to draw a conclusion.

2 Begin reading a story to the children and then stop and ask them what they think will happen next. To answer this question, the children must take a look at the facts that have been presented or the events that have been read, and then predict what is going to happen. This requires the children to draw conclusions by making inferences. Continue reading the story to see if the children's predictions were right. Help the children realize that all inferences are not correct by discussing the fact that we make inferences based on our experiences. As we have experiences with many people, places, and things, we become better at making inferences.

3 Practice in classifying objects also helps children draw conclusions. Name four objects and then ask the children which one does not belong with the others. For example, if you say *chairs, beds, cake,* and *bookcase,* the children would tell you *cake* did not belong because it is not furniture. Skill in classifying helps children see relationships and thus put things together, a prerequisite for drawing conclusions.

4 Find some reading selections the students can read at their instructional or independent levels. Ask them to read the story to find out how each character feels. After drawing their conclusions, have them read aloud the sentences in the story that led them to draw their conclusion about the character's feelings.

Learning Center Activities to Help Children Draw Conclusions

1 Cause Clauses. Appendix Item 52 consists of five pairs of clauses for children to match by drawing conclusions. The children will be able to check their answers and probably will enjoy making their own cause clause puzzles.

2 Write a Riddle. Perhaps one of the favorite activities of children who are learning how to draw conclusions is that of saying riddles to each other. You might get a book of riddles, write some of them on index cards, and place the cards in a "riddle box." The children can read riddles to each other and see if they can guess the answers. Of course in doing so,

they must draw conclusions. Children generally enjoy making some of their own riddles to add to the riddle box.

3 Analogies. Write some analogies on index cards and put them in an "analogy box." Make a master list of answers or write the answers on the backs of the index cards if you want the children to correct their responses.

1. **Boy** is to **girl** as **he** is to _____.
2. **One** is to **I** as **two** is to _____.
3. **Robin** is to **bird** as **red** is to _____.
4. **Boat** is to **water** as **car** is to _____.
5. **Day** is to **night** as **old** is to _____.
6. **Water** is to **glass** as **coffee** is to _____
7. **Pencil** is to **write** as **crayon** is to _____
8. **Needle** is to **sew** as **knife** is to _____
9. **Two** is to **four** as **eight** is to _____.
10. **Mother** is to **Mom** as **Father** is to _____.

4 What Would Happen If? Write some "what would happen if" questions on index cards and put these into a box for the children to answer. For example, if you have the question, "What would happen if we did not have clocks?" the children would have to draw conclusions about the function and value of having clocks. You can structure this activity by making answers available; however, the children might be more creative in their responses if definite answers are not provided. The different responses can be shared when the skill group meets. Other sample questions are:

1. What would happen if it never rained?
2. What would happen if schools did not exist?
3. What would happen if we did not have shoes?
4. What would happen if all televisions were destroyed?
5. What would happen if you did not have a name?

5 **Don't Forget Me.** List three related words on an index card and ask the children to add one more word that is related to the first three. If you list **pedal, handlebars,** and **chain,** the children might add **seat, horn, fender,** or some other part of a bicycle. Possible responses can be written on the back of the index card if the children are going to check their answers. Encourage the children to make additional cards for this activity. Other samples are:

red	six
orange	one
green	two
hot	pencil
cold	crayon
sunny	magic marker
hammer	river
screwdriver	pond
saw	ocean
horse	bed
goat	dresser
cow	hamper

6 **How Do You Know?** Write simple stories for the children or select paragraphs from readers and then provide questions concerning relationships in the story. To answer the questions, the children will have to see the relationships and draw conclusions. An example follows:

Betty said, "Can you come over to my house to play?"

"Yes, if my mother will let me," said Josephine. "I will ask her when she gets home at five o'clock."

"Do you think she will mind?" asked Betty.

"I don't think so," said Josephine. "She will probably be glad because she is always tired when she gets home. I'll call to let you know."

Questions:

1. How do you know Betty and Josephine are friends?
2. How do you know both girls have a telephone?
3. How do you know Josephine listens to her mother?
4. Where do you think Josephine's mother is? How do you know?
5. Do you think the girls will be able to play together? How do you know?

Did you notice that some of the questions were based entirely on facts presented in the selection while others required the students to make inferences before drawing conclusions? As you write your questions, try to include both types. Discuss the children's answers when the skill group meets. During the discussion of questions that require inferences you can learn much about the child's background if you listen carefully.

7 **Why Words.** Provide **Weekly Readers,** children's magazines, and selections from old textbooks and direct the children to circle words that tell "why." The children will soon learn to spot words such as **so, since, because,** and **therefore.** Direct the children to write a sentence using each one of these words. The children's sentences can be read orally and discussed when the skill group meets.

CRITICAL READING

What Children Should Learn
Children must learn that they cannot believe everything they read. At the elementary school level we begin to teach critical reading skills by helping students (1) separate fact from opinion, (2) recognize bias, (3) detect propaganda techniques, (4) realize words have connotations, and (5) judge the competence of the authors.

Many times young children believe anything that appears in print is true. "It says so" is a common response when children are asked why they believe certain things. As adults we have learned the importance of critical reading. Some authors are not well informed, people do have biases, and many dubious techniques are used to persuade us. It is our task, then, to make children aware of these realities by helping them develop critical reading skills. Of course, this is not done in one easy lesson; however, if the critical reading skills are only taught incidentally, chances are children will not develop them or integrate them: specific lessons are needed.

Diagnosing Critical Reading Skills
The following questions can be asked after children have read something to determine if they can evaluate what they have read:

1. Do you really think that happened?
2. Who do you think wrote this? What should her qualifications be?
3. What is true in this story? What is make-believe?
4. What are the exaggerations in the story?
5. Which statements are fact and which ones are opinion?
6. When was the information written? Do you think this is still true today?
7. What are the author's beliefs?
8. How did the author try to influence you?

Again it is not necessary to ask every question; however, many examples are included for variety and because different questions might be more appropriate for different types of selections.

Skill Group Activities for Teaching Critical Reading Skills

1 Read two stories to the children, one that is a tall tale or an exaggerated story, and another that is true. Ask the children to tell you which story is true and which one is pretend or make-believe. Introduce the words *fiction* and *nonfiction* in the discussion. Provide short selections for the children to read and classify as fiction or nonfiction.

2 Children of elementary school age should be aware of some of the propaganda techniques they are exposed to frequently on TV and in magazines. Introduce the "bandwagon technique" (i.e., everybody is doing it, so you had better do it, too) and have the children try to spot this technique in magazine advertisements or TV commercials. Ask them to keep lists or cut out examples.

Another propaganda technique frequently used to influence children is the appeal to be like a popular person or sports hero. Have children cut out advertisements from magazines and cereal boxes, and think of advertisements from TV where such a person is used to advertise a product in hopes that the children will want to be like this person and will thus buy the product. Summarize these activities by helping the children realize authors try to influence readers to do or believe certain things.

3 Point out to the children that some statements they read are opinions while others are facts. Explain that facts are statements that have been proven to be true. Opinions are statements of belief that may be true or false. Tell them you are going to read some statements and ask them to listen carefully to determine whether each statement is a fact or an opinion. The following examples can be used:

Fact or Opinion

1. The Miami Dolphins have the best football players.
2. Harry's hair is too short.
3. All teachers love children.
4. Palm trees grow in Florida.
5. Every family should have a pet.
6. Two plus two equals four.
7. Horses are animals.
8. The President is doing a nice job.
9. Cigarette smoking is dangerous to your health.
10. Children should get to bed at seven o'clock.

After you have read several statements, have the children write two statements, one that is a fact and one that is an opinion. They can read these aloud to see if other students in the group can determine which statements are factual and which are opinions. Summarize by discussing the importance of determining whether the information they are reading consists of facts or opinions.

4 Help the children realize that words have connotations in addition to their exact meanings. Explain that some words, such as *vacation, mother, apple pie,* and *candy,* may have pleasant connotations. Other words, such as *homework, ugly, sad,* and *spinach,* may have unpleasant connotations. Lead the children to realize that connotations are feelings people have about words, rather than part of their actual definition. For example, the word *vacation* means "a period of rest from work," yet many people define vacation as a happy time.

Read some words to the children and have them indicate the connotations they have by responding with "mmmmm," or "yuk." The following words can be used:

prisoner	girl	ice cream
sly	boy	reading
money	slavery	bicycle
peace	communism	dolls
war	democracy	spanking

Summarize the activity by helping children realize we associate feelings with words. Tell them authors use different words to arouse our emotions and make us feel certain ways without realizing it. As we read we should try to notice if an author is trying to influence us by using words with connotations.

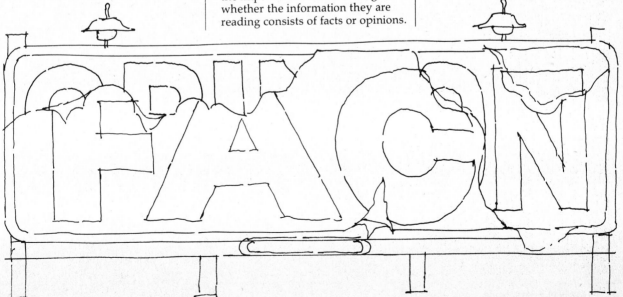

1 **Mmmm–Yuk–Blah!** Duplicate and hand out the activity in the Appendix (Item 53). Tell the children to read each word and then classify it according to its connotation. The children should make a happy face for **mmmm** words, a sad face for **yuk** words, and a straight face for **blah** words. It is not possible to provide answers for this activity because children may have different connotations for some words; therefore, you may want to discuss these differences when the skill group meets.

2 **Yes or Maybe.** Write some statements on a piece of tagboard, put a blank in front of each statement, and then laminate the tagboard. Direct the children to put a **Y** (for **yes**) in front of the statements that are definitely true and an **M** (for **maybe**) in front of the statements that may be true. Write the answers on the back if you want the children to check their answers. The following examples may be used:

_____ 1. Dogs make good pets.
_____ 2. Tennis is a fun game.
_____ 3. People like planes better
than cars.

3 **Try It, You'll Like It.** Ask the children to bring to school the empty boxes from their favorite cereal and labels from canned goods. Place these at the learning center and ask the children to read them to notice how the manufacturers are trying to influence them. Discuss the children's ideas when the skill group meets.

4 **Tall Tales.** Provide some tall tales at the learning center and ask the children to make a list of the exaggerations and the facts after reading the selection. You might want to provide answers; however, some discussion in the skill group might be more appropriate. You can structure this activity by preparing a ditto master with two columns labeled "exaggerations" and "facts."

5 **Buy Me!** Provide magazines and newspapers for this activity. Direct the children to find advertisements that illustrate different propaganda techniques and paste them in a scrapbook under such headings as "jump on the bandwagon," "testimonials by famous people," "slogans," and "appeals to status." Use the scrapbook in the skill group to explain and clarify.

6 **Is There a Difference?** If possible, obtain several different editions of a science, health, or social studies book. Have the children discover how the treatment of the same topic varies from one edition to another by noticing how much space is devoted to the topic, whether or not the accounts of the events differ, and how the facts are presented. Children might compare the authors, copyright dates, and publishing companies to determine reasons for the differences they discover.

7 **My Beliefs.** Ask the children to write paragraphs with their beliefs about topics of interest, such as cars, roles of women, favorite sports figures, bedtimes, reading, and favorite TV programs. Direct the children to bring these to the skill group to read to others. The listeners should try to detect bias by noting facts and opinions. Lead the children to realize opinions are acceptable if they are based on facts.

8 **Words Have Emotions?** Tell the children to find in their textbooks, readers, and magazines words that express emotions. As they find words, ask them to try to determine why the author used those particular words. Direct the children to bring their favorite passages to the skill group and share them with others.

VOCABULARY DEVELOPMENT

What Children Should Learn

The importance of vocabulary as a prerequisite for comprehension is clearly evident. Vocabulary accounts for approximately 60% of comprehension. Comprehension is only possible when the reader has knowledge of the concepts words represent. Students who have very limited vocabularies certainly will not be able to comprehend much of what they read.

Technically speaking, students have four vocabularies: listening, speaking, reading, and writing. The first vocabulary to be developed is the listening vocabulary. The infant acquires a listening vocabulary before learning to speak. As the listening vocabulary is being acquired, children learn to speak. Finally the reading and writing vocabularies are developed. Our task is to help the students develop each vocabulary so they can be better listeners, speakers, readers, and writers.

In addition to learning *new* vocabulary words, students need to expand their knowledge of the relationships of the words they are learning and know. Students learn synonyms, antonyms, and homonyms as a part of vocabulary development. Likewise, we teach students about word origins and about the multiple meanings and connotations of words.

When helping children increase their vocabulary, it is necessary to deal with both pronunciation and meaning. The emphasis in this chapter is on word meaning. Consult Chapter 3 for ideas on how to teach pronunciation.

Diagnosing Students' Vocabulary Needs

There are several ways of identifying students who need additional instruction and enrichment activities to improve their vocabularies. An informal technique is to listen to the students talk. Notice those students who use many words as compared to those who have a very limited speaking vocabulary. The speaking vocabulary is related to the reading vocabulary and is generally larger than the reading vocabulary at young ages. If you notice students in your room who have a very limited speaking vocabulary, you can assume that their reading vocabulary is limited, also.

Another informal way to determine students' vocabulary needs is to read graded selections to them and then check their listening comprehension. After reading the selections ask questions to see if the students comprehend at least 75% of what they heard. Students who have difficulty when listening and trying to comprehend may need extra help with vocabulary.

Teachers frequently use "vocabulary" questions that ask students to define words used in the passages. As you work with the children ask questions such as:

1. What does _____ mean in the passage?
2. Can you use _____ in a sentence?
3. What is another word for _____?
4. What is the opposite of _____?

Another method for determining students' vocabularies is to give them a test that includes words commonly found in their content area materials. These specialized vocabulary words are generally in boldface print or in italics. The format of the vocabulary test could be matching, fill in the blank, or multiple choice. Using vocabulary from content materials will enable you to determine which students may encounter difficulty in completing and comprehending school assignments.

In addition to the above-mentioned techniques for determining students' vocabularies, you may want to use the informal vocabulary tests found in many of the basal series, in the teacher's guide for some encyclopedias, such as the *World Book Encyclopedia*, and in *Weekly Readers*. Again these may be used to determine those students who are especially weak in vocabulary and need some extra instruction to increase vocabulary.

Skill Group Activities for Helping Students Increase Their Vocabulary

1 Write the following sentence on the board and ask the students to read it: "I ate a *bammer*." Ask them to explain what the word *bammer* means in this sentence. Of course they will not be able to tell you the meaning of *bammer* because it is a nonsense word. They may be able to determine from the context that a *bammer* is edible, but they will not be sure how it looks, tastes, smells or feels. Help the children see that, before they can understand what they read, they must know the meanings of many different words.

Ask the children how we learn words. For example, if the children were going to learn the meaning of *bammer*, how would they learn it? The children will probably point out that, if you have a picture of a *bammer* or a real *bammer*, they could learn about it by seeing it. If it is edible, they might like to taste it to develop a further understanding of the word. Likewise, if there is a smell or particular texture, they might notice it and develop a better understanding of *bammer*. In other words, help the children realize we learn the meaning of words through our five senses.

If we want to be able to read the word, we notice the letters in it and make an association between the printed symbols and what they represent. Later when we see the printed symbols again, we form a mental picture. Likewise, if we want to learn to use the word when we talk, we make an association between the sounds and our concept of the word. Tell the children that in this skill group you are going to be helping them increase their vocabularies so that, when they read, they can understand more. Explain that they will be using their five senses to learn more about words and then they will be making "matches" or associations between the printed form of the word and what it represents.

2 When meeting with the skill group on vocabulary, introduce at least one new word each day. Of course, you must adjust the rate of vocabulary development to the children's abilities; however, if the children feel they are learning many new vocabulary words, they will be motivated to learn more. You can have a continuing activity called "The Word for Today." Select and introduce one new word, then use it informally during the day. Encourage the children to use their five senses to discover the meaning of the word.

3 Many of the phrases in the English language are considered as figures of speech or idioms in that the meaning of the phrase cannot be literally interpreted from the words. Children must be taught these idioms or figures of speech in order to understand what they mean. You may want to tell the children that sometimes in our language we have words that are used as expressions. They really do not mean exactly what the words say. You might use an example such as "down in the dumps" in the sentence, "He did poorly on the test and was down in the dumps." The children of course will realize the boy was not really in the dump yard, but rather he was feeling bad or depressed. Tell the children we have many phrases like this in our language and you will help them learn some of these so that when they read the expressions they will know the meanings. The following expressions might be used as examples:

The children might want to put each phrase on a 3" x 5" index card, use the phrase in a sentence, and write its meaning on the back of the card. These cards might also be put in their "word boxes" as they work toward joining a ten, twenty, or thirty word club.

4 If children are having a difficult time associating a particular word with its meaning, have them use the kinesthetic technique. The kinesthetic technique involves tracing the word, in addition to seeing it and hearing it, while associating it with its meaning. Lead the children in following these directions to learn words that are particularly difficult for them to remember.

1. Use the word in a sentence or review its meaning.
2. Say the word and write it on paper, making the letters approximately 2 inches high. As you write the word, say each syllable. When the word is completed, say it again.
3. Trace the word with your index finger. As you trace the word, say it in syllables rather than saying each letter. Pronounce the word correctly after tracing it.
4. Remove the copy of the word and then write the word on another sheet of paper.
5. Check the writing of the word to make sure it is correct. If you make an error, retrace the word. Do not erase to correct your errors. Repeat the steps until you can write the word from memory.

1. to make a scene	to create a disturbance
2. to go scot free	to escape without punishment
3. to put one's hands on	to find
4. know the ropes	to be familiar with some situation or place
5. in the dark	not aware of the facts
6. red tape	bureaucratic procedure, especially as marked by excessive concern with detail and by delay
7. by hook or by crook	by any means
8. take down a peg or two	to lower the pride of, to humiliate
9. in the limelight	the center of attention

Learning Center Activities to Help Children Increase Vocabulary

1 **Find the Hidden Words.** Duplicate Appendix Item 54. Direct the children to find at least 20 words on the doughnut by following the direction of the arrow. The children can list the words they find and bring their lists to the skill group. Some words they will find on the doughnut are: **man, an, and, scared, scare, car, are, care, came, red, do, dog, eat, at, ate, eaten, ten, tent, tenth, thin, think,** and **gum.** Remind the children that the words must be formed by using letters in sequence.

2 **Run for Your Life.** Duplicate Appendix Item 55 for this activity. Direct the children to spin a spinner or roll a die, then move the number of spaces indicated by correctly reading each word along the way. If they cannot read a word, they stop on the space before that word. The first one to the finish line is the winner.

3 **Simple Word Puzzles.** This activity will help children increase their knowledge of synonyms and antonyms and at the same time help them learn to do crossword puzzles. Write definitions for the children such as, "the opposite of

day" on a ditto master and after each one place the exact number of squares needed to write each letter of the word defined (see Figure 25). You may want to provide clues by filling in one letter.

1. The opposite of day

| | i | | | |

2. To be nice

| | | | | | d | |

3. Very different from others

| o | | | | | | |

4. The opposite of love

| | | | e | |

Figure 25. Simple word puzzle.

Of course, if your children are more advanced, they may be able to tackle the crossword puzzles in children's magazines.

1. to make amends
2. to make a mountain out of a molehill
3. to stir up a hornets' nest
4. to stick to one's guns
5. with tongue in cheek
6. to put the cart before the horse

7. to draw in one's horns
8. out of hand
9. to look a gift horse in the mouth
10. a horse of a different color

4 **Building With Words.** Direct the children to write a long word they know and then, using the letters in that word, see how many other words they can build by adding letters as in Figure 26. If competition is desirable, have all the children begin with the same word and add letters for a specified period of time. Ask them to bring the words they have built to the skill group.

5 **Matching Expressions.** Some 5" x 8" index cards are needed for this activity. On each card write an idiom or familiar expression and its meaning. Then cut the cards in half so one half of the card contains the idiom and the other half contains its meaning. Tell the children to put the cards together, matching the idioms and their meanings. Some of the idioms you may want to use are:

to compensate
to treat a trifle with importance
to cause serious trouble
to maintain that you are right
insincerely or not really meaning it
reverse the logical order so the last thing is first
to reduce one's demands or expectations beyond control
to be critical of some gift
an entirely different situation or person

Figure 26. Building with words.

l
a make automobile rubber
b a t o again i h n
too see p n going
t i
n
t

RATE OF COMPREHENSION

What Children Should Learn

There are many students who believe an excellent reader is a fast reader. When directing silent reading, teachers often notice children having an unofficial race to see who can finish first. Likewise, many students read as rapidly as possible when asked to read orally. Our objective, then, is to help children realize that an effective reader is not necessarily a fast reader. An effective reader is one who can adjust his rate to his purpose and to the type of materials he is reading.

We teach children to read at three different

rates. The *normal* rate is used when reading to find answers to questions, to note details, to solve problems, and see the relationships of details to the main idea. The normal rate is also used when trying to appreciate the author's writing style or the nature of the literature.

A *rapid* rate of reading is used when skimming to find a particular answer, to determine the main idea of a selection, or to review something that was read previously. For example, children employ a rapid rate of reading when trying to find a word in the dictionary, telephone book, or encyclopedia, or when locating specific information in a textbook, newspaper article, or other literature.

The third rate of reading is the *careful* or *study* rate of reading. The study rate of reading is used when trying to memorize or master content, evaluate materials according to certain criteria, to note the particular sequence of events, or to follow directions for an experiment or in a recipe. A careful rate of reading is also necessary when using study skills such as outlining and note-taking.

The task of the teacher is twofold: first to teach the children that we need different rates for different types of materials, and then to help children develop these different rates. These objectives are usually emphasized during the intermediate grades.

Determining Students' Rates of Reading

To find the students' normal rate of reading, use the graded selections such as in the Comprehension Skills Test (Appendix Items 43-48). Count the number of words in each selection. Ask a child to read one selection silently and then divide the number of words by the number of minutes re-

APPENDIX ITEMS 43-48

quired to read it. The quotient is the number of words a child can read per minute. For example, if a child reads a 100-word selection in 2 minutes, he has read approximately 50 words per minute.

If the selections require less than a minute to read, simply divide the number of words by the number of seconds necessary to read the selection, then multiply by 60 to convert to minutes. For example, if it took a child 20 seconds to read a selection of 50 words you would divide 50 by 20. Then you would multiply the quotient by 60. In this case you will find the child is reading about 150 words per minute.

When determining students' rates of reading, be sure you ask questions to check their comprehension. A rapid rate of reading is useless if the student is not comprehending.

Skill Group Activities for Helping Children Improve Their Rate of Comprehension

1 Begin this skill group by telling the children a good reader has three different reading rates. Explain each rate to them and give examples of materials or have them suggest materials they would read at each rate. You might actually provide materials, such as a social studies textbook, stories from a basal reader, newspaper article, directions for a science experiment, a play, or an article from an encyclopedia, and have them tell you what reading rate is most appropriate for comprehending each one.

You can make an analogy to help children further understand why we use different rates. Explain that, when their mothers or fathers are driving an automobile, they use different speeds. One speed is used on the expressway, one speed is used on the neighborhood streets, and another speed is used in heavy traffic. The good driver, like a good reader, must be able to adjust his speed to the situation. Tell the children in this skill group you will be helping them develop careful,

normal, and rapid rates of reading, and teaching them how to adjust their reading rate to the situation.

2 One way to help children develop a rapid rate of reading is to teach them to read in phrases rather than word by word. When a child looks at each word and fixates on it, his reading rate is hindered.

Conversely, if we teach children to look at more than one word, and to read in phrases, their rate of reading can be improved. You can help children realize the value of reading in phrases by giving them a reading selection that has been divided into phrases, such as the one that follows. After they have read this or a similar selection, discuss the value of reading in phrases.

These words
are arranged
in columns
of phrases
to help you
realize the
importance of
reading phrases.
You should
try to read
each line

as a unit
rather than
reading
each word
as a unit.
This will
help you read
more smoothly,
more rapidly,
and with
better comprehension.

Your eyes
can see
several small words
at a time.
As you develop
you will be able
to read longer phrases.
Now it's time
for you to tell
why you should
read in phrases.

3 In teaching children to read at a study or careful rate, you will need to provide mathematical problems, science experiments, technical information from social studies or health textbooks, or recipes. Have the children read the selections as quickly as they can, and then ask questions concerning the directions or details in the selection. Of course, they will not be able to answer all of your specific questions. Have the children read the materials again carefully to note the specific details and sequence. Again ask the questions. The children will readily see that a slow rate of reading is important. Conclude by asking the children what other materials should be read at a slow rate.

4 One way to help children increase their rapid rate of reading is to teach them to skim. Help children look for key words in selections. Help them notice that these words are usually nouns and verbs. The adjectives, adverbs, prepositions, and conjunctions are important, but not as important when reading rapidly. Lead the children to realize that the key words give them the essence of the selection.

The children can make a homemade controlled reader by taking a 4" x 6" or 3" x 5" index card and cutting a small window in the middle of it. The hole should be no more than the space of 16 letters. Have the children place the card on the material they are reading and move it along as quickly as they are able to comprehend. This will help the children increase their attention span for symbols and thus enable them to read more rapidly.

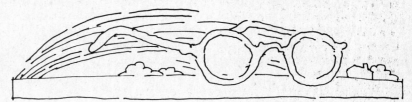

Learning Center Activities to Help Children Develop Flexible Rates of Comprehension

1 Obey the Speed Limit! For this activity you will need to duplicate Appendix Items 56 and 57. Cut out the cards on Item 57 following the dotted lines. Place the cards in a stack. Direct the children to take turns drawing cards. They must follow the directions on the cards to move their tokens. The first one to reach home is the winner. In playing this game, children become more aware of the different rates of reading and when they are appropriate.

2 Where Are the Phrases? Provide newspapers, magazines, or other consumable materials on which children can write. Direct the children to use slashes to divide the sentences into phrases. The children can bring their work to the skill group to read to others in phrases.

3 Where Is Your Name? Provide an old telephone book and make some word cards with the names of people. Tell the children to turn over each word card and find the name in the telephone book as quickly as possible. The children can have a race if they keep records of the time required to locate their name. This activity can be adapted for dictionary words or encyclopedia topics.

4 Time Find. Word cards from some of the other activities can be used for this game. Direct the children to place the word cards face up on the center of the table. One child reads a word and the others try to find it as quickly as possible. The children can compare the number of cards to see who found the most words.

5 Helpful Fingers. Normally we try to teach children not to use their fingers when reading, yet when skimming, it is very appropriate to "let the fingers do the walking." Direct the children to skim by moving their fingers down the center of a page to find the main idea or key words. Ask them to use their textbooks and make a list of the key words found on each page. Discuss this technique when the skill group meets.

You can adapt this activity by having the children circle the five key words in each paragraph. This limit is imposed to make sure they look at the most important words in the selection.

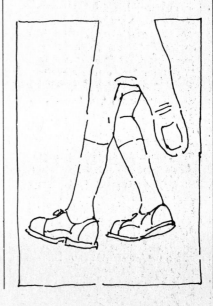

What Children Should Learn

We help children develop many interrelated reading skills so they can read well orally. Children learn to pay attention to punctuation marks, and to identify and express the moods of the selection by varying the rate, pitch, and volume. We want children to read in phrases, rather than word by word, and yet articulate each word. Oral reading then requires the children to "put it all together" so that others can comprehend.

In addition to developing the appropriate oral reading skills and habits, we need to help children understand the advantages and limitations of oral reading. We teach children that oral reading can be an aid as well as a hindrance to the process of getting meaning. Oral reading seems to aid comprehension when the reader does not understand something he is reading. All of us have probably reread complicated directions to get the meaning. It seems as though another modality—that of hearing—enables us to understand.

Oral reading can be a hindrance to comprehension when "sounding good" rather than getting meaning is emphasized. Children must understand that reading is getting meaning and not simply calling words; therefore, it is essential that they think as they read. Again we are concerned about attitudes as well as skills when we work with the children.

Diagnosing Student's Oral Reading Skills

The checklist in Figure 27 can be used to guide your observations as you listen to and observe your students reading orally. Remember that, before students read a selection orally, they should have a chance to read it silently. Silent reading is essential so the children can express the mood or tone of the story. Silent reading also gives students a chance to apply their word recognition skills to figure out words that may at first seem unfamiliar. After the students have silently read the selections on the Comprehension Skills Test, use the checklist to determine their specific oral reading skill needs.

_____ 1. Determines the mood or tone of the selection (humor, sadness, excitement, suspense, etc.)
_____ 2. Reads in thought phrases or units.
_____ 3. Observes punctuation marks.
_____ 4. Reads smoothly without jerkiness or hesitation.
_____ 5. Uses appropriate volume.
_____ 6. Enunciates clearly and distinctly.
_____ 7. Uses a suitable pitch and voice quality.
_____ 8. Is free from strain, tension, or nervous habits.
_____ 9. Reads at an appropriate rate so the listeners can understand.
_____ 10. Does not omit words, substitute words, repeat words, or insert words.
_____ 11. Holds the material properly (14 inches from the eyes is typical).
_____ 12. Keeps his place without difficulty.

Figure 27. Oral reading skills checklist.

Skill Group Activities to Help Children Improve Their Oral Reading Skills

1 Discuss the importance of oral reading with your students. Ask them why and when it is necessary for them to read well orally. Help them realize we must read orally when only one copy of the material is available. You might also point out that oral reading may sometimes help them understand what they are reading. Give them an example of when you used oral reading to help you figure out what to do. Also, tell them you have them read orally to determine what words they can read and how well they can read to others. After they realize the purposes of oral reading, ask them what a good oral reader does. They can make a checklist similar to the one in Figure 27.

2 Have the children read a selection as you tape record it. After a few children have read, play the tape and ask the children to evaluate each other by using the checklist in Figure 27 or one they have made. Help the children realize that we do not all have the same strengths and weaknesses. Likewise, we are not all the same height, do not have the same color of eyes, and so forth. The idea of this group is to discover the strengths and weaknesses of each student and to help each one improve so he can read effectively to others. Find one skill for each child to emphasize as you point out the skills they have mastered.

3 Read a few selections to the children and ask them to evaluate as you read. Have them point out when and why you read slowly, change the pitch or volume, and so forth. For example, if the mood was one of excitement, have the children notice that you read faster. If the mood was one of sadness, indicate you read a bit slower and lowered your voice. Happiness can be illustrated by reading at a higher pitch and perhaps

more rapidly. Draw guidelines for pitch, rate, and voice quality for expressing different moods. Then have the children do a choral reading so they can use the appropriate phrasing, expression, pitch, and voice quality together.

4 Review the punctuation marks with the children so they understand

how these influence their oral reading. Have them point out that a period means stop, a comma indicates pause, a question mark tells them they should raise their voice at the end of a sentence, and an exclamation mark indicates they should use strong feeling in reading that sentence. Also review quotation marks to help them determine who is saying what. Choral readings can again be used for practice.

Learning Center Activities to Help Children Develop Skill in Reading Orally

1 **Markers Can Help.** Suggest using markers to those children who use their fingers to keep their place as they read. Markers are preferred to fingers because the child is looking at the entire line when using a marker, rather than pointing to each word. A child who uses his fingers to keep his place often reads word by word because he points to each word in the selection.

2 **Let Me Entertain You.** Invite children from other classrooms to your room to read orally to the children who are attempting to improve their oral reading skills. Your students will learn by hearing the models provided by excellent readers. Likewise, students from your classroom may want to go to other rooms to read stories they have been practicing.

3 **Kinds of Sentences.** Write different kinds of sentences on index cards for this activity. Some of the sentences may be questions, some might relate strong feeling, some might be command sentences, and others might be simply declarative sentences. Have the children read the sentences the way they think they should be said. They will soon realize

sentences can be read at different rates and pitches, and with different voice qualities, to emphasize different meanings. When the skill group meets, have the children read the selections in as many different ways as possible. Sample sentences are:

1. I would like to do it.
2. I said shut the door.
3. You are really nice.
4. I am having a birthday party again.
5. Did you watch television last night?
6. Sharpen your pencil.
7. That makes me feel sad.
8. Who said that I did that?
9. That is news to me.
10. Why on earth did you ever tell her I said that?

4 **Radio Plays.** One way to help children read orally effectively is to have them read plays. Many of the basal series have plays for children to read or you may want to have them write one of their own. The children can practice the play while at the learning center.

5 **Play It Again.** A tape recorder should be made available at this learning center or at some other place in the room. Direct the children to take turns reading a selection into the tape recorder. After doing so, they should listen carefully to notice what they are doing well and what needs improvement. Have them reread the same selection using their own suggestions, or ideas from other children.

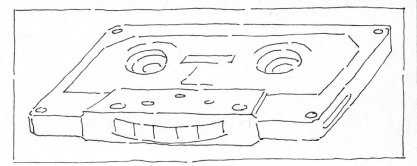

FUNCTIONAL READING SKILLS

Readers have two very important purposes: to gather information and to derive pleasure. This chapter emphasizes those skills that enable children to use reading as a tool for learning and source of recreation. The first seven sections of the chapter deal with the skills required to "read to learn"; the final section—and to some the most important section—concerns reading for recreation.

The first section deals with reading *symbols and abbreviations*. Reading is the process of getting meaning from *symbols,* which is more inclusive than just reading words. Every day children see symbols in math, music, science, and social studies. In addition to teaching letters and words, we must help children learn common symbols.

There are many special skills required to read *maps*. In the intermediate grades, reading materials in content areas frequently include *graphs, diagrams, and tables*. If children are able to read these special ways of presenting information, they will be able to obtain more information from their reading. Too often children skip maps, tables, diagrams, and charts because they do not know how to read them.

Teaching children how to use different *parts of a book* is the topic for the fourth section. Children will be able to get more information from books if they are able to use the title page, table of contents, preface, bibliography, appendices, and other aids that are commonly included.

The next section of this chapter concerns *reference skills*. Elementary school children are introduced to many types of reference books. In addition to developing skill in selecting and using them, we want children to develop favorable attitudes toward them. "Looking something up" will not be a burdensome task if children realize where and how to locate the information.

Many elementary schools have libraries; therefore, it is necessary that children learn skills needed to use the *library* efficiently. The sixth section of this chapter includes ideas that will enable children to locate the books and materials they desire.

The foundation for higher level *study skills and habits* is built in the elementary grades. Children are taught to employ effective study strategies to get more from their content area books. Emphasis is also on helping children develop appropriate study habits.

The final section of this chapter concerns *recreational reading*. If children learn to read, and yet dislike reading, we have failed. Our goal is to help children realize the value of reading as a recreational activity and thus to find hours of pleasure between the covers of books. You can establish many different learning centers based on the separate functional reading skills, but make one center a "reading for fun," so children have time to enjoy reading as they apply their newly acquired skills.

READING SYMBOLS AND ABBREVIATIONS

What Children Should Learn

Elementary school children should soon learn we have many symbols and abbreviations in our language to represent particular concepts. They must learn to make the associations between these symbols and concepts in many different content areas. Add to this the number of abbreviations found in each content area, and one begins to understand why reading in the content areas is difficult. For example, consider this brief list of some of the common symbols children need to know in order to succeed in math.

APPENDIX ITEM 58

$	¢	#	%	+	−	×
−	≠	>	<	0	'	"
I	V	L	C	D	M	in.
ft.	yd.	mi.				

These are only a few symbols from one content area. In addition, every content area, such as music, science, social studies, and physical education, has symbols representing concepts. It is necessary for teachers to focus on reading abbreviations and symbols as well as words.

Diagnosing Children's Skill in Reading Symbols and Abbreviations

A skill test is provided in the Appendix (Item 58) and can be used to see if children can match common symbols and abbreviations with their meanings. Direct the children to crack the code by matching each abbreviation or symbol with its meaning. You may want to prepare similar tests to see if the children know the symbols and abbreviations that are commonly used in other subject areas. Item 58 only deals with symbols and abbreviations in mathematics.

Skill Group Activities for Teaching Children to Read Symbols and Abbreviations

1 Ask the children to name some symbols and abbreviations and tell why we have them. Help the children realize that symbols are actually shortcuts in that they save us from writing out many words. Write a math problem such as 16 + 7 on the board using first numerals and then words (sixteen plus seven). Provide other examples to help the children realize the value of symbols. Summarize the activity by telling the children you will help them learn some of the most common symbols so they will be able to read and write them quickly.

2 Symbols and abbreviations are learned by making associations. You can help the children understand this by writing a word such as *cat* on the board. Ask the children what they think of when they see the word *cat*. After they have responded, tell them they have made an association between the symbols and some mental picture or visual image. Give other examples using *dog*, a plus sign, a period, and so forth. Lead the children to realize that, when they see a particular symbol, they can read or get meaning from it if they have made the association.

Tell the children the way they learn symbols is to first understand what the symbols mean and then to memorize the sign or symbol that stands for this understanding. Share some techniques people use for memorization, such as writing and saying, or simply looking and thinking.

Select a symbol to teach the children. First, explain what the symbol represents and then write the symbol. Summarize the activity by asking the children how they plan to memorize this association.

3 Abbreviations are generally easier to teach children because they usually contain some of the letters from the words they represent. Write some words on the board and then write the abbreviation for each word. If possible, have the children circle the letters that make up the abbreviations. You might ask why those letters were chosen to form the abbreviation. Also, point out that abbreviations usually consist of consonants rather than vowels; therefore, if the children want to make some of their own abbreviations for note-taking, they should use consonant letters. Introduce the word *mnemonic* device and give examples of mnemonic devices you use to help you remember. Perhaps the children can suggest some good mnemonic devices for the symbols and abbreviations they are learning. For example, they may be able to remember the symbol for division because the line *divides* or separates the two dots (÷). Have the children suggest others.

Learning Center Activities for Teaching Symbols and Abbreviations

1 **Symbol Concentration.** Make a set of flash cards with symbols and another set with the meanings of these symbols. This game is played as regular concentration. The cards are arranged face down in rows on the floor or table. In turn each player turns over two cards. If the two cards match, that is, if the symbol and its definition are turned up, the player keeps them and takes another turn. If the two cards do not match, he turns them over in the same place and the next player has a turn. The player with the most pairs is the winner.

2 **This Means.** A deck of cards with a symbol or abbreviation written on one side and the meaning or word written on the other side is needed for this activity. Direct the children to shuffle the cards and put them into a deep box. Each player draws a card, looks at the side with the symbol or abbreviation, and says what the meaning or word is. If successful he scores one point. Players alternate turns until all cards have been used. The players with the most points win.

3 **All Aboard.** You can help the children get an idea of how many symbols they encounter by having them make a train car for each symbol. The train car can be made of matchboxes or other small boxes. Direct the children to write the symbol on the outside of the train car, then put a piece of paper with the definition or the meaning of the symbol inside the car. Of course the same can be done with abbreviations. The object of this activity would be to see how long the children can make the train by adding cars. Once the train is made, the children can take out the definitions, mix them up, and then put them back in the appropriate car.

List 19. Two-Letter Abbreviations for State Names

Alabama	AL
Alaska	AK
Arizona	AZ
Arkansas	AR
California	CA
Colorado	CO
Connecticut	CT
Delaware	DE
Florida	FL
Georgia	GA
Hawaii	HI
Idaho	ID
Illinois	IL
Indiana	IN
Iowa	IA
Kansas	KS
Kentucky	KY
Louisiana	LA
Maine	ME
Maryland	MD
Massachusetts	MA
Michigan	MI
Minnesota	MN
Mississippi	MS
Missouri	MO
Montana	MT
Nebraska	NE
Nevada	NV
New Hampshire	NH
New Jersey	NJ
New Mexico	NM
New York	NY
North Carolina	NC
North Dakota	ND
Ohio	OH
Oklahoma	OK
Oregon	OR
Pennsylvania	PA
Rhode Island	RI
South Carolina	SC
South Dakota	SD
Tennessee	TN
Texas	TX
Utah	UT
Vermont	VT
Virginia	VA
Washington	WA
West Virginia	WV
Wisconsin	WI
Wyoming	WY

4 **USA.** Help the children learn the abbreviation for each state name by giving them a map of the United States and having them write the correct abbreviation in each one. Provide a model at the learning center. Go over the maps with the children when the skill group meets. The two-letter abbreviations approved by the U.S. Postal Service are given in List 19.

5 **Montage.** Provide old magazines, textbooks, and newspapers and direct the children to cut out symbols and abbreviations. The children can make a montage by pasting their findings on a large sheet of poster board. You can use the montage to go over the symbols and abbreviations when the children come to the skill group.

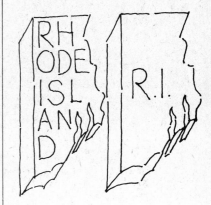

6 **It's a Small World.** The children can realize how valuable symbols and abbreviations are and practice learning them by comparing the symbols and abbreviations to the words they represent. Provide index cards that have been cut into fifths so the pieces are 3" x 1" rather than 3" x 5". Direct the children to see if they can write from one to one-hundred on the small card. Also, ask them to try to write all fifty states. It will not take them long to realize the value of abbreviations.

What Children Should Learn

Reading teachers and social studies teachers share the responsibility for helping children develop the skills and knowledge required to read maps. Again it is important to realize that many skills are necessary to get meaning from maps. Specifically, elementary school children begin to:

1. note the directions on maps according to the eight major compass points (N, S, E, W, SE, SW, NE, NW)
2. locate places on maps by using latitude and longitude lines
3. learn symbols commonly used on maps
4. trace routes of travel by different means of transportation
5. notice scales to determine distances
6. draw inferences based on the information presented on the map
7. learn the kinds of maps for different purposes

In addition to developing these skills and knowledge, we want children to form favorable attitudes toward reading maps. If children realize maps are pictures and are used as devices to present information in a concise and clear fashion, they will value maps rather than avoiding them when reading.

Diagnosing Students' Map Skill Needs

The questions used to determine students' skills in reading maps depend upon the kind of maps you ask them to read. Select different types of maps (population maps, road maps, product maps, and so forth) which are commonly found in elementary school classrooms and textbooks. Write questions such as the following to determine the children who can obtain information from maps and those who need instruction:

1. What does this map show you?
2. List four symbols used on this map. Write the meaning of each symbol.
3. What is the scale of this map?
4. How far is it from _____ to _____?
5. What country is south of _____? (political map)
6. What city is located at _____ degrees latitude and _____ degrees longitude? (political)
7. What area has mountains? (geographical)
8. Why does this country have so much _____? (product)
9. Why do so few people live in _____? (population)
10. Where do most of the people live? _____ Why? (population)
11. What is the best route to get from _____ to _____ by car if you are in a hurry? (road map)
12. How are the major cities alike in terms of location?

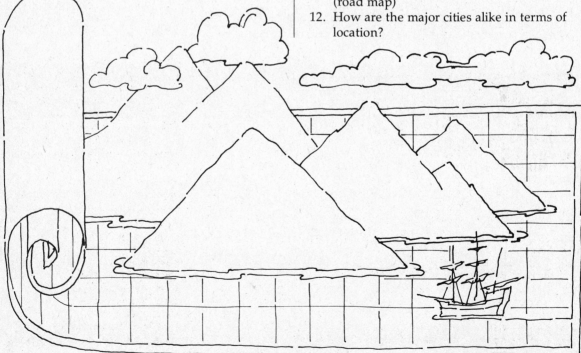

Skill Group Activities to Help Children Read Maps

1 One of the first skill group lessons should concern why we have maps. Help the children realize the value of maps by showing different kinds of maps and asking what information each one provides. Discuss other ways of presenting this same information. For example, could paragraphs be used to present the information found on road maps? Are maps really necessary? What would it be like to not have maps? Summarize this activity by having the children list the values of maps.

2 Introduce the children to an atlas if they have never seen one. Have them notice the symbols used on different maps. Ask the children why symbols are used on maps. Begin making a booklet of common symbols. Have each child draw the symbols, tell what they mean or represent, and locate them on maps.

3 Direct the children to notice the lines of latitude and longitude on maps and the globe. Ask the children what the lines might be. Explain that they are imaginary lines to help us locate places. Tell the children the lines that are parallel to the equator and used to measure the distance north or south of it are called latitude lines. The lines that run from pole to pole and measure the distance east or west of the meridian that passes through Greenwich, England, are called longitude lines. Have the children look at the index in the atlas and notice that places are listed according to their latitude and longitude. Direct the children to locate particular places by using the latitude and longitude lines. Conclude the activity by asking children what it would be like if we did not have such lines on maps.

If your children are not ready to learn how to locate places by using latitude and longitude lines, you can teach the same principle by having them use the letters and number key usually found on road maps. the procedures above can be adapted.

4 Have the children look at a particular geographical map in their social studies book to notice the scale, symbols, and information shown. Ask them to make as many "because statements" as they can by noticing the location of particular cities. For example, the children might say, "One reason Cleveland became a large city is because it is near a large body of water." Lead the children to make inferences by combining the information they see on the map with other information they have learned. Other questions that can be used for a map of the United States are:

1. Why do so many people like to go to Miami Beach in the winter?
2. Why is Chicago such a large city?
3. Why is Atlanta, Georgia, becoming a large city?
4. Why are there miners in West Virginia?
5. Why is Columbus the capital of Ohio?
6. What do Baltimore, Philadelphia, and New York have in common?
7. Why don't many people live in Nevada?
8. How are Houston and New Orleans alike?

Learning Center Activities for Map Skills

1 **Monster Map Symbols.** Duplicate Appendix Item 59 on tagboard and laminate. You will need two copies. Direct the children to cut the cards apart. All the cards except one of the Monster cards should be shuffled and dealt to the players. Play this game as you do Old Maid. The players take turns drawing a card from the person on their left beginning with the dealer. The object of the activity is to form pairs by matching map symbols. When a player has a pair of symbols, he places them on the center of the table. The person who ends up with the Monster is the loser.

2 **Map Puzzles.** Obtain some road maps or other kinds of maps that are free and paste each one on tagboard or cardboard. Laminate them if possible. Cut them apart to form puzzles the children can put together to learn different places. In doing so, the students will be noticing symbols and the lines of latitude and longitude (or number and letter key).

3 **Salt and Flour Maps.** Maps can be made with salt and flour. Tell the children to:

1. Outline the map.
2. Make a dough of two cups of flour, one cup of salt, and one cup of water. (Use less salt on damp days or in regions where humidity is high because the salt absorbs water from the atmosphere.)
3. Mold the mixture to show the desired features and let dry.
4. Color the different features with cold water paints.

4 **NE-NW-SE-SW.** Provide a map and questions concerning the location of particular places that are two directions from a reference point. For example, "If you were in St. Louis and wanted to go to Cleveland, in what direction should you travel?" Write the questions on index cards and the answers on the back so the children can check their responses. Again the students may want to make some of their own questions for others to answer.

5 **Map Time Find.** Ask the children to find certain places on the map as quickly as possible using the index. Provide index cards with names of obscure places and two maps. Children can compete against one another or against a timer or clock. The fastest finder is the winner. If you have a road map of Florida, you may want to write these places on an index card for the children to locate: Thomas City, Pirates Cove, Picnic, Lilly, Dills, Cabbage Grove, and Bruce.

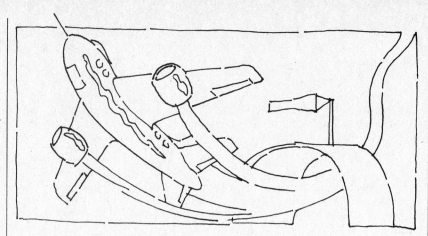

6 **Jet Set.** Provide a map of the United States with the names of large cities on it. Write "travel plans" on index cards and direct the children to go from one city to the next city following a straight line as an airplane would do. Have them add the total miles of their trip by using the scale. The children can make other routes for trips which can then be calculated by their peers. An example follows:

You left the Cleveland, Ohio, airport and flew to Miami, Florida, for some sunshine. After getting a good tan, you decided to go snow skiing in Denver, Colorado. On your way home from Denver, you stopped to see an old next-door neighbor in St. Louis, Missouri. Finally, you returned to Cleveland. How many air miles did you travel?

You can adapt this activity by providing a road map and directions to a certain destination on the index cards. For example, "Begin in Baltimore, Maryland. Take I95 south 39 miles. Where did you go?"

7 **Where Are You?** Write the location of cities by listing only the lines of latitude and longitude on an index card. Direct the children to use the map provided to locate the city at those particular lines of latitude and longitude. Write the name of the city on the back of the index card if you want the children to check their responses. For example, if you provide a map of the United States, you may want to list 34.00 N and 118.15 W (Los Angeles).

READING TABLES, DIAGRAMS, AND GRAPHS

What Children Should Learn

Many times elementary school children skip rather than read diagrams, tables, and graphs. This is unfortunate because many social studies, art, science, and health textbooks present information by these means. If elementary school children learn how to read the tables, diagrams, and graphs, they will be able to get more information from their reading; therefore, it is imperative that we help children learn to read these special ways of presenting information.

There are many skills required to read tables, diagrams, and graphs. To gain information from a table, the student must know the purpose of the table, be able to locate the information by following lines until they intersect, and draw conclusions from the information presented. In reading graphs the student must understand the purpose of the graph, determine the units of measure, summarize, and infer meanings. To read diagrams the child is required to identify parts and be able to see the relationships among them.

Diagnosing Children's Skill in Reading Tables, Diagrams, and Graphs

Sample questions are presented in the paragraphs that follow to help you develop diagnostic devices to determine if your students can read tables, diagrams, and graphs. You will need to provide tables, diagrams, and graphs that are appropriate for your children.

To construct a skills test for reading tables, find

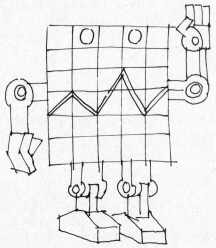

a representative table in the students' social studies, health, or science book. Ask the children to read the table, then answer such questions as

1. What is the title of the table?
2. What units of measure are being used?
3. What are the column headings?
4. What are the side headings?
5. How can you use this information?

In addition to asking these general questions concerning the table, you will need to write questions to see if the children can follow the lines to where they intersect, and then interpret the information. For example, if the graph concerns the number of children who buy their lunch and the number of students who bring their lunch, you might ask (1) why this information is needed, (2) how many children bring their lunch during a certain month as compared to another month, (3) why more children eat in the cafeteria during a certain month as compared to another month, and (4) what other information, such as the total number of students in the school, can be derived from the table.

To construct a skills test for reading diagrams, select a diagram from a health or science book the children are using. Direct the students to look at the diagram and tell

1. What is pictured in the diagram?
2. Why the authors included this diagram?

Also prepare specific questions dealing with the location of the different parts and relationships of the separate parts. For example, if you are using a diagram of the human body, you might ask what part connects the head to the shoulders, or why the knee is an important part of the body.

To construct a skills test for reading graphs, provide a bar graph, a circle graph, and a line graph. Ask some general questions, such as

1. What type of graph is being used?
2. What information is presented?
3. What is the unit of measure?
4. What symbols are used? What does each one mean?
5. What is the importance of the information presented in the graph?

In addition to these general questions, ask specific questions concerning the information presented on the graphs.

Skill Group Activities to Teach Children to Read Tables, Diagrams, and Graphs

1 Make a table and a graph of the number of different pets the children have. After doing so have the children dictate the same information in paragraph form as you write it on the board. Lead the children to discover that tables and graphs are used to present information in a concise form. Help them realize when information is presented in a graph, it enables them to form a mental image of the information. Tables provide the information in outline form. Compare both the graph and table to the wordiness of the paragraphs. Summarize by discussing the value of tables and graphs.

2 Have the children locate diagrams in their health or science textbooks. Help them realize a picture can be "worth a thousand words" by having them describe the diagram as you write in paragraph form the information illustrated in the diagram. The children might want to use a diagram concerning the

parts of their body, a flower, a tree, or the parts of a car. Compare the diagram with the written description of what is in the diagram. Have the children discuss the advantages of the diagram as compared to the paragraph. The children should readily see that diagrams clarify by providing a picture and showing how the parts are interrelated. Summarize this activity by discussing the authors' purposes in using diagrams.

3 Use a table of the temperatures in major cities and show the children how this same information can be put on a graph. Begin with the simple bar graph if appropriate. Have the children look at the table and the graph and compare the advantages of each one. Help them realize many times bar graphs can give us a *picture* of the facts which makes them easier to remember. If possible put the information on a line graph and again compare this to a

bar graph. Discuss the advantages and limitations of each type of graph.

4 Generally children do not have too much difficulty in learning how to read tables, diagrams, and graphs; however, it is perplexing for them to make inferences and draw conclusions about the information presented. Make tables or graphs that include information children are interested in knowing, such as how many children bought their lunch on a particular day in a month. The children may be able to draw conclusions about why the lunch count was so high on some days and so low on others. Perhaps the kind of food that was served was a factor. Also, if you teach in a community where payday is near the beginning of the month, you may notice that more children buy their lunch at the beginning of the month than near the end. By using the students' background of experience, you can help them make inferences and draw conclusions.

1 **Making Graphs.** Children generally enjoy making graphs and can learn to read graphs by constructing them. Duplicate Appendix Item 60 and direct the children to gather the information and fill in their graphs. They may want to find and illustrate other information, such as the number of brothers and sisters, or the kinds of pets class members have. They can bring their completed graphs to the skill group to share and to be checked.

2 **Making Tables.** Provide newspapers and direct the children to make tables of sports standings, temperatures, or rising food prices. The students' work can be checked when the skill group meets and then displayed for the other children.

3 **A Thousand Words.** Elementary school children generally like to trace diagrams from their health or social studies books. Make the children aware of the different diagrams in their books and then provide sheets of tracing paper or onionskin for them to use. Have them copy their favorite diagrams and label the parts. Perhaps they would like to make a "pictures are worth a thousand words" bulletin board to display the diagrams they have copied.

4 **What We Do.** Direct the children to make a circle graph of what they do when they are in school. You can structure this activity by providing dittoed copies of a circle divided into six hours to represent the school day (Figure 28). The

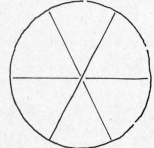

Figure 28.

children can complete the graph by drawing lines indicating what portion of the school day is devoted to each activity.

5 **Graph Grab.** Provide a graph and index cards with questions about the information presented. The graph might be drawn or glued on the front of a piece of tagboard and the questions kept in an envelope glued to the back (Figure 29). Also, make a master list of answers to the questions. Direct the children to divide into two teams and take turns drawing and answering a question. The team that answers the most questions by reading the graph wins.

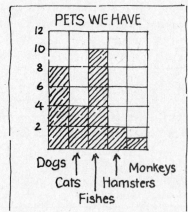

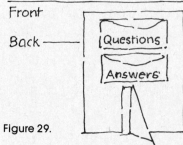

Figure 29.

6 **I Like Facts.** Provide an almanac and social studies books. Have the children make tables about the states according to their population, their area, and the year they were admitted to the Union. The children may want to staple the pages together to make a booklet of facts about the United States. This activity can be adapted to professional football or some other interest if the information is available. For example, the children may want to use the newspaper or a football program to make tables with the leading rushers, kickers, passers, and so forth. The children will enjoy making the tables if the information is interesting to them.

7 **My Favorite Players.** Provide an almanac and questions about sports figures. Direct the children to read each question and then locate the information in the almanac to answer the question. This information is presented in the almanac in table form; thus, the children will have practice in reading tables. You can provide a master list of answers if you want the children to check their responses. Competition can be added by dividing into teams and setting a time limit for finding the answer. Some questions you might want to use are:

1. Who won the men's single badminton championship in 1974?
2. What team won the NBA championship in 1974?
3. In 1976 which players had the best percentage for free throws in the NBA?
4. Who won the Super Bowl in 1969?
5. Who was the leading pass receiver in the AFL in 1970?

8 **A Trip Across the USA.** An almanac and a game board that lists every state are needed for this activity (Figure 30). You may want to use the abbreviations for the state names if the children are learning these. Direct the children to place their tokens on start and then spin a spinner or roll a die to see how many spaces they can move. When they land on a space, they should (1) read the name of the state, and (2) look at the table in the almanac that indicates the highest and lowest temperature ever recorded in the state. If the player reads the table correctly, he can stay on that state. If not, he must return to his original place. The first player to cross the finish line is the winner. Of course, any information tabulated by state can be used for this game.

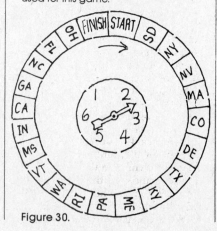

Figure 30.

PARTS OF A BOOK

What Children Should Learn

Books have many valuable aids we help children learn to use. The *title page* helps the reader select books by noticing the title of the book, author or editor, and edition. Further information concerning the appropriateness of a book can be gathered by looking at the *table of contents* and *preface*.

If the book contains many *tables, figures, maps, or pictures*, a list of these is usually included at the beginning of the book. Sometimes *bibliographies* are included at the end of each section or chapter to aid the reader in finding more information about particular topics. Likewise, some books, especially textbooks, include *questions* for discussion or *suggested activities* that aid the learner's understanding.

A *glossary* of specialized words is often found in textbooks. The definitions in the glossary are the ones for the vocabulary words as they are used in

the book; thus, the reader has some assistance in selecting the appropriate meaning. The *index* can help readers locate specific information quickly. Finally, some books include *appendices* which contain valuable supplemental material.

One of the important objectives of the elementary school reading program is to help children become aware of the *many different aids* in books and to guide development of the skills needed to use these aids. Children will be able to "get more mileage" from books, save time, and enjoy books more if they have the knowledge and skills required to use them.

Determining Students' Knowledge of the Parts of Books

A skill test (Appendix Item 61) is included to determine if students are aware of the different parts of books. Ask the children to use one of their

APPENDIX ITEM 61

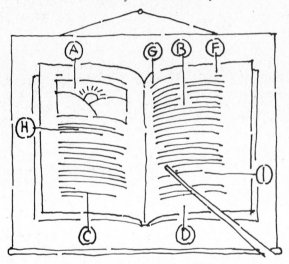

content books, such as their social studies, health, or science book, to complete the test. When evaluating the responses, notice which parts of the book the children know and do not know. This test might also be used as an activity for introducing textbooks to children. Again remember that many of the diagnostic tests and learning center activities in this book are interchangeable.

Skill Group Activities for Teaching Children the Parts of a Book

1 Ask the children to bring their social studies book to this skill group. Have them skim the book to find the different special sections such as the title page, preface or acknowledgments, the list of tables, maps, or figures, table of contents, the index, bibliographies, and appendices. Discuss the purpose of each of the different parts briefly by asking the children why they are included and how they can help us. The children should draw the conclusions that (1) we can get more out of the textbook if we know the

different parts of the book, (2) we can judge if the book is what we need, and (3) if we know how to use the different parts of the book, we will save time.

2 Go back to each part of the book on different days and have the children find the four *W*'s and *how*. *What* is the name of each part of the book, *why* is it included, *when* should it be used, *where* is it usually located, and *how* does one use it. Ask them

what it would be like if that part of the book were missing. Would it really hinder the use of the book? For example, concentrate on the table of contents during one of the sessions. Have the children notice the chapter titles along with the subtopics. Ask the children why certain subtitles are needed. Have them locate the different subtitles and see if these are helpful. Divide the group into two teams and play a game by suggesting a subtitle in the table of contents and seeing who can find the page number first.

3 Have the children bring a content textbook that includes an index. Examine the topics included in the index. Have the children notice the subheadings under the major topics in an index. Help them realize that, in using the index, they need to know the key word or major topic, then look for subheadings included under the major heading. Have the children refer to the "see also" statements and read the sections to which they were referred to see why there was a cross reference. Again you might divide the group into two teams and give them topics to locate in an index and see who can find the pages first. When doing so,

begin by using major headings and then some of the subheadings.

Children are sometimes confused when they notice that some page numbers in an index are separated by commas while others have hyphens between them. Direct the children to find examples of commas and hyphens. Have them locate the pages to notice that a comma after a page number indicates the last page concerning that topic; whereas, a hyphen between numbers indicates a series of pages concerning the topic. Have them apply this knowledge by asking questions about how many

pages concern a particular topic.

4 Have the children bring to skill group textbooks that have appendices. Ask the children when they might refer to these. Also, ask why the author included this information in the appendices rather than in some chapter. Adapt your procedures to the nature of the appendices. If their reading book includes a list of new words, talk with the children about how they can use it. For example, they might want to use it as a checklist to see if they have learned the new words in the book, or to show to their parents the new words they are learning.

Learning Center Activities to Help Children Learn the Parts of a Book

1 B Is for Book. Duplicate Appendix Item 62 for this game. Also duplicate a few copies of the question cards for the game (Appendix Item 63) and have the children cut them apart. Direct the children to see if they can move around the letter **B** by moving the number of spaces indicated by the spinner. If a child lands on a space that has a question, he must answer the question correctly or move back to the nearest free space. If a player lands on one of the "super question" spaces, he must draw a card from the top of the deck and answer the question on the card. If he answers the question correctly, he moves forward 2 spaces. If not, he stays on the question mark. The first one to move all the way around the **B** is the winner. You may want to make a master list of answers for the "super questions" so this activity can be self-correcting.

2 My Book. One of the best activities for helping children learn the parts of a book is to have them actually make a booklet. The idea for making the booklet can be introduced in the skill group, while most of the work can be done independently. Have the children select a topic such as animals and then list the kinds of information they would like to include in their booklet. As they develop the book, they will see the need for a table of contents. An index may be necessary if they have many details in their descriptions of the animals. After they have completed the book, they can make a title page, preface, a list of the pictures, and so forth. Have the children bring their booklets to the skill group periodically to check their progress.

3 Categories: Names of. The children can practice categorizing objects by playing the game "Categories: Names of." To play the game, seat the children in a small circle. The person designated to go first names a category, such as cars, states, food, trees, and so forth. After naming the category, he names one object in the category. For example, if he says cars, he could say Chevrolet. Each child in turn names a different object in the category. The idea of the game is to move as far around the circle as possible. This activity may help the children expand their knowledge of main headings and subheadings.

4 Newspapers. Provide a copy of the Sunday newspaper and ask the children to locate information by using the "Where to Find" table. Sample questions follow. Write the answers on the back if you want the children to check their responses.

1. On what pages can you find sports?
2. On what pages can you find what movies are being shown at local theaters?
3. What pages are devoted to comics?
4. If you wanted to buy a dog, on what pages would they be listed?
5. Where is the local news found?

5 Index Race. For this activity you will need to have the children make cards with topics from their indexes in the content books. To play the game, the children should turn over a card and find the topic in the index quickly. The child who finds the topic first wins. You can adapt this activity by providing sentences on index cards. Direct the children to read the sentence, determine the key word, and locate the topic in the index. Sample questions from a social studies book follow.

1. What is the capital of California?
2. What is the most important crop in Florida?
3. Who is the governor of Ohio?
4. Where do the Seminole Indians live?
5. What is the population of Miami?
6. How does corn grow?
7. Who invented the telephone?
8. Why do robins migrate to the South in the winter?

6 Use the Bibliography. Have the children use the bibliography at the end of chapters in their different content books by going to the library to locate the suggested books. The children might then want to set up a learning center to display the books they have found concerning a certain topic.

7 Why Copyrights? Have the children find out what a copyright is by reading an almanac or by writing to one of the local governmental agencies. The children might want to send for the forms authors complete to obtain a copyright. Have them discuss why an author would like to have a copyright. After the children have gathered this information, they may want to write a television program or create a bulletin board to inform others about copyrights.

REFERENCE SKILLS

What Children Should Learn

The amount of knowledge mankind has increases daily. It has become impossible for specialists to keep up-to-date in their fields, let alone to have children learn all of the information that is available and valuable. The need to refer to the appropriate book for information becomes greater each year.

In the elementary school we try to teach children to use many different types of reference materials: encyclopedias, almanacs, atlases, dictionaries, thesauri, and telephone directories. Our objectives are twofold: (1) to teach children what information is presented in the different types of reference materials and (2) to help children develop skill in locating desired materials. This section of the chapter is devoted to helping children learn the kinds of information found in the various types of reference materials. The common skills (alphabetical order, use of guide words, using the index, skill in selecting the key words) required to use these reference materials were presented in the Dictionary Skills section of Chapter 3 and in the preceding section of this chapter.

In conducting the skill group activities and using learning center activities, you should remember that one of the most important goals is to help children develop favorable attitudes toward reference materials. Too often children learn to hate reference books because they are told to "go look it up" without having the knowledge of where to look and how to locate the information. This initial introduction to reference materials should be pleasant so children will value these sources of information as well as develop skills in selecting and using them.

Diagnosing Students' Knowledge of Reference Materials

A skill test is provided in the Appendix (Item 64) to determine if children know what kind of information is found in different types of reference books. Direct the children to match the information desired with the reference material that would most likely be the best source of that information. In evaluating responses notice what kinds of reference books the children are aware of in terms of content.

APPENDIX ITEM 64

Skill Group Activities to Help Children Learn About Reference Materials

1 Obtain copies of different reference books and give one to each child. For an example, you may distribute telephone books, almanacs, atlases, different volumes of encyclopedias, thesauri, or dictionaries. Ask each child to look through his book and be ready to tell what information is in it and when he might need that information. Tell the children that in this group you will be helping them find out more about what the different books contain.

2 During some sessions concentrate on encyclopedias. Distribute a volume to each child and ask the children to look through and find the most interesting information they would like to share with the class. Provide time for the children to find something and briefly share the information. By doing so, the children will get an idea of what kinds of information they are most likely to find and when this information might be valuable. Have the children notice the volumes are arranged in alphabetical order and guide words are provided. You might show them the index to help them see where they would go to find particular information. Have them see that the index is organized in a similar fashion to the indices in their social studies and science textbooks. Review the importance of knowing the key word when using an index. Summarize the activities by asking the children why we have encyclopedias.

3 During one of the sessions with this skill group introduce the almanac. If possible get a copy of the almanac for each child and ask them to look through it to find something that is interesting to them. Provide the children with an opportunity to share this information with others in the class. Have the children notice that the index for the almanac is at the front of the book. Ask them why this is so. Also, have them look at the major topics and subheadings on a particular page of the index. After they have had a chance to become familiar with the organization of the index ask them where they would find certain topics such as the following:

1. The population of California
2. How old one has to be to get married in New Hampshire
3. How many farms are in Ohio
4. The population of Carson City, Nevada
5. The population of the United States in 1890 and 1970

Conclude the activity by asking children why we have almanacs and why a new edition is presented each year.

4 Use one of these skill group sessions to emphasize the telephone book. If the children are aware of the fact that names and addresses are found in the telephone book, refer them to other pages. For example, ask them where they would find information on how to make a long distance call. Have them refer to the yellow pages to see particular advertisements. Again point out the guide words. Ask the students how people go about selecting a medical doctor, a flower service, an appliance store, car dealer, or toy store. Summarize the lesson by asking the children what it would be like if we did not have telephone directories.

Learning Center Activities to Help Children Become Aware of Reference Materials

1 **My Personal Directory.** Provide telephone books for the children to make personal telephone directories with numbers of interest to them. Duplicate Appendix Item 65 for this activity.

2 **My Favorite Is.** Elementary school children generally have favorite flowers, animals, and other objects which are usually presented on colored plates in encyclopedias. Ask the children to complete Appendix Item 66 by finding their favorites. Again the children will be seeing that encyclopedias do contain interesting information.

3 **Our Class Almanac.** Direct the children to make an almanac of facts about the students in the class or school. For example, they may gather information concerning who has pets, what kind they have, and how many they have; who lives on what street; who has a television set, radio, and telephone; who has brothers and sisters and how many they have; where the different children were born, and so forth. This booklet of facts can be indexed like a regular almanac and will help children realize what an almanac is and how the information in it is gathered and organized.

4 **Call Me Roget.** Have the children make a miniature thesaurus of slang words and expressions. Direct them to write the slang word or expression at the top of the page and a synonym and antonym below it. Illustrations can be drawn if they desire. Have the children bring their booklets to the skill group to share and be evaluated. The children may want to display their booklets in the library.

5 **How Many in the City?** Have the children find out the populations of the cities having baseball or football teams. After determining the populations, ask the children to rank the teams according to their city's populations.

6 **Do You Know?** Make a deck of index cards with questions about which the children might have some curiosity. Direct the children to use the appropriate reference material to find the answer. If you want to make this a self-correcting activity, write the type of reference material and the page number on which the answer is found on the back of a card. After the children have a chance to use all of your questions, have them

make some of their own. The following questions might be used as examples:

1. What products are made with oil?
2. How is paper made?
3. What were the first schools like?
4. What is the telephone number of the court house?
5. What number would you call if you needed to report a fire?
6. What minerals are found in the United States?
7. How many types of sharks are there?
8. What is a synonym for crazy?
9. How did the game of basketball begin?
10. When is the best time to see meteors?

7 **The 100 Yard Dash.** For this activity you will need a strip of paper divided into 100 parts plus a starting and a finish line. You will also need to make a set of index cards with words on them that the children are learning. Direct the children to put a token on the starting line and in turn take a card from the deck. Each child reads his word and then, referring to a thesaurus, names as many synonyms and antonyms as possible in a specified period of time (e.g., 3 minutes). He moves his token as many spaces as the number of synonyms and antonyms he is able to name. The next player turns up another card and does the same thing. Of course the object of the game is to run the 100 yard dash as quickly as possible. The first player to the finish line is the winner.

LIBRARY SKILLS

What Children Should Learn

Many elementary schools have central libraries in addition to small classroom libraries. It is necessary then for elementary school children to begin to master the skills needed to use the library efficiently. The children need to learn to use a card catalog, to understand how library books are arranged, to develop skill in using the *Reader's Guide to Periodical Literature*, and to become aware of proper library behavior.

The card catalog is perhaps the most important aid children should learn to use to locate books. Students need to learn the three basic types of cards (author, subject, and title) found in a card catalog. In addition, they learn that the cards provide information to help them locate books. They learn that capital *B* tells that the book is a *biography* and is classified under the last name of the person whose story it tells. A capital *R* means *reference*. They also learn there are no markings on cards for fiction books, but rather these are classified by the author's last name. They need to understand the numbers found on cards of nonfiction books arranged by the author's last name are usually classified under the Dewey decimal system or, in larger libraries, according to the Library of Congress *A*-to-*Z* system.

In using a card catalog, the children must learn more about alphabetical order in that books are arranged in alphabetical order by the title except when the title begins with *the*, *a*, or *an*. In these cases, the next word in the title is considered in

placing the book in alphabetical order. Likewise, children must be made aware of small deviations, such as that *Mc* is treated the same as *Mac* when alphabetizing books. They also must realize that numbers are always written out when considering alphabetical order. Of course, abbreviations are not considered in alphabetical order. For example, the children must learn that, if they are looking for a book whose title begins with *St.*, they must look under *Saint*.

Some elementary school libraries are fortunate to have journals and thus also purchase the *Reader's Guide to Periodical Literature*. Children should understand why a guide to periodical literature is necessary and also develop skill in using it.

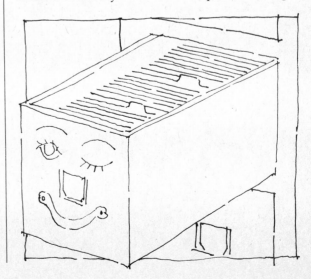

This is especially appropriate for intermediate grade children who are interested in particular topics or are required to do reports. Children should learn that magazines usually have more up-to-date information than books because it takes more time to publish books.

In addition to developing the library skills, elementary school children should develop appropriate library behavior habits. We do believe that libraries are to be used by the children and we want them to be comfortable places. At the same time the children must realize that some people read in the libraries and need quiet areas. A discussion of taking care of books, as well as returning books on time, would certainly be a part of the instruction concerning library skills.

Diagnosing Students' Library Skills

A skill test is provided in the Appendix (Item 67) to determine the students' accomplishment of some of the library skills. The first part of the test is designed to see if children know alphabetical order as it applies to book titles. The second part deals with the card catalog, what information is found in it and why we have it. You may want to develop a skill test to determine what children know about using the *Reader's Guide to Periodical Literature* if available.

APPENDIX ITEM 67

Skill Group Activities for Teaching Library Skills

1 Perhaps the best way to begin this skill group is to talk first about why we have libraries, where the money comes from for libraries, and standards for using library books. Help the children understand it is not possible for each individual to buy every book he would like to have; therefore, we all pay money (taxes) to have books available. Because these books are available to everyone, it is necessary to have certain rules or standards to make sure everyone has a chance to use the book. This is why we have deadlines concerning how long a person may keep a book and why it is also necessary to have some kind of fine or punishment if the book is not returned on time. Also discuss the importance of taking care of books since they belong to everyone and each person would like to find a book in good condition.

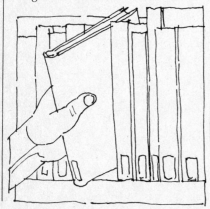

2 If possible take the children to the library to teach them how to use the card catalog. If this is not possible, you should have some cards available to show the children. You might want to make transparencies of these so you can use an overhead projector to display them on a screen while you discuss them. Have the children look at each card to see whether it is the author card, title card, or subject card. Ask the children why we have three cards on each book.

When the children are aware of the three cards, ask them to name some of their favorite topics, authors, or book titles. Have them use the card catalog to see if the school library holds the book. If so, point out the information on the cards so they can locate the books.

3 After the children are aware of the three different cards, introduce the call numbers and other information found in the upper left-hand corner. Help the children understand what a biography is by referring to some biographies you may have read to them. Likewise, teach the difference between fiction and nonfiction by giving examples of certain stories you have read already or that you know the children have read. Explain to the children that each library has an area for fiction books and these books are arranged

in alphabetical order by the author's last name. The nonfiction books have numbers and are classified by the Dewey decimal system. Take the children to the library and show them where books in each category are located.

4 Have the children notice the *R* on cards of reference books and talk with them about the kinds of reference books that can be found in a library. Also discuss with them why certain books must be used in the library and cannot be taken out. You might help them see that, if one volume of a reference collection is missing, this will hinder the use of the entire set of materials. Point out the cost of reference materials in explaining why some books must remain in the library.

5 Children may need some work with alphabetical order because knowledge of alphabetical order is needed to locate books. Ask them to arrange the following titles in alphabetical order and tell why their answer is correct. Reteach as necessary.

20,000 Leagues Under the Sea
The Little Story for You
Thomas Jefferson
St. Mary's Secret
Dr. Doolittle Rides Again
An Animal Can Be Fun

Learning Center Activities for Library Skill Development

1 Where Do I Belong? Duplicate Appendix Item 68 for this activity. Direct the children to read the titles at the bottom of the page and then determine whether each book is a reference, biography, fiction, or nonfiction book. The children should write the titles of the book on the appropriate shelf in alphabetical order.

2 Making Card Catalogs. One way to help children realize what information is included in a card catalog is to have them actually make cards for some books. Make available approximately 10 to 15 books, along with three 3" x 5" index cards for each one. Direct the children to make an author, title, and subject card for each book. Display examples for the children. If the same books are in your school library, the children can go to the library and compare their cards with those found in the card catalog.

3 Find Me as Quickly as You Can. Provide several lists of five books for the children and direct them to go to the card catalog in the school library and find the books as quickly as possible. The first child to find all five books on his list is the winner. Those children who try to find the books without using the card catalog will soon realize the value of it. Likewise children will learn there are sometimes disappointments in trying to find a book that is on loan.

4 All About. Make a list of topics that are interesting to the children in your class. Direct the children to go to the library and use the subject cards in the card catalog to see which books the library has. The children can then locate the books and see if they are appropriate for their needs.

5 Magazines and Audio-Visual Materials. If your library subscribes to some of the children's magazines, ask the librarian to meet with the children to show them where current and back issues are located. Likewise, many elementary school libraries have expanded to include different types of media: filmstrips, posters, pictures, films, and so forth. Obtain the cooperation of the librarian to teach the children how to locate these materials. Allow time for the children to survey materials that seem attractive.

6 Our Library. Have the children organize the books in the classroom according to the four major categories and arrange them in alphabetical order. They may want to use colored tape to simplify the catalog system. Children will develop many of the library skills by actually serving as librarians.

STUDY SKILLS AND HABITS

What Children Should Learn

Elementary school children should develop efficient study skills and habits to read materials in health, science, social studies, mathematics, and other areas of interest. Many of the functional reading skills introduced previously, such as using different parts of books and reading maps and graphs, are needed to study efficiently. In addition, students must develop some study strategies and appropriate habits. Elementary school teachers have the responsibility of (1) introducing the various study strategies, and (2) guiding the development of appropriate habits so students can use and later refine these skills.

One of the most popular study strategies that can be taught in the elementary school is called SQ3R. SQ3R is an acronym that represents the five steps employed in the study strategy (survey, question, read, recite, review). This study method was suggested by Francis Robinson.[1] Another popular strategy introduced by Spache[2] is called PQRST which also involves five steps when studying (preview, question, read, summarize, and test).

The first step in SQ3R is to survey the material to determine what it concerns and how much time will be involved in reading it. In the PQRST formula, the first step is the same, but it is called a different name: preview. In both cases the children are trying to develop a frame of reference for what they are going to be reading. When children survey or preview, they look at the pictures, major headings, number of pages, and other aids provided in the reading material.

The second step in both strategies is to develop questions. Perhaps the easiest way of doing this is to try to change the headings into question form. For example, if the major heading or subheading is "Products of Venezuela" the children would say, "What are some products of Venezuela?" This step helps the children develop purposes for their reading and thus improves comprehension.

1. F. P. Robinson, "Study Skills for Superior Students in Secondary School," in L. E. Hafner, ed., *Improving Reading in Middle and Secondary Schools*, 2d ed. (New York: Macmillan, 1974).

2. G. D. Spache, *Toward Better Reading* (Champaign, Ill.: Garrard, 1963).

The third step in each method is to read to answer the questions. Generally children employ the study rate or slow rate when reading content materials.

The fourth step in the SQ3R step is to recite answers to the questions which were formulated; whereas, the fourth step in the PQRST method is to summarize what was read. The purpose of these steps is to help the children evaluate whether they did in fact concentrate and comprehend as they were reading.

The final step in the SQ3R study method is to review. Step five in the PQRST method—test—is similar to the fourth step in the SQ3R method. The SQ3R method varies in that now review is suggested to aid retention of the material.

The task of elementary school teachers is clear. Rather than having children develop the habit of reading an assignment by beginning at the first paragraph, without previewing, asking questions, reading at a slow rate, summarizing, and reviewing, we need to help children develop strategies that include these procedures.

Another skill that is required when studying is that of outlining. Children in the elementary school learn a simple form of outlining by using Roman numerals for the main topic, capital letters for the main ideas, and Arabic numerals for specific details or supporting details. Outlining helps children recognize main ideas and the supporting details, and perhaps see cause-and-effect relationships.

Many elementary school children have difficulty when taking notes from content books, encyclopedias, or other reference books. They tend to copy every word rather than to select key words and the information that is most important to them. Note-taking is another skill that is introduced at the elementary school level and refined in secondary schools. The role of the teacher is to help children realize it is not valuable or desirable to copy every word the author says unless a direct quotation is needed.

In addition to guiding the development of these study skills, elementary school teachers try to help students develop appropriate study *habits*. Emphasis is on helping children realize the importance of a place for studying, setting time limits for study activities, and developing schedules that have a balance of recreational and study activities.

Diagnosing Students' Study Skills and Habits

A checklist is provided in the Appendix (Item 69) and can be administered to the children to determine what study skills and habits they have developed. You can also use this checklist as you observe the children when they are studying.

APPENDIX ITEM 69

Skill Group Activities to Teach Study Skills and Habits

1 The most effective way of teaching students to use SQ3R is to actually go through the steps with them on some study assignment. Obtain some textbook all the students can read at their independent or instructional reading level and select three or four pages you can use to demonstrate SQ3R or PQRST. As you go through each step, ask the children why the step is important. For example, why is it necessary to survey or preview the material? Why is it important to raise questions? Why is it important to use a slower rate of reading? Why review or summarize? Why recite the answers to yourself? Helping the children realize the reasons for each step will help them realize the value of each study method. Summarize the activity by telling the children that it does take more time to study when they first use SQ3R, but soon the steps will become automatic and will save them time later.

2 Using the same selection, or another selection that is appropriate, help the children identify the major points that would be included in an outline. You might begin by having them indicate the major topic of the selection and then the major ideas presented in the selection. After doing so, see if the children can find details concerning the main ideas. Introduce the simple format for outlining in which Roman numerals are used for the central topics of the entire selection, capital letters are used for the main ideas, and Arabic numerals are used for supporting details. Conclude the activity by talking to the children about the kinds of materials they may need to outline.

3 Discuss the importance of having a place to study where all the study tools, such as paper, pens, paper clips, and so forth, are readily available. Ask the students what happens if a definite place for study has not been established. Also discuss the importance of setting a time limit for studying. Tell the children research indicates students do better when they say they are going to study a definite time length and try to finish their studies within that time. Conclude the discussion by having the children write a list of appropriate study habits.

4 Another study aid is that of predicting outcomes. As the children survey the major topics and look at the pictures, they should try to guess what is going to happen. By predicting some outcomes, the students will concentrate more because they will be reading to see if their predictions come true. Have the children look at some of the stories in basal readers, library books, or other books that include pictures and try to predict what happens in the story. After the children have finished reading the selections, discuss their predictions and how these helped them concentrate.

Learning Center Activities for Helping Children Develop Study Skills and Habits

1 Take Five. Duplicate Appendix Item 70 on tagboard and cut apart the cards. Shuffle the cards and place them in a box. Each player in turn draws five cards, reads them, and determines his score for the round. The cards are then placed back in the box and the next player takes a turn. The player with the highest score at the end of the round is the winner.

2 Practice, Practice, Practice. Children need practice in developing the SQ3R or PQRST study method. Provide different content books with interesting selections. Direct the children to use the five steps in reading the selections. You might want to have the children write questions for some of the selections. If so, ask them to put their questions in the book so other children can compare the questions.

3 Study Skills Booklet. The children in this skill group might want to work as a group at the learning center to make a study skills booklet. For example, one child can describe a good place for studying. Another child might want to do some illustration or write something that explains the importance of setting a time limit for study. Another child can illustrate the steps of different study techniques. When the children have completed the booklet, it could be used for review during the skill group.

4 SQ3R BB. Direct the children to make a bulletin board that illustrates the steps involved when using SQ3R or PQRST. Provide old textbooks the children can cut if they decide to include real selections in their illustrations. Use the bulletin board as a teaching device when it is complete.

5 Outlining Is Helpful. Provide dittoed copies of the outline format explained earlier. Direct the children to read specific pages in their books or certain interesting selections in the encyclopedias and then complete the outline. Provide answers by completing the outlines and making them available to the students.

6 Unfinished Stories. One way to help children develop skill in predicting outcomes is to provide unfinished stories for them to complete. There are many commercial materials available for this activity or some of the children might want to write the beginnings of stories and have other children finish them. Make the unfinished stories available at the learning center and direct the children to complete them and bring them to the skill group for discussion.

7 Make a Note of It. Select articles from children's magazines which include information children want to remember. Ask the children to read the articles and take notes by noticing the five W's: who, what, when, where, and why. Again a dittoed worksheet that lists these key words can be provided to structure the activity. Direct the children to bring these notes to the skill group to be evaluated.

8 I Predict. Provide articles or suggest specific pages in books for children to read. Direct the children to survey or preview the material and then predict what information is going to be included. Provide 3" x 5" index cards for the children to write their predictions on before reading. Ask the children to then read the selection to see if their predictions are true. Discuss the predictions and values of predicting when the children come to the skill group.

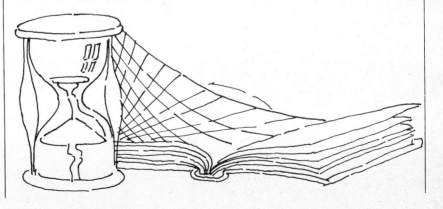

What Children Should Learn

If we teach children all the skills involved in reading, but do not teach them to love or enjoy reading, we have failed. One of the major goals of the elementary school reading program is to help children enjoy reading as a leisure time activity and as a technique for gathering information of interest. Recreational reading is also important in the elementary school program because children become better readers by reading, reading, and reading. Reading is similar to other skills: if you don't use it, you will lose it. The child who reads frequently continues to improve his vocabulary, rate of comprehension, and other reading skills.

One of the most effective ways of helping children enjoy reading as a leisure time activity is to provide reading materials concerning their interests. We must determine and expand interests so children will desire more information. Perhaps reading would be a natural activity if children had interests and were aware of what books and other reading materials are available to help satisfy these interests. Children who are interested in cars, shells, animals, sports, sewing, or whatever can be easily influenced to read if these materials are available at their reading level. Our task is to help children expand their interests and make them aware of appropriate reading materials concerning their interests.

Diagnosing Interests and Needs in Recreational Reading

Because the most effective way of encouraging children to do more recreational reading is to make sure there are materials available concerning their interests, it is necessary to determine the interests of children. A two-part interest inventory is provided in the Appendix (Items 71 and 72) to find out what interests children have and what recreational activities they enjoy. You can ask your children to complete these or simply use them as a guide for informal talks and/or observations. After determining the major interests of your children, gather books, pamphlets, and other materials that coincide with these interests. Perhaps you will want to keep a separate chart of the children's interests. This will be particularly valuable if you decide to have interest groups. Again simply list the names of the children down the left-hand column and the possible interests along the top of the chart. Put a check mark by the child's name under the most current interests he has.

APPENDIX ITEMS 71 AND 72

Skill Group Activities for Increasing Recreational Reading

1 Perhaps one of the most effective ways of increasing recreational reading is to establish a recreational reading room in your classroom. This might be a section of the room that is partitioned and includes more comfortable furniture, such as covered chairs, couch, beanbag chairs, or throw pillows. Have the children design the room and also establish the rules for using it. As the children look for materials for the area, you might ask them to consider baseball or football cards, pamphlets from their vacations, postcards, newspapers, maps they like, games they enjoy playing, books related to interests, jokes they have written, and other things that would "turn them on" to reading. Parents can help by supplying used furniture, carpet, shower curtains, and other things to make the area pleasant and private.

2 It is important to discuss why reading is necessary. Children soon realize learning to read is something that is expected in our society, yet they are not sure why reading is all that important. Help the children understand they will become more independent when they are able to read well. For example, they would be able to read the comics by themselves, put models together or bake cakes, find restrooms, and avoid danger by noting signs and labels. Ask the children to give other examples. Conclude by summarizing the reasons we learn to read. Perhaps the group would want to make a bulletin board to inform other students of why reading is important. The bulletin board might consist of labels and signs that are commonly found. Some of these

signs might be important for the children's safety, such as the poison sign. The bulletin board might also include cartoons, directions for making a model, candy wrappers, and so forth.

3 Read some unusual and very exciting reading materials to the children, such as comic books, baseball cards, jokes, adventure stories, and some of your favorite children's stories. Closed books in libraries are not very exciting. Open the books for your children by reading about interesting people, sad and dangerous events, and happy moments that send chills up and down the spine. Children will not value books unless they know what they are like, yet, too often we stop reading to children after first grade. Find and read spellbinding selections to your students!

4 Some teachers have used songs successfully to increase students' desire to read. Ask the children what some of their favorite songs are and type or print the words to these songs. The children can have fun singing the songs as they are learning the correct words. Some of the children may enjoy writing their own songs or words to songs. Perhaps skill group members will want to make a booklet of their favorite songs.

Learning Center Activities to Increase Recreational Reading

1 **Reading the Newspaper.** There are many interesting newspaper activities elementary school children can do. Duplicate Appendix Item 73 and then provide copies of newspapers for the children. The children will enjoy the newspaper as they try to locate the information necessary to answer the questions on the learning center activity sheet.

2 **Books Can Help Me.** Display books or articles to help children understand more about themselves. Ask the librarian what books are available concerning belonging, boasting, death, discontentment, disobedience, family life, friendship, frustrations, getting along with others, physical handicaps, heartaches and hurt feelings, loneliness, honesty, love and understanding, manners, kindness, temper, and working cooperatively. Suggested books can be located at this center.

3 **Look What I Read.** Direct the children to make some product to share the major ideas of some book they have read. Perhaps the children will want to make a radio announcement, telegram, picture, diorama, mobile, mural, book cover, or a poster to illustrate the book. These can be shared with others in the class during the skill group and hopefully influence them to read or listen to that book.

4 **What Can I Do Now?** Provide books that have simple directions for making crafts and pamphlets. For example, you may want to get **What To Do When There's Nothing To Do** (Boston Children's Medical Center), **1001 Ways to Have Fun with Children** (Jeanne Scargall), and **838 Ways to Amuse a Child** (June Johnson). Direct the children to select projects, follow the directions, and share the results with others.

5 **Interest Group Centers.** Perhaps there are some children in the room who want to be in a special interest group. For example, you might have an interest group on horses, sports, industrial arts, sewing, games, collecting rocks and shells, and so forth. The children in the interest groups could meet and gather more information about their special interests. Of course, all the activities would not be reading, but in most cases some helpful written materials will be available. Direct the children to set up interest centers to display products, books and articles, pictures, or other materials that may influence others to develop the interest.

The children can prepare oral reports to inform others of their hobbies or interests. By organizing and sharing this information, they will be helping others expand interests and at the same time have an opportunity to feel special. Provide the following outline to help children prepare reports for others. Remember, the major purpose of this activity is to increase and expand interests so children will have some need for recreational reading.

Suggestions for Preparing a Report

1. What is your topic?
2. List the major ideas or facts you want others to know.
3. Can you show pictures, models, objects, or other things to help others understand? Which ones?
4. Can you involve the class in making something? What materials are you going to need?
5. How are you going to begin the presentation to make sure you get everyone's attention?
6. How are you going to conclude the presentation?

---

6 Profiles. You can make a profile of each child by using the light from the overhead projector. Simply have the child stand between the light and paper on which you trace the profile. Give the children a star to put on their profile to indicate books, articles, or other materials they have read. Vary the requirements for the stars according to the reading capabilities and interests of the students. Remember, success breeds success. Ask the children to keep you informed of their independent reading by talking with you and/or completing a form such as the one that follows:

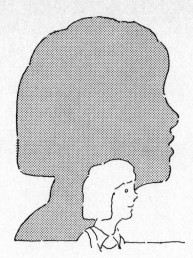

I read _____

The most interesting _____

Other students should read this because _____

New words I learned:

        word   meaning

_____   _____

_____   _____

7 Mad Magazines. Children's magazines have many activities and games, such as follow the dots, find the hidden pictures, vocabulary puzzles, riddles and jokes, things to make, and games based on a holiday. Provide magazines in the recreational room for use by the children. If you do not want them to mark the copies, have them use a transparency and a grease pencil. Encourage the children to put some of their favorite stories in the magazine on tape so they can be enjoyed by others who may find the selections too difficult. You can structure the activity by providing specific directions such as, "Do you like jokes and riddles? You can find some funny jokes and riddles at the back page of every issue of **Boy's Life**." You

should also remember to read some of the selections from the popular magazines to children during your read aloud time. By seeing what the magazines contain, the children will be motivated to use them.

8 My Book About _____. Direct the children to make some of their own books for others to read. Ask the children to select a topic of interest to them, gather information, and make illustrations or find appropriate pictures. For example, boys who really enjoy football may make a book about their favorite football players. In doing so, they could find pictures in discarded football programs or newspapers. Information

concerning the rules of football can be found in the encyclopedia. Display the books for others to read.

9 Creative Writing. Ask the children to write some of their own stories or poems to be read by others. Provide story starters or topics to motivate the children. Direct the children to bring their stories to the skill group to read to others and to be evaluated. Give suggestions and help the children understand authors do much rewriting before getting the final product. Suggestions for stories, such as those in List 20, can be written on 3" x 5" index cards.

List 20. Story Starters

1. What would you do if school were canceled?
2. Describe a bammer.
3. What could happen to Mr. Baddottle?
4. You just received two free tickets. What are the tickets for and what are you going to do with them?
5. The U.S. Supreme Court just outlawed all cars, buses, airplanes, and other vehicles. Describe the situation.
6. This is your "special day." What are you going to do?
7. Your dog was as big as a horse when you woke up this morning. What happened?
8. All the children in this class moved into your house for one week. What was it like?
9. What would happen in the game of basketball, golf, tennis, or football if all the balls were square instead of round?
10. You are the manager of the school cafeteria. What would you do?

FINAL COMMENT

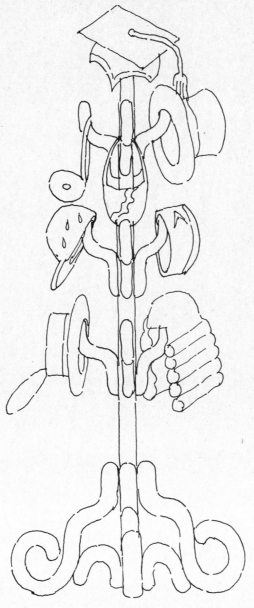

Only A Teacher

You are a scholar, *you are well aware of the skills children must develop in order to read.*

You are a diagnostician, *you use many devices to determine individual needs.*

You are an accountant, *you have records to keep while others enjoy evenings of peace.*

You are a sociologist, *you form many groups that you try to meet.*

You are an interior decorator, *you have lots of ideas to make the room neat.*

You are a reservationist, *trying to schedule children so they won't be late to eat.*

You are an instructor, *you have lots of children to teach.*

You are a judge and informant, *with information and suggestions that others should heed.*

You are only a teacher, *you understand why you are beat, yet others will never realize what makes you weep.*

Only you know what it is like to teach!

Have faith and fortitude as you help others learn to read, only you can enjoy the benefits others never reap!

APPENDIX

READY-TO-DUPLICATE
MATERIALS
TO INDIVIDUALIZE
READING INSTRUCTION

Students' Needs in Reading

	12.	11.	10.	9.	8.	7.	6.	5.	4.	3.	2.	1.	Names of Students	
													Visual	PREREADING
													Auditory	
													Sequencing / Memory	
													Motor	
													Vocabulary	
													Concepts	
													Readiness for Books	
													Letters	
													Sight Words	WORD RECOGNITION
													Consonants	
													Sound Patterns	
													Vowels	
													Syllabication / Accent	
													Context Clues	
													Structure	
													Dictionary	
													Main Idea	COMPREHENSION
													Details	
													Sequence of Events	
													Drawing Conclusions	
													Critical Reading	
													Vocabulary Development	
													Rate	
													Oral	
													Symbols / Abbreviations	FUNCTIONAL
													Maps	
													Tables / Diagrams / Graphs	
													Parts of a Book	
													Reference Skills	
													Library Skills	
													Study Skills	
													Recreational Reading	

This card is from **The Reading Corner** © 1977 Goodyear Publishing Company, Inc. and Harry W. Forgan, Jr.

This Week in Reading

Name _____

Week of _____

A. I will enjoy reading:

1. _____

2. _____

3. _____

B. To be a better reader, I'll work on: | What I'll Do

1.

_____

2.

_____

3.

_____

4.

_____

C. Here is a list of new words I am learning:

Monday _____

Tuesday _____

Wednesday _____

Thursday _____

Friday _____

D. How I feel about what I am planning to do this week.

This card is from The Reading Corner ®1977 Goodyear Publishing Company, Inc. and Harry W. Forgan, Jr.

Dear Parents:

One of the most difficult and important tasks teachers have is that of providing for the individual differences of students. Many materials are needed for the children who are working independently until they meet with the teacher. Teachers have been making many academic games and activities for independent use; however, there is not enough time to make all the materials that are needed. We need your help.

On _____, _____, from _____
to _____ o'clock, _____ will meet parents to make academic games and materials. All the materials and directions will be provided. We simply need helping hands. Please check below if you are able to attend this session.

You also can help by sending any of the following materials which will be used in making some of the activities.

___coffee cans   ___cardboard boxes   ___egg cartons   ___gift boxes
___milk cartons   ___old buttons   ___magazines   ___newspapers
___chips or tokens   ___spinners from games   ___catalogs with   ___fabric scraps
   from old games   pictures

                                    Sincerely,

Child's Name _____

Parent's Name _____

_____Yes, I am able to work.

_____No, I am not able to work.

This card is from The Reading Corner ©1977 Goodyear Publishing Company, Inc. and Harry W. Forgan, Jr.

Name _____

Self-Evaluation Report

Directions: Tell about your week in "reading" by completing these sentences.

Week of _____

1. I really enjoyed _____

2. I did not like _____

3. I read _____

4. I would like to read more about _____

5. Some new words I learned are _____

6. In one group I _____

7. The learning center activity I liked best was _____

8. The story I liked best was _____

9. It was fun to _____

10. I am a better reader because _____

11. I wish my teacher would help me _____

12. I want to _____

13. At home my parents _____

14. When I came to a word I did not know _____

15. This week reading was _____

16. Next week I _____

This card is from **The Reading Corner** ©1977 Goodyear Publishing Company, Inc. and Harry W. Forgan. Jr.

Individual Progress Record

Name _____

Address _____

Birth Date _____

Phone _____

1. **Reading Levels** ____Independent ____Instructional ____Frustrational

2. **Reading Skills**

   Prereading ____Visual ____Auditory ____Sequencing and Memory ____Motor ____Vocabulary ____Concepts
   ____Readiness for Books ____Letter Names

   Word Recognition ____Sight Words ____Consonants ____Vowels ____Sound Patterns ____Accents and Syllables
   ____Context Clues ____Structure ____Use of Dictionary

   Comprehension ____Main Idea ____Details ____Sequence of Events ____Drawing Conclusions
   ____Critical Reading ____Vocabulary Development ____Rate of Comprehension
   ____Oral Reading

   Functional ____Parts of a Book ____Symbols and Abbreviations ____Graphs and Tables ____Maps
   ____Reference Skills ____Library Skills ____Study Habits ____Recreational Reading

   (Check those that have been mastered. Star those that are being emphasized now.)

3. **Major Interests** _____

   _____

4. **Factors Influencing Learning** (Ask parents for more information.)

   Physical (vision, hearing, health) _____

   _____

   Language (speech, spelling, sentence structure) _____

   _____

   Educational (previous school experience, attendance, success) _____

   _____

   Aptitude (interest in reading, visual memory, auditory memory) _____

   _____

   Social–Emotional (self-concept, relationships with others) _____

   _____

   Environmental (experiences, books available) _____

   _____

This card is from **The Reading Corner** © 1977 Goodyear Publishing Company, Inc. and Harry W. Forgan, Jr.

This card is from **The Reading Corner** © 1977 Goodyear Publishing Company, Inc. and Harry W. Forgan, Jr.

Dear Parents,

Some of you are probably wondering what your role is in helping your child learn to read. I realize you are concerned about your child's reading achievement, and therefore want to provide you with some general guidelines as to your responsibilities. During the school year I shall be sharing other more specific suggestions to enable you to help your child.

One basic responsibility is that of helping your child value books and reading. Research has shown that parents who read to their child and provide many books and magazines, or make use of the public library, help their child develop an interest in and love for reading.

A second major responsibility is to show interest in your child's reading. Reading is considered to be a task that all children should achieve. As with other basic tasks, children want you and other significant people to notice their achievements. Look at your child's school papers when they are brought home. Show interest in your child by practicing some of the new reading skills being learned. I hope you will feel free to come to the school for a conference to discuss your child's reading achievement.

The final responsibility you have is to provide for the physical, social, emotional, and language needs of your child. Physical factors, such as good vision, hearing, and health, are essential for effective growth in reading. I hope you will help your child maintain his health by getting the proper rest and diet. Likewise, if you accept and love your child as he is, chances are he will do better in school. Another way you can accept this responsibility is by providing a variety of experiences for your child. Generally, the more experiences a child has the better reader he is. Parents who do many things with their child and talk about the experiences they are having are actually helping their child learn to read.

If you look back at the three basic responsibilities of a parent, you will notice the initial letters in the key words form the acronym VIP. The first responsibility is for parents to help their child value books and reading. Second, parents should show interest in their child's reading. Finally, parents should provide basic necessities that are needed for achievement in reading. You are a VIP. Let us cooperate together to help your child learn to enjoy reading.

                                        Professionally,

Taken from Harry W. Forgan, **Help Your Child Learn to Read** (Toronto: Pagurian Press Limited, 1975).

Dear Parents,

Some parents express a desire to help their child in reading. This letter includes some suggestions on how you can help your child develop readiness for reading. You will notice that the ideas can be used in informal situations without turning your house into a miniature school. I hope you enjoy using these activities with your child. Be patient and praise your child as you have fun together. If you would like additional ideas, please contact me.

1. <u>Dinner Time.</u> Often natural opportunities arise during the dinner hour to help your child learn new words. As different members of the family describe their activities, words are used which are new to the child. When your child asks what a particular word means, give a brief explanation and then try to use the word later on in the evening or on the following day. Remember that your child needs many meaningful repetitions of the word to make it his own.

2. <u>Listening to Stories.</u> Reading stories to your child is a very valuable activity. This helps him develop listening comprehension in addition to expanding concepts and providing hours of enjoyment. Stop as you read and ask questions about the pictures, characters, or events in the story. You might also have your child dramatize part of the story or retell his favorite part. Take your child to the store or library with you when you select books. Use books with many pictures so the child can develop concepts as you read.

3. <u>Using Synonyms.</u> You can help your child expand his vocabulary by using a new word and then later on in the sentence, or in the following sentence, using a familiar word that means the same as the new word. Let us suppose you are eating breakfast with your child and he says, "My eggs are still hot." You might respond by saying, "Yes, eggs do retain their heat for a long time," and follow this with the sentence, "They hold their temperature for a while." In doing so, you will be helping your child realize that retain and hold are synonyms. Do this frequently throughout the day as you take advantage of teaching moments.

4. <u>Experiences Make the Difference.</u> Children develop concepts by experiencing many situations. The child who has visited a fire station forms mental images of what fire engines are like. If he has seen firemen fighting a fire, his concepts or visual images of fire engines are extended in that he knows how the equipment on the trucks is used. There are many valuable experiences that help your child develop concepts. As you go to the grocery store, hardware store, post office, bank, and garage, your child is learning the functions of these places. Special excursions, like a trip to the zoo, police station, beach, or junkyard, and vacations are valuable too. Many common experiences at home, such as working in the yard, helping you in the kitchen, and watching television, will help your child form concepts and thus he will be able to create many visual images when he reads.

Professionally,

Taken from Harry W. Forgan, **Help Your Child Learn to Read** (Toronto, Pagurian Press Limited, 1975).

This card is from **The Reading Corner** © 1977 Goodyear Publishing Company, Inc. and Harry W. Forgan, Jr.

Dear Parents,

Some parents express a desire to help their child in reading. This letter
includes some suggestions on how you can help your child recognize words.
You will notice the ideas can be used in informal situations without turning
your house into a miniature school. I hope you enjoy using these activities
with your child. Be patient and praise your child as you have fun together.
If you would like additional ideas, please contact me.

1. How Do You Spell ---? As your child develops an interest in writing
    words, he will be asking you how to spell different words. Sometimes
    simply respond by telling him the letters. Other times, repeat the word
    and say, "What sound does it have at the beginning?" If your child is
    able, also help him to hear the sounds in the middle and the end of the
    word. This activity will help your child develop more independence in
    spelling because you are teaching him to listen to the sounds and think
    of the letters that represent them.

2. What's This Word? When your child is reading and encounters an unfamiliar
    word, ask him if he sees any familiar sound patterns such as at, ill, or
    ake. Often children can pronounce a word that appears difficult if they
    analyze it. Point out the sound patterns by covering other letters.
    Encourage your child to look at the beginning and ending sounds, too.

3. How Many Words Can You Make? Provide your child with several plastic
    alphabet letters or letters that you have written on index cards. Ask him
    to see how many words he can make using the letters. Time limits of 5 to
    10 minutes make this activity enjoyable. The activity is also more
    exciting if you take a turn at making some words. In doing so, you may
    want to introduce some new words to your child.

4. Word Baseball. To play this game, designate one corner of a room as home
    plate and the other three corners as first, second, and third base. You
    can be the pitcher by flashing sight words to your child. If he pronounces
    a word correctly within 3 seconds, he may go to first base. If he says the
    next word, he may go to second base, on the next turn he goes to third base,
    and then scores a homerun when he gets the fourth word correct. If he is
    unable to pronounce a word, he is out and then goes back to bat again. The
    game is over after 3 outs. The object is to see how many runs your child can
    score in each game.

5. Guidance Helps. As your child is reading and comes to a word he does not
    know, tell him to skip it and read the rest of the sentence to determine
    what it is. If he cannot, simply pronounce the word for him. If he says
    a word, but it is incorrect, have him look at the sounds of the word. One
    advantage of having your child read to you is that you can guide his
    development of word recognition techniques. Remember not to become so
    involved in the recognition of words that you forget to see if your child is
    comprehending and enjoying the story. By suggesting techniques to your child,
    and praising him sincerely when he uses them, you will be helping him develop
    effective reading habits.

                                             Professionally,

Taken from Harry W. Forgan, Help Your Child Learn to Read (Toronto: Pagurian Press Limited, 1975).

This card is from The Reading Corner ©1977 Goodyear Publishing Company, Inc. and Harry W. Forgan, Jr.

Dear Parents,

Some parents express a desire to help their child in reading. This letter includes some suggestions on how you can help your child comprehend what he reads. You will notice the ideas can be used in informal situations without turning your house into a miniature school. I hope you enjoy using these activities with your child. Be patient and praise your child as you have fun together. If you would like additional ideas, please contact me.

1. What Was Your Favorite Part? After reading a story to your child, or after he reads a story to you, ask him what his favorite part was. Listen carefully to what he says, as this will give you an indication of whether or not he can determine the main idea or whether he tells you every fact without saying something about the central thought. As you listen to his description of the favorite part, keep this information in mind as it will help you select other appropriate materials for your child.

2. Survey First! You can help your child develop the habit of surveying materials before he reads them. When surveying materials, have your child notice the pictures, major headings, and perhaps even read the summary if there is one. By surveying, your child is developing a frame of reference for what he will be reading. Of course, this also helps him develop purposes for reading and thus aids concentration.

3. Follow Directions. The next time you put a toy or model together according to particular directions, have your child assist you. Ask him to read some of the directions to you or point to the picture that illustrates the direction you are reading. When your child gets a new game, give him an opportunity to figure out the directions independently. These activities not only help your child find important details, but emphasize that reading can be very useful.

4. Feelings. As you read to your child, or as your child reads to you, ask him how the different characters feel. Have him tell you why he has drawn this conclusion by pointing to significant facts or events in the story. If your conclusions differ, reread appropriate parts of the story to explain how you arrived at your conclusions.

5. Tell Me Why. One of the most important things you can do to help your child draw conclusions is to talk to him about things that he sees. For example, as you are taking a walk or riding in the car, you might ask him why cars have tires, why trees need rain, or why we have expressways. The more concepts the child brings to the reading situation, the more he gains from it. Remember that you are still helping your child learn to read by using many of these activities that do not even deal with written words, but rather with thinking skills. Reading is a thinking process.

Professionally,

Taken from Harry W. Forgan Help Your Child Learn to Read (Toronto: Pagurian Press Limited, 1975).

This card is from The Reading Corner ©1977 Goodyear Publishing Company, Inc. and Harry W. Forgan, Jr.

Dear Parents,

Some parents express a desire to help their child in reading. This letter
includes some suggestions on how you can help your child develop more interest
in reading. You will notice the ideas can be used in informal situations
without turning your house into a miniature school. I hope you enjoy using
these activities with your child. Be patient and praise your child as you
have fun together. If you would like additional ideas, please contact me.

1. <u>Subscribe to Children's Magazines.</u> Many birthday and holiday presents
   are broken before the special day is over, but for a fairly reasonable
   price you can get your child a magazine subscription that will last throughout
   the year. Most of the magazines for preschool and elementary school children
   include many reading activities in addition to good stories.

2. <u>Develop the Library Habit.</u> Take advantage of the library story hours,
   book clubs, and plays, in addition to checking out books for your child
   and yourself. Ask the children's librarian what books and activities
   she recommends most highly for your child.

3. <u>Continue Reading Those Stories.</u> I believe the most valuable way you can
   help your child desire to learn to read is by reading stories to him.
   Children soon discover there are many adventures in books which cannot
   be found on television and are available at times when television programs
   are not. In addition, books have the advantage of being able to be read
   again and again. By reading to your child, you are helping him value reading
   and books. Save time for this very important activity. In addition to
   getting books from the library, buy some books for your child so he can
   begin his personal libary.

4. <u>Let's Find Out.</u> Topics such as insects, planets, plants, animals, or events
   may come up as you are watching television or working in the yard. For
   example, if your child asks, "How do TV pictures get into our house?" you
   can find out together by using encyclopedias. Often parents complain because
   they have spent a lot of money on a set of encyclopedias that their child
   never uses. But remember, it is necessary to show your child how to use it!
   As you locate information "think out loud," so your child will realize why
   you select a certain volume of an encyclopedia. Point out cross references
   and other aids, such as the index.

5. <u>How To.</u> Many "how to" books are available for doing such things as binding
   books, knitting, sewing, and playing sports. If your child is interested in
   learning any of these new skills, you might purchase a book for him or borrow
   one from the library. If he is unable to read it, read it to him. This will
   help him see the value of books.

                                        Professionally,

Taken from Harry W. Forgan, **Help Your Child Learn to Read** (Toronto: Pagurian Press Limited, 1975).

This card is from The Reading Corner © 1977 Goodyear Publishing Company, Inc. and Harry W. Forgan, Jr.

One Point Is Like the Center

Directions:
1. Look at the center of each star carefully.
2. Look at the points on each star.
3. Find the point that looks the same as the center of the star.
4. Color the two parts of the star that are alike.

This card is from **The Reading Corner** © 1977 Goodyear Publishing Company, Inc. and Harry W. Forgan, Jr.

Name

Appendix Item 12
Learning Center Activity Sheet
for Visual Perception

Haunted House

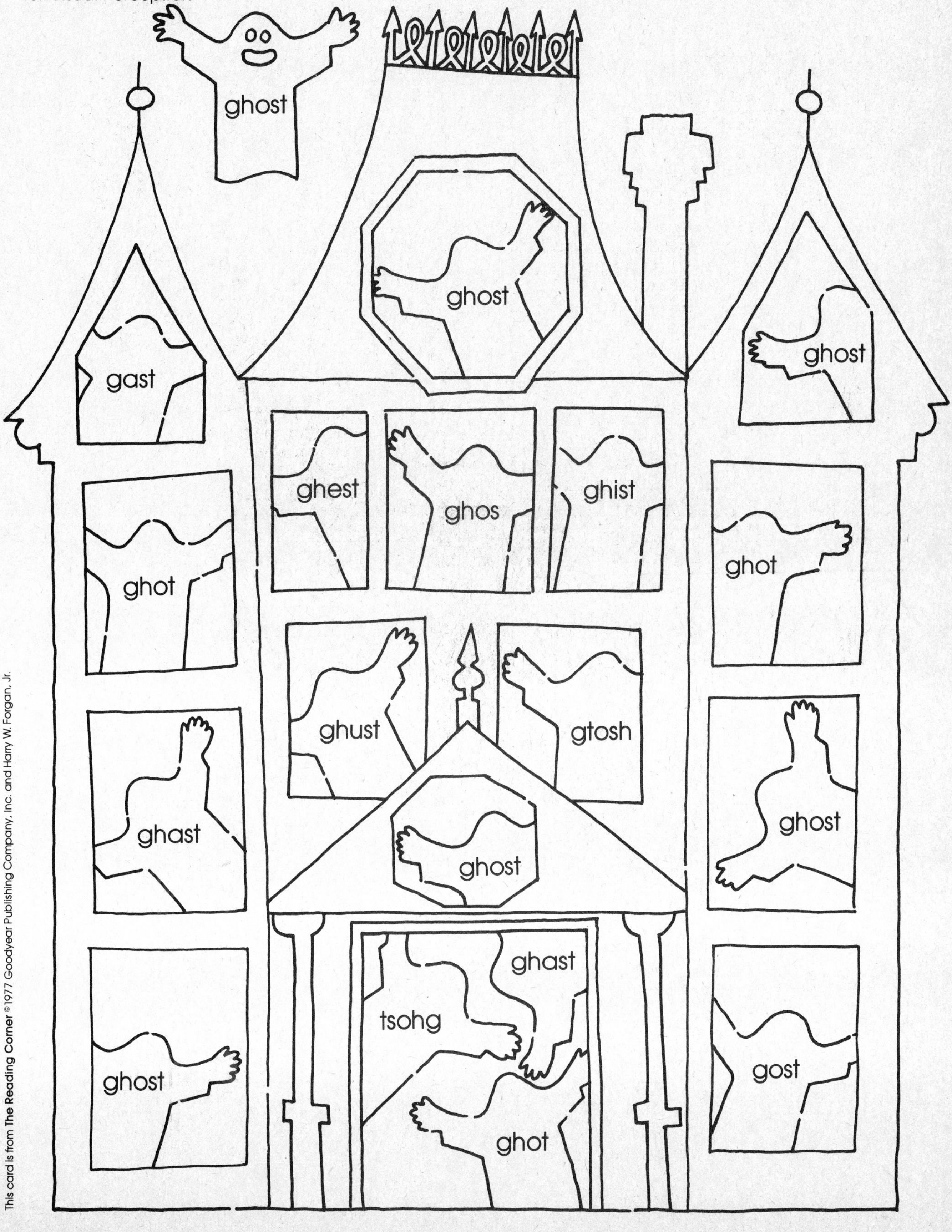
ghost
ghost
gast
ghost
ghest
ghos
ghist
ghot
ghot
ghust
gtosh
ghast
ghost
ghost
ghast
tsohg
ghost
gost
ghot

This card is from **The Reading Corner** ©1977 Goodyear Publishing Company, Inc. and Harry W. Forgan, Jr.

Name _____

Auditory Perception Response Sheet

| 1. | | Yes | 🙂 | No | 🙁 |
| 2. | | Yes | 🙂 | No | 🙁 |

| 3. | | Yes | 🙂 | No | 🙁 |
| 4. | | Yes | 🙂 | No | 🙁 |

| 5. | | Yes | 🙂 | No | 🙁 |
| 6. | | Yes | 🙂 | No | 🙁 |

| 7. | | Yes | 🙂 | No | 🙁 |
| 8. | | Yes | 🙂 | No | 🙁 |

| 9. | | Yes | 🙂 | No | 🙁 |
| 10. | | Yes | 🙂 | No | 🙁 |

This card is from **The Reading Corner** ©1977 Goodyear Publishing Company, Inc. and Harry W. Forgan, Jr.

Appendix Item **14**
Game Board for Auditory Perception

On The Way Home

Directions:
1. Get a die or spinner and markers.
2. Spin the spinner or roll the die to see how many spaces to move.
3. When you stop on a space, you must say a word that begins like the picture.
4. If you can say a word you stay there until your next turn.
5. If you cannot say a word, move back until you can.
6. To get home, you must say a word that begins with /h/.

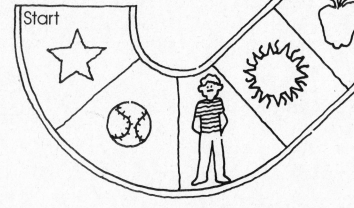

Start

Home

This card is from **The Reading Corner** ®1977 Goodyear Publishing Company, Inc. and Harry W. Forgan, Jr.

e t f

w p s t

s g t o h

p u l f t s

q r t i h v y

This card is from **The Reading Corner** ©1977 Goodyear Publishing Company, Inc. and Harry W. Forgan, Jr.

Appendix Item **16**
Skill Test for Visual-Auditory
Sequencing and Memory

Response Sheet

1

f t e	e t f	t e f	e f t

2

w s p t	s p w t	w p s t	t s p w

3

s g o t h	o s g t h	h o t g s	s g t o h

4

p u l f t s	s t f l u p	p u t f l s	t u p f l s

5

y v h i t r q	q r h i t v y	q r t i h v y	h v y q r t i

This card is from The Reading Corner ©1977 Goodyear Publishing Company, Inc. and Harry W. Forgan, Jr.

Name _____

I can read.
My name is _____.

This card is from **The Reading Corner** ©1977 Goodyear Publishing Company, Inc. and Harry W. Forgan, Jr.

m	l	n	i	M	a	n	a

c	y	e	a	s	e	r	d

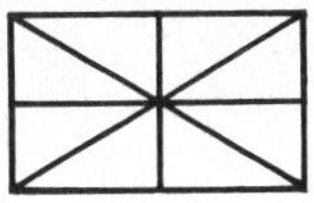

This card is from **The Reading Corner** ©1977 Goodyear Publishing Company, Inc. and Harry W. Forgan, Jr.

Appendix Item **18**
Skill Test for Visual-Motor Perception

Just Like Mine

1 ◯

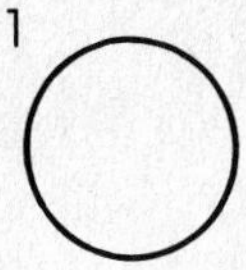

2 □

3 △

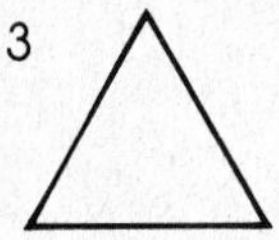

4 d

5 N

6

Appendix Item **19**
Learning Center Activity Sheet
for Visual-Motor Perception

Name

Bicycle
Obstacle Course

Time

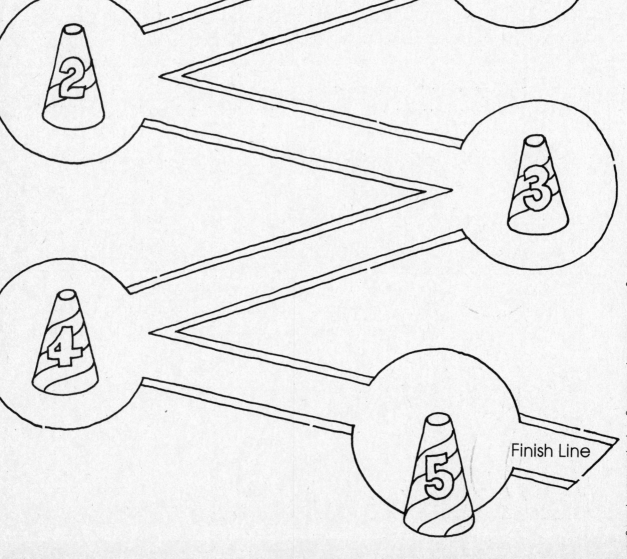

Finish Line

This card is from *The Reading Corner* ©1977 Goodyear Publishing Company, Inc. and Harry W. Forgan, Jr.

This card is from **The Reading Corner** ©1977 Goodyear Publishing Company, Inc. and Harry W. Forgan, Jr.

Name _____

Appendix Item **20**
Learning Center Activity Sheet
for Developing Listening and Speaking
Vocabularies

Puppet Cutouts

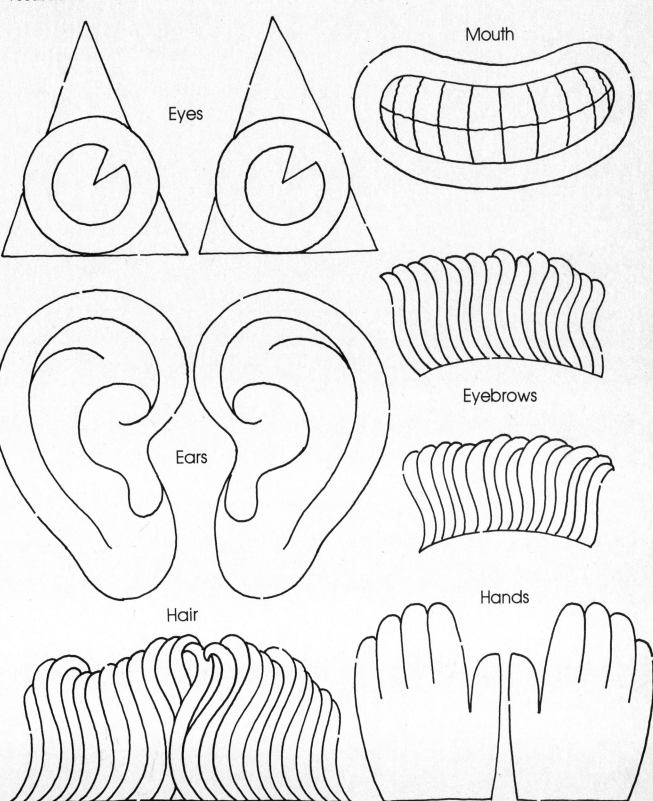

Eyes

Mouth

Ears

Eyebrows

Hair

Hands

The Weirdies

This card is from **The Reading Corner** ©1977 Goodyear Publishing Company, Inc. and Harry W. Forgan, Jr.

This card is from **The Reading Corner** ©1977 Goodyear Publishing Company, Inc. and Harry W. Forgan, Jr.

Appendix Item **22**
Learning Center Activity Sheet
for Concept Development

Find and Tell

apple
pear
squirrel
cup
school
turtle
spoon
butterfly
swan
fish

Name _____

Lucky Letters

1 a o / c e	2 i t / p h	3 b d / p q	4 g y / j l	5 n o / p r
6 r t / d k	7 z r / s e	8 g q / j l	9 c o / e a	10 d p / b f
11 u n / m o	12 h k / l t	13 k i / j l	14 l m / j k	15 i e / a o
16 k j / m g	17 b q / p d	18 y z / g k	19 w m / u z	20 a o / u x
21 p d / q t	22 u v / w x	23 k t / l d	24 z y / x g	25 w o / m u

This card is from **The Reading Corner** ©1977 Goodyear Publishing Company, Inc. and Harry W. Forgan, Jr.

Appendix Item **24**
Game Board for Letter Names

Letter Land

Directions:

1. Pick up a paper cup.
2. Count the paper clips and move that many spaces.
3. Read the name of the letter on the space where you land. If you cannot read it, you must lose your next turn.
4. The first person to reach the Letter Factory is the winner.

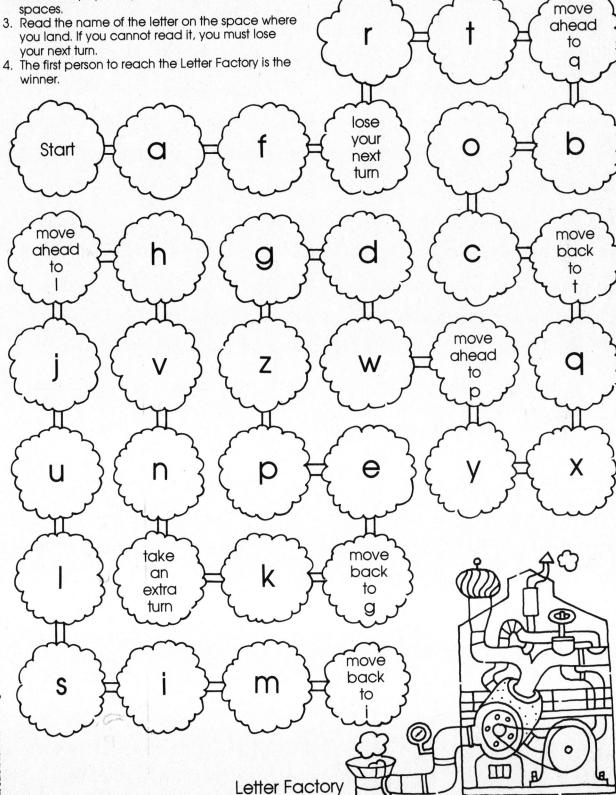

Start | a | f | lose your next turn

r | r | t | move ahead to q

o | b

move ahead to l | h | g | d | c | move back to t

j | v | z | w | move ahead to p | q

u | n | p | e | y | x

l | take an extra turn | k | move back to g

s | i | m | move back to i

Letter Factory

This card is from **The Reading Corner** ©1977 Goodyear Publishing Company, Inc. and Harry W. Forgan, Jr.

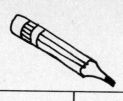

Appendix Item **25**
Skill Test for Sight Words

1. are all an and	2. me we be he	3. is it if in	4. new not no upon	5. as any ask at
6. on to no so	7. call could can cut	8. am are an any	9. or on of out	10. the this too three
11. here him help have	12. green gave goes good	13. after around about again	14. then when went which	15. now no so on
16. may made my many	17. never every seven very	18. because been before better	19. think they them there	20. from funny for find
21. good got go so	22. was were saw done	23. one over our out	24. made may make draw	25. hurt hot his him
26. shall show shoe she	27. see saw said say	28. want work who what	29. gave good give grow	30. little look book like
31. red ride ran run	32. think thing this their	33. friend from for find	34. pull play put pick	35. work want went wash

This card is from **The Reading Corner** ©1977 Goodyear Publishing Company, Inc. and Harry W. Forgan, Jr.

Touchdown!

Touchdown   0   Team 2 Start Here

90	10
80	20
70	30
60	40
50	50
40	60
30	70
20	80
10	90

0

Team 1 Start Here   Touchdown

Place cards
face down
here

Discard
here

This card is from **The Reading Corner** ©1977 Goodyear Publishing Company, Inc. and Harry W. Forgan, Jr.

Auto Racing

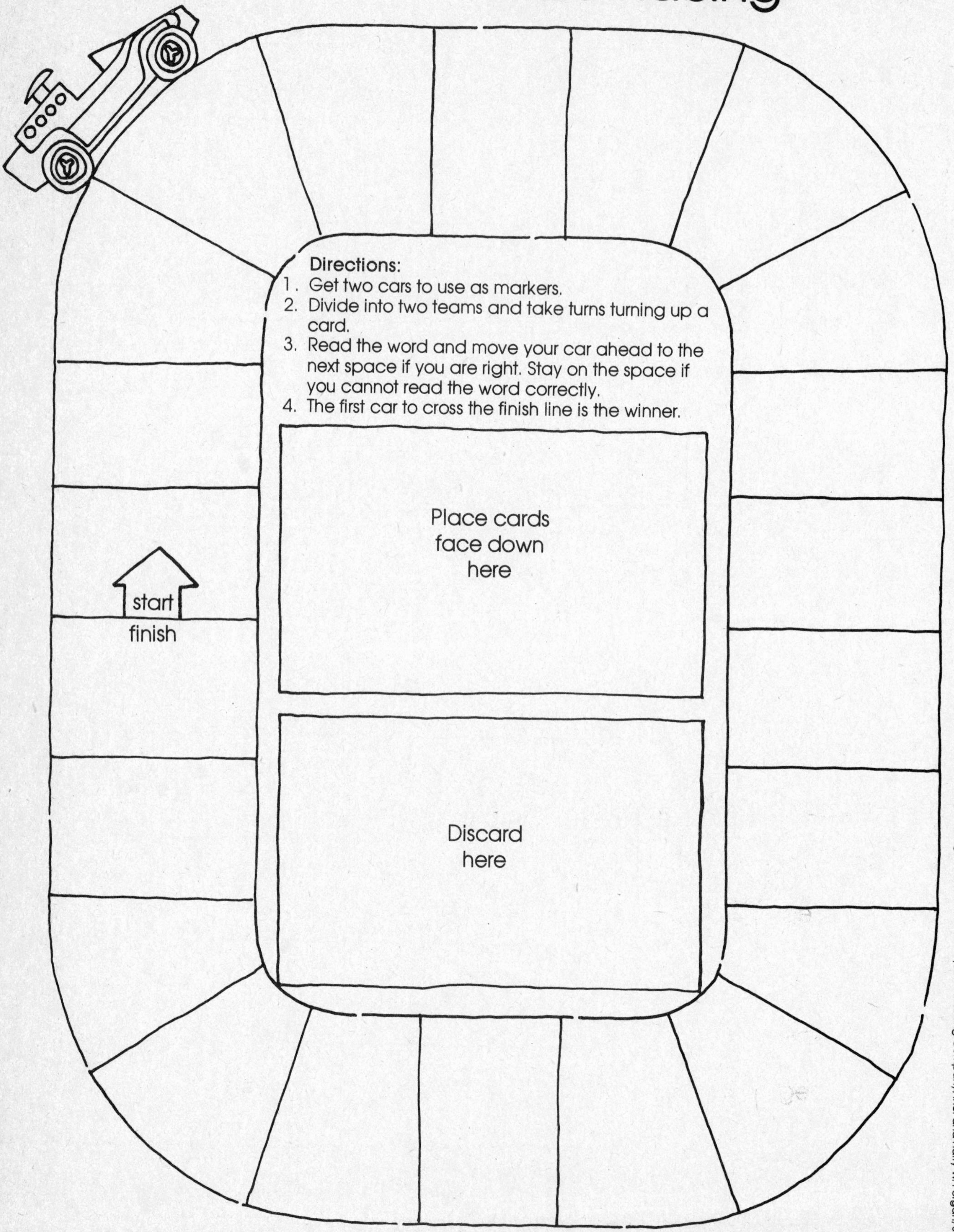

Directions:
1. Get two cars to use as markers.
2. Divide into two teams and take turns turning up a card.
3. Read the word and move your car ahead to the next space if you are right. Stay on the space if you cannot read the word correctly.
4. The first car to cross the finish line is the winner.

Place cards
face down
here

Discard
here

start
finish

This card is from **The Reading Corner** © 1977 Goodyear Publishing Company, Inc. and Harry W. Forgan, Jr.

Appendix Item **28**
Skill Test for Consonant Sounds

Name the Pet Rocks!

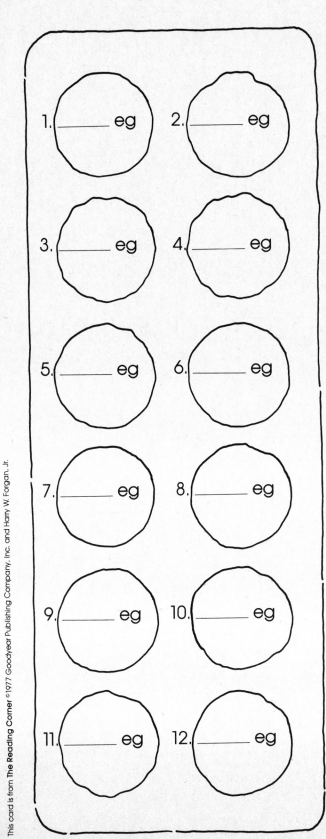

1. _____ eg   2. _____ eg

3. _____ eg   4. _____ eg

5. _____ eg   6. _____ eg

7. _____ eg   8. _____ eg

9. _____ eg   10. _____ eg

11. _____ eg   12. _____ eg

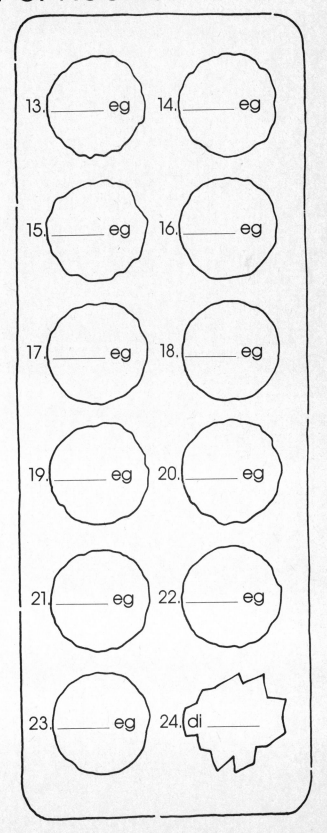

13. _____ eg   14. _____ eg

15. _____ eg   16. _____ eg

17. _____ eg   18. _____ eg

19. _____ eg   20. _____ eg

21. _____ eg   22. _____ eg

23. _____ eg   24. di _____

This card is from **The Reading Corner** ©1977 Goodyear Publishing Company, Inc. and Harry W. Forgan, Jr.

Pg 44

Name _____

Silly Pops

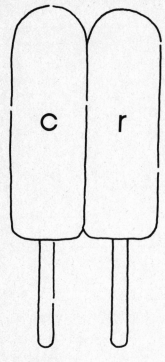

cryberry
cr _____

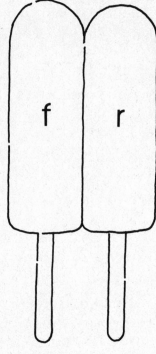

frogberry
fr _____

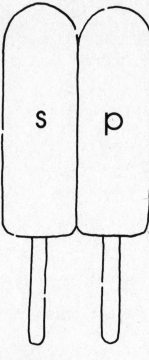

spotberry
sp _____

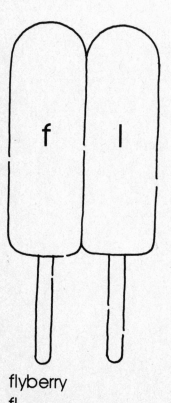

flyberry
fl _____

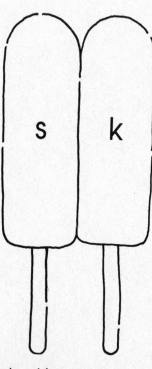

snowberry
sn _____

skunkberry
sk _____

This card is from *The Reading Corner* © 1977 Goodyear Publishing Company, Inc. and Harry W. Forgan, Jr.

Appendix Item **30**
Skill Test for Sound Patterns

Name _____

Number the
Pool Balls

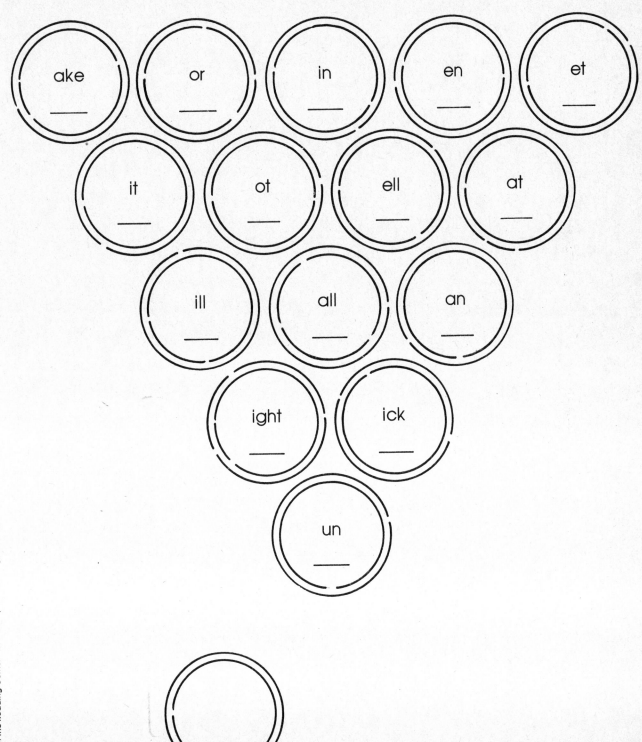

This card is from **The Reading Corner** ®1977 Goodyear Publishing Company, Inc. and Harry W. Forgan, Jr.

Name _____

New Words

	a	t
b	h	th
f	m	p
r	s	ch

This card is from **The Reading Corner** ©1977 Goodyear Publishing Company, Inc. and Harry W. Forgan, Jr.

Bowling

Score

Game	Player 1	Player 2	Player 3
1			
2			
3			
4			
5			
6			
7			

Directions:

Get five chips and place them on the circles. Each player flicks the five chips to land on the sound patterns. A chip touching any part of one circle is worth one point if you can say a word that has that sound pattern. If the chip is touching more than one circle, you can get additional points for correctly making words using the sound patterns in the touched circles. The person with the highest score wins.

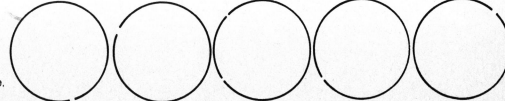

Place the chips here.

This card is from **The Reading Corner** ©1977 Goodyear Publishing Company, Inc. and Harry W. Forgan, Jr.

Name ____________________

Appendix Item 33
Skill Test For Vowel Sounds

The Three Blind Mice

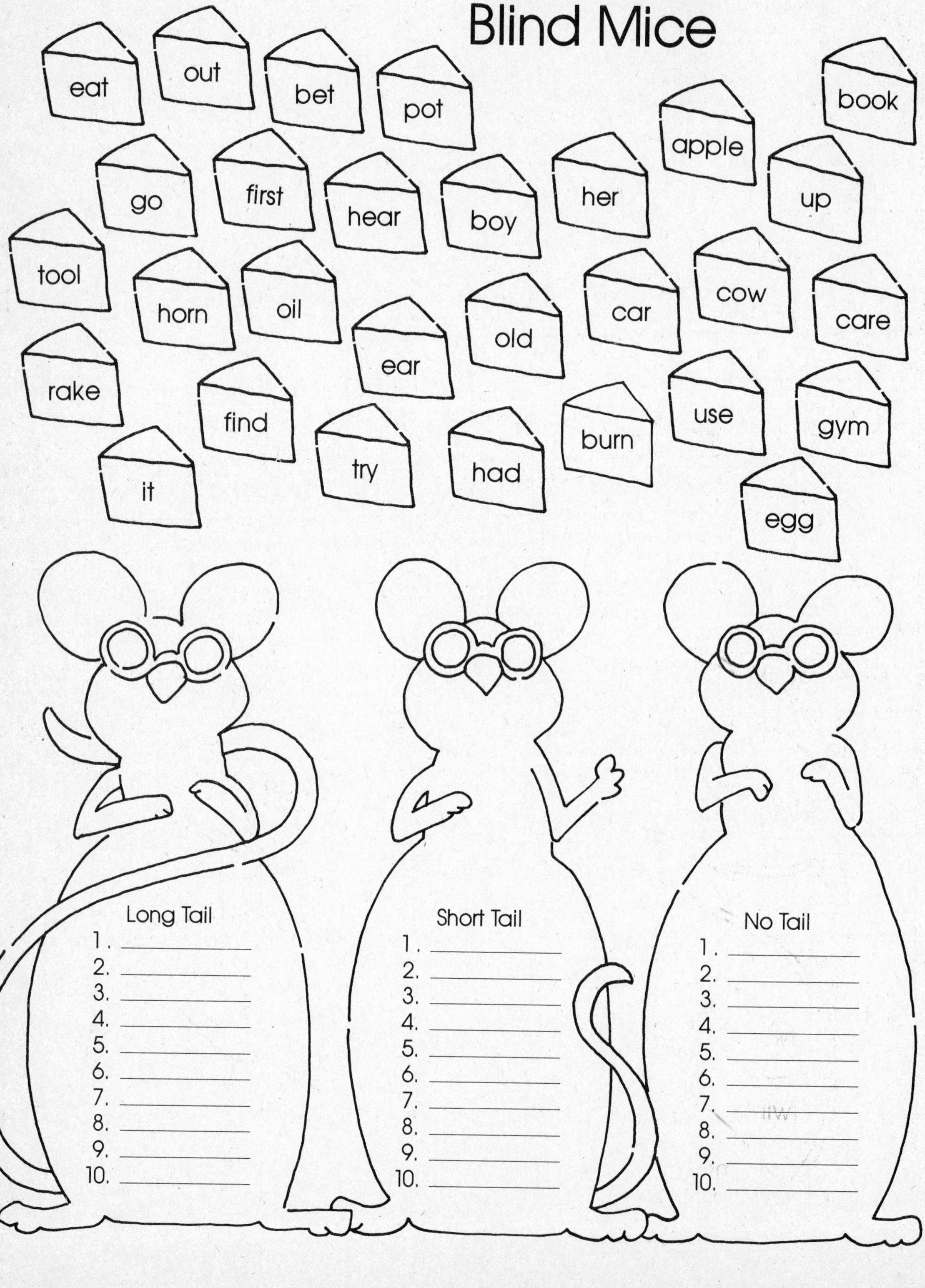
eat
out
bet
pot
book
apple
go
first
hear
boy
her
up
tool
horn
oil
ear
old
car
cow
care
rake
find
try
had
burn
use
gym
it
egg
Long Tail
1. ____
2. ____
3. ____
4. ____
5. ____
6. ____
7. ____
8. ____
9. ____
10. ____
Short Tail
1. ____
2. ____
3. ____
4. ____
5. ____
6. ____
7. ____
8. ____
9. ____
10. ____
No Tail
1. ____
2. ____
3. ____
4. ____
5. ____
6. ____
7. ____
8. ____
9. ____
10. ____

This card is from The Reading Corner ©1977 Goodyear Publishing Company, Inc. and Harry W. Forgan, Jr.

Scat or Skate

Directions:
Spin a spinner to see how many spaces you can skate. To move you must read the word on the space on which you land. If you cannot read the word, you scat back until you come to a word you can read. Follow the arrows when you land on SCAT or SKATE. The first one to land on the word WIN is the winner!

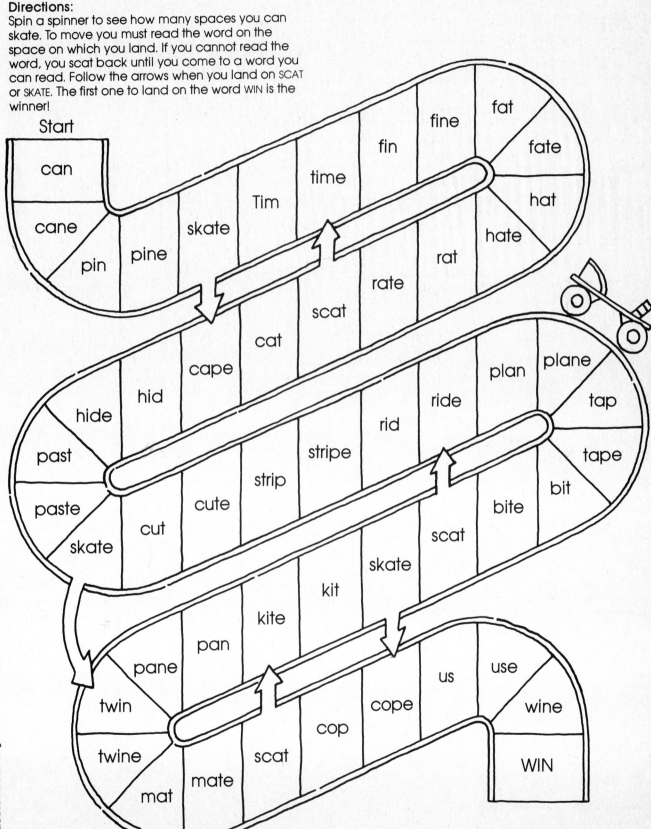

This card is from **The Reading Corner** ©1977 Goodyear Publishing Company, Inc. and Harry W. Forgan, Jr.

Follow that Sound!

Start	say	her	fat	toy	or	year	eat
book	rope	hair	pie	last	count	arm	burn
mean	point	now	first	ice	Finish!	cute	oil
tar	fear					tool	like
us	cut					egg	bed
for	her					home	dirt
town	joy					soil	cow
care	us					sir	cook
ate	blue	sore	is	more	pod	room	boat
bar	our	on	zoo	cute	hurt	boil	it

Directions:
Drop a button on the circle. Move to the first word that contains the type of vowel sound on which your button lands (SHORT, LONG, BOSSY R, or DIPHTHONG). Continue moving around the board in this fashion. To cross the finish line, you will need a SHORT.

Short	Long
Bossy R	Diphthong or oo

This card is from **The Reading Corner** ©1977 Goodyear Publishing Company, Inc. and Harry W. Forgan, Jr.

Obey the Speed Limit

Directions:
For this game, you will need tokens and playing cards. Take turns drawing cards. Follow the directions on each card, but never move back beyond start. The winner is the first one to reach home.

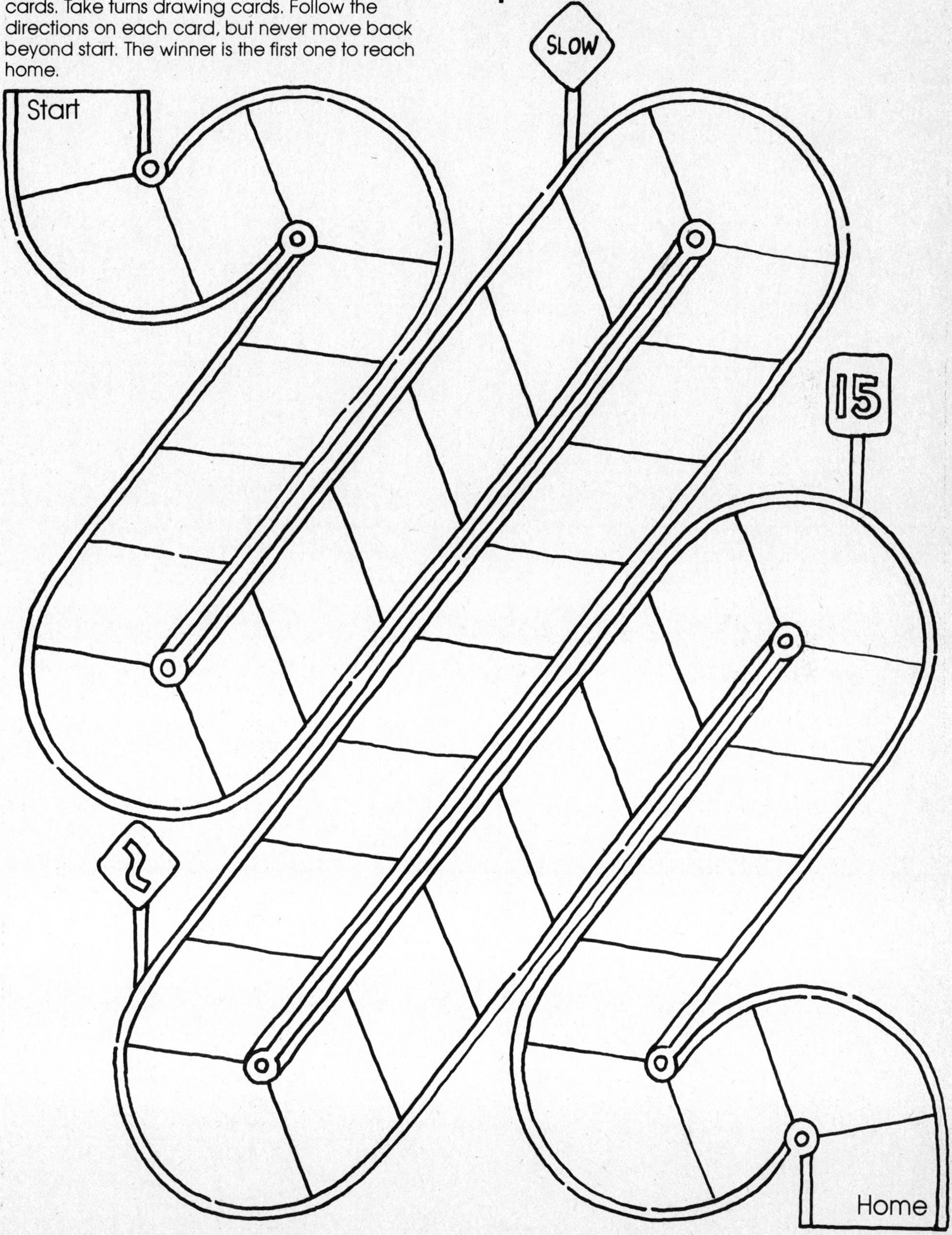

Start

SLOW

15

2

Home

This card is from **The Reading Corner** ©1977 Goodyear Publishing Company, Inc. and Harry W. Forgan, Jr.

Run for Your Life!

Directions:
1. Cut out one of the markers at the top of the page and color it your favorite color.
2. Spin a spinner to see how many spaces you can move.
3. Run to that space by reading each word along the way.
4. If you miss a word, you have fallen and must go back to the last word you read correctly.
5. The first one to the finish line is the winner.

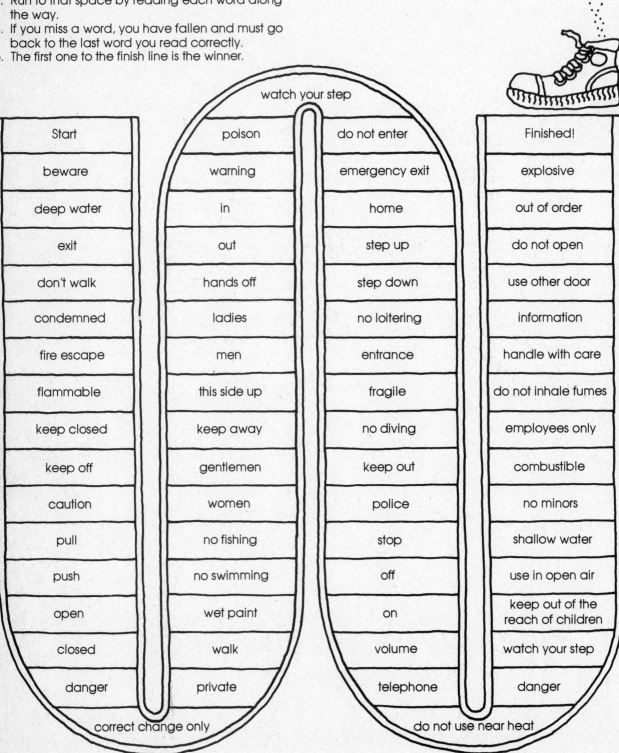

watch your step

Start	poison	do not enter	Finished!
beware	warning	emergency exit	explosive
deep water	in	home	out of order
exit	out	step up	do not open
don't walk	hands off	step down	use other door
condemned	ladies	no loitering	information
fire escape	men	entrance	handle with care
flammable	this side up	fragile	do not inhale fumes
keep closed	keep away	no diving	employees only
keep off	gentlemen	keep out	combustible
caution	women	police	no minors
pull	no fishing	stop	shallow water
push	no swimming	off	use in open air
open	wet paint	on	keep out of the reach of children
closed	walk	volume	watch your step
danger	private	telephone	danger

correct change only   do not use near heat

This card is from **The Reading Corner** ©1977 Goodyear Publishing Company, Inc. and Harry W. Forgan, Jr.

This card is from The Reading Corner ©1977 Goodyear Publishing Company, Inc. and Harry W. Forgan, Jr.

Appendix Item **53**
Learning Center Activity Sheet for Critical Reading

Name

Mmmm–Yuk–Blah

Directions:
Make a face for each one of the words listed below. If you have **mmmm** feelings toward the word, make a smiling face. If you have **yuk** feelings toward the word, make a sad face. If you have **blah** feelings toward the word, make a straight face.

window

plate

television

sewing

dogs

reading

school

sister

peanut butter

church

spoon

brother

dolls

cats

cars

dancing

candy

swimming

bowling

baseball

breakfast

camping

checkers

fishing

Appendix Item **54**
Learning Center Activity Sheet
for Vocabulary Development

Hidden Words
Doughnut

Directions:
There are more than 20 words on this doughnut.
Follow the direction of the arrow. Write each word
you find on a line below. You will need to use most
of the letters in more than one word.

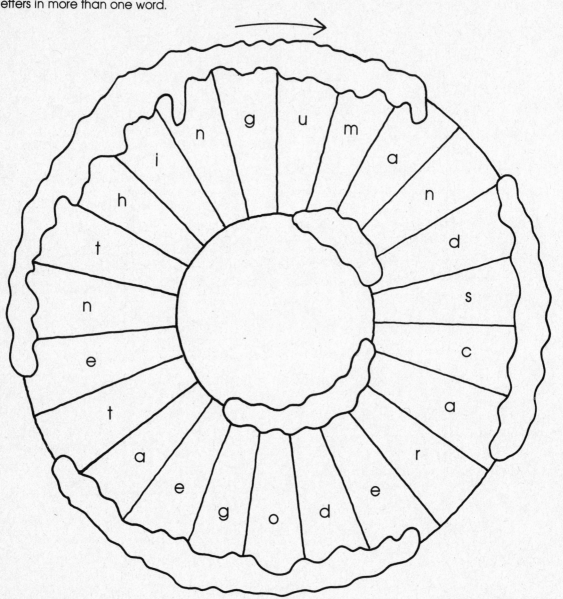

I found these words:

1. _____   6. _____   11. _____   16. _____

2. _____   7. _____   12. _____   17. _____

3. _____   8. _____   13. _____   18. _____

4. _____   9. _____   14. _____   19. _____

5. _____   10. _____   15. _____   20. _____

This card is from **The Reading Corner** ©1977 Goodyear Publishing Company, Inc. and Harry W. Forgan, Jr.

Appendix Item **36**
Skill Test for Syllabication and Accent

This card is from **The Reading Corner** ©1977 Goodyear Publishing Company, Inc. and Harry W. Forgan, Jr.

Name _____

Target Practice

Directions:
Draw arrows between the syllables in each word.
Put a bullet or dot over the accented syllables.

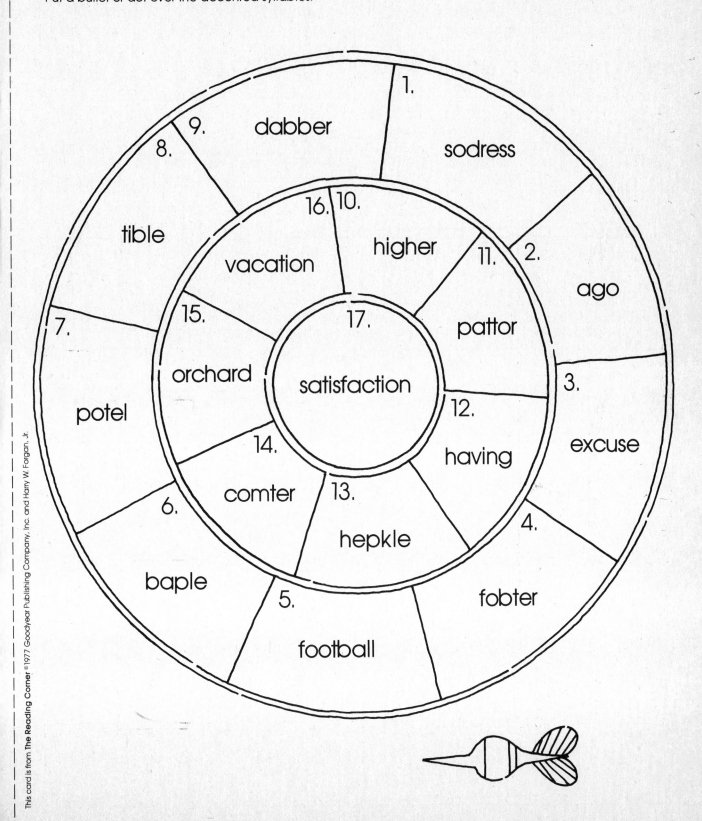

1. sodress
2. ago
3. excuse
4. fobter
5. football
6. baple
7. potel
8. tible
9. dabber
10. higher
11. pattor
12. having
13. hepkle
14. comter
15. orchard
16. vacation
17. satisfaction

Syllabication Walk

Start

Finish

Directions:
Shuffle a deck of cards with words on them. Place them face down on the game board. Take turns drawing a card. Move your token as many spaces as the word has syllables. Move an extra space if you can say which syllable is loudest. The first player to finish is the winner.

Place cards
face down
here

Discard
cards here

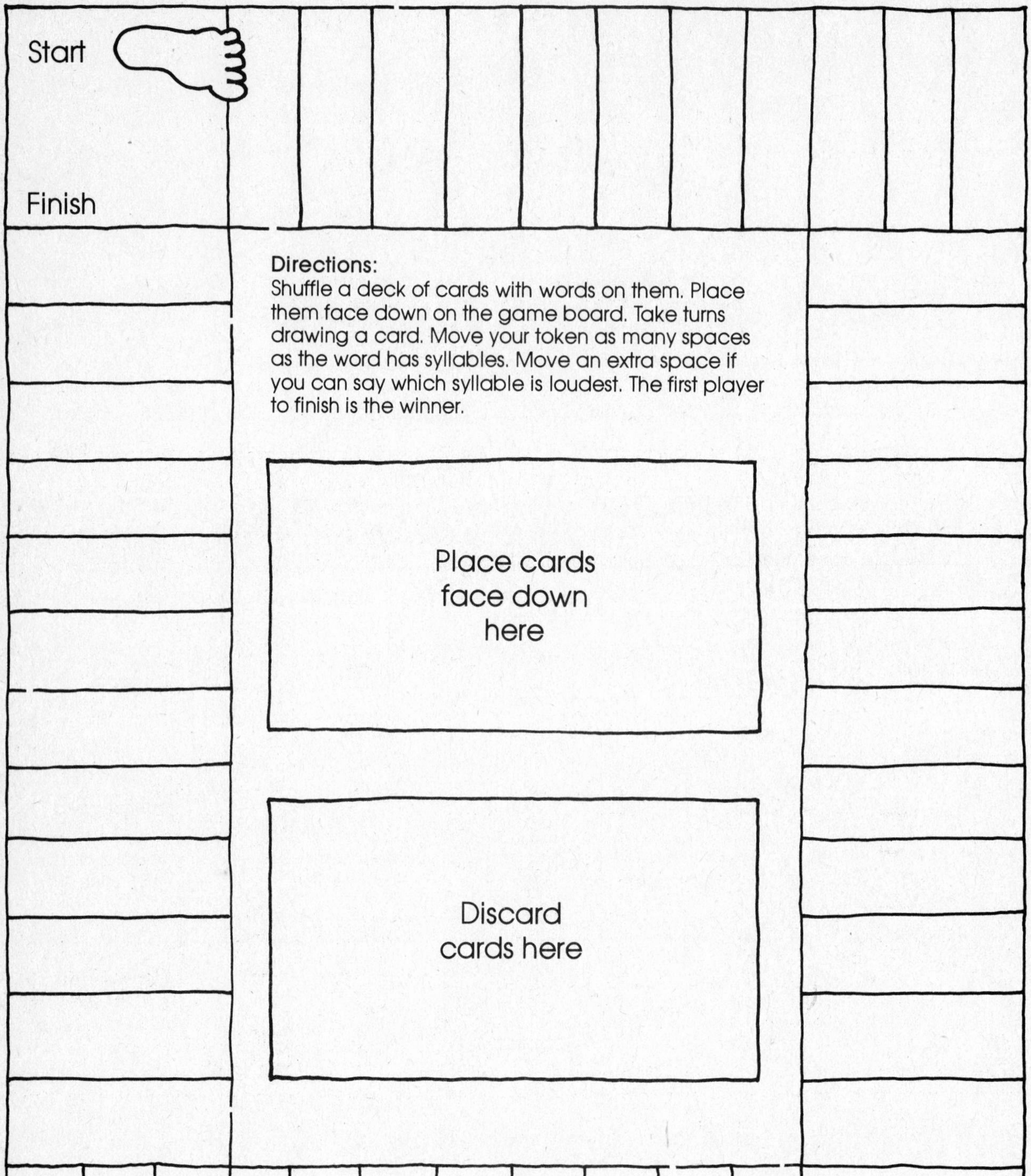

This card is from **The Reading Corner** © 1977 Goodyear Publishing Company, Inc. and Harry W. Forgan, Jr.

Name _____

These Cars
Need Repairs!

**Carol's
Compound Words**

Directions:
All of these cars are having trouble. The cars with compound words should go to Carol's Compound Words. The cards with contractions should go to Carl's Contractions. The cars with prefixes should go to Pearl's Prefixes. The cars with suffixes should go to Sam's Suffixes. The cars that do not belong in any garage should go to the Junk Yard. Look at the words on the cars, then write each of these words on the right garage or the Junk Yard.

**Carl's
Contractions**

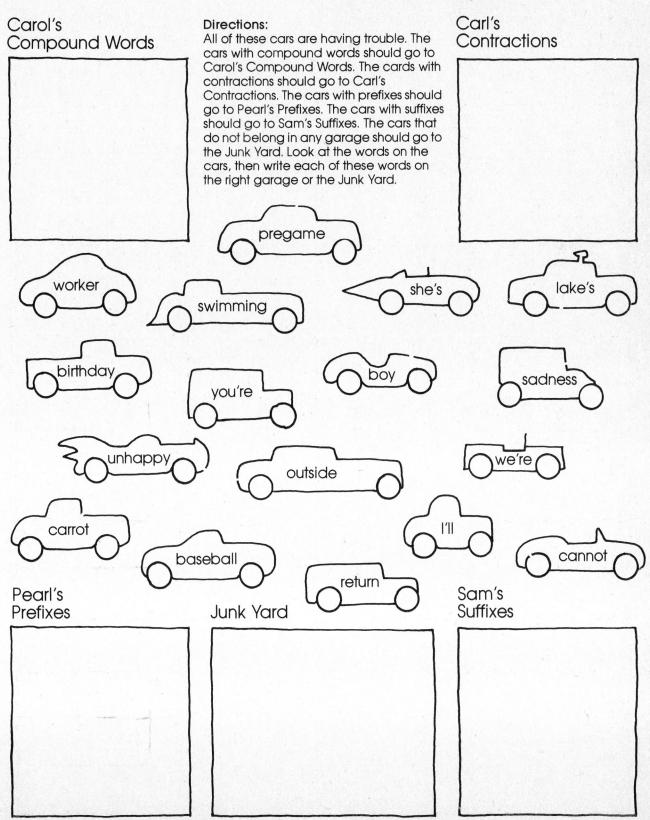

**Pearl's
Prefixes**

Junk Yard

**Sam's
Suffixes**

This card is from **The Reading Corner** © 1977 Goodyear Publishing Company, Inc. and Harry W. Forgan. Jr.

Movin' On

Directions:
Get a spinner and four tokens of the same color (red, yellow, blue, or green) for each player. Take turns spinning the spinner and moving. If you land on a word you must use it correctly in a sentence. Try to get all four of your tokens home to be the winner.

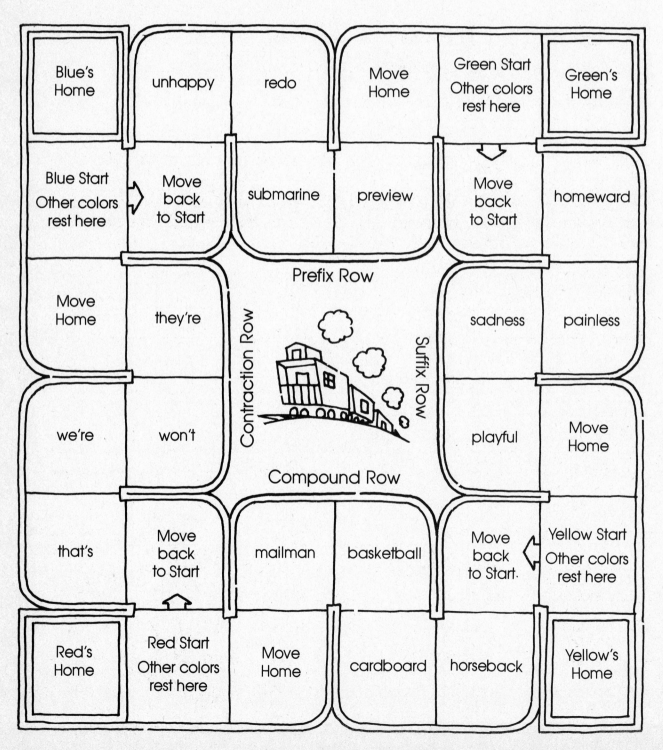

Blue's Home	unhappy	redo	Move Home	Green Start — Other colors rest here	Green's Home
Blue Start — Other colors rest here	Move back to Start	submarine	preview	Move back to Start	homeward
Move Home	they're			sadness	painless
we're	won't			playful	Move Home
that's	Move back to Start	mailman	basketball	Move back to Start.	Yellow Start — Other colors rest here
Red's Home	Red Start — Other colors rest here	Move Home	cardboard	horseback	Yellow's Home

Prefix Row

Contraction Row

Suffix Row

Compound Row

This card is from **The Reading Corner** ©1977 Goodyear Publishing Company, Inc. and Harry W. Forgan, Jr.

Appendix Item **40**
Dictionary Skills Test

Part 1: Quarters of the Dictionary
Directions:
Put a 1, 2, 3, or 4 on the line in front of each word to tell if the word would be located in the first, second, third, or fourth quarter of the dictionary.

_____ late	_____ noon	_____ you	_____ men
_____ dog	_____ jack	_____ hit	_____ appear
_____ take	_____ apple	_____ queen	_____ under
_____ many	_____ elephant	_____ boy	_____ flat
_____ fat	_____ gave	_____ want	_____ over
_____ seat	_____ zoo	_____ kite	_____ car
_____ ate	_____ bake	_____ date	_____ rat
_____ read	_____ not	_____ open	_____ vase

Part 2: Guide Words
Directions:
Put a check mark in front of the words that would appear on the page in the dictionary if the guide words were **ski** and **spot**.

ski   **spot**

_____ slope	_____ smooth	_____ skunk
_____ soft	_____ sure	_____ square
_____ sharp	_____ step	_____ solo
_____ silent	_____ some	_____ spotless
_____ sting	_____ shave	_____ slight
_____ submarine	_____ sky	_____ sheep
_____ silk	_____ snow	_____ sketch
_____ snake	_____ skin	_____ steer
_____ statue	_____ star	_____ spring
_____ soap	_____ slap	_____ speed

This card is from **The Reading Corner** ©1977 Goodyear Publishing Company, Inc. and Harry W. Forgan, Jr.

Appendix Item **40**
Dictionary Skills Test (continued)

Part 3: Interpreting Diacritical Marks
Directions:
Use the following pronunciation key to determine and circle the correct respelling of the numbered words.

Pronunciation Key

făt	câre	lāte	ärm	ȧgain	wē	bĕt	hēr	hīde
ĭt	ōld	ŏctopus	ôr	ūse	ŭs	bûrn	mo͞on	fo͝ot
oil	out							

---

1. horse

    hôrs   hers   hôrz   hōrs

2. mine

    mīn   mĭn   mīnē   mĭnē

3. foil

    foil   fōl   fŏl   fo͞ol

4. book

    bo͞ok   bo͝ok   bōk   bŏk

5. radio

    rā dĭ ŏ   rā′dē ō   rā′dĭ ō   ră dĭ ō

6. safety

    săf′tĭ   săf′tĭ   sāfē tĭ   sāf′tē

7. holder

    hōld′ĕr   hōl′dĕr   hŏldĕr   hŏld′ĕr

8. snake

    snăk   snākē   snāk   snak

9. beast

    bēst   bēȧst   bĕst   bĕāst

10. north

    nōrth   nŏrth   nôrth   nērth

Part 4: Alphabetical Order
Directions:
Put the 10 words in alphabetical order.

1. _____

2. _____

3. _____

4. _____

5. _____

6. _____

7. _____

8. _____

9. _____

10. _____

This card is from **The Reading Corner** © 1977 Goodyear Publishing Company, Inc. and Harry W. Forgan, Jr.

Appendix Item 41
Learning Activity Sheet for Dictionary Skills

The Champion
Is _____?

Directions:
Here are guide words from the top of a page in a
dictionary. Look at each word listed below and
decide if the word would be on, before, or after this
page. Write the word on the correct ribbon. Decide
which player (Before, On, or After) is the winner.
Write first, second, or third on each ribbon to show
the champion, the runner-up, and the loser.

Pear   Rest

Do these words come before, on, or after the page with these guide words?

1 . open   6. peach   11 . over   16 . pier

2. rake   7. restaurant   12. pretty   17 . take

3. stairs   8. pearl   13. quiet   18 . rat

4. queen   9. ride   14. set   19 . sat

5. table   10. party   15. quilt   20. peace

This card is from **The Reading Corner** ©1977 Goodyear Publishing Company, Inc. and Harry W. Forgan, Jr.

The Winner Is _____

Directions:
Get a deck of word cards and a dictionary for each player. Each player chooses a number from which to start. Turn one word card up. Each player tries to find in the dictionary the word on the card as soon as possible. The player who finds it first puts an **X** on the first box under his number. The first player to get six **X's** is the winner.

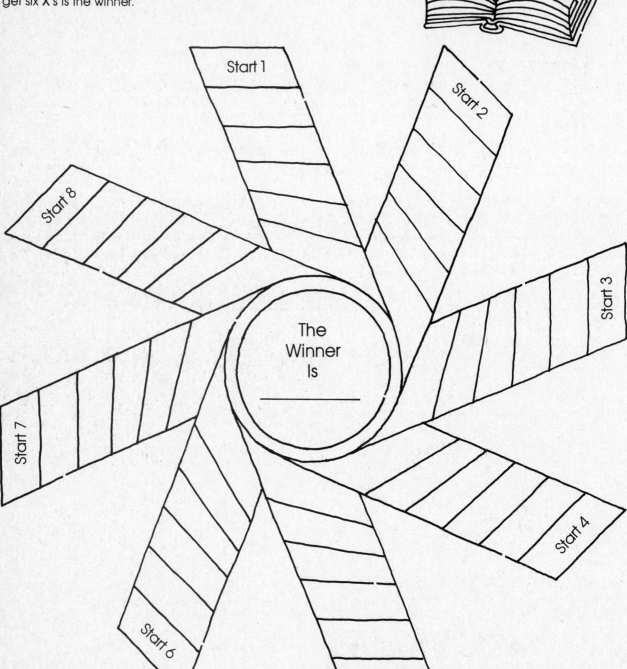

Motivation Statement:

This story is about a child's dog. Read it to find out what the child does with the dog.

Selection:

I love my dog. He is brown and white. I call him Happy. I like to play with him.

Happy likes to run. He runs after me. He can always catch me. He runs and jumps over things.

I take care of my dog. I give him food and water. Sometimes I give him a bath. He gets me all wet.

My dog is four years old. I got him when I was two years old. We are great pals.

Answer These Questions:

1. A good name for this story is _____

2. Happy likes to _____

3. Happy gets the child all wet when _____

4. The child in the story is _____ years old.

5. "Pal" means _____

6. "Happy" is a good name for this dog because _____

_____

This card is from **The Reading Corner** ©1977 Goodyear Publishing Company, Inc. and Harry W. Forgan, Jr.

Motivation Statement:
Nearly everyone loves puppies. Read this story to learn more about puppies.

Selection:
     When puppies are born they are blind and deaf. Their mother keeps them warm and feeds them. In about 14 days their eyes open. In about 21 days their ears open and they can hear things.
     Puppies begin to walk when they are 3 weeks old. It is easy to become friends with them when they are 6 to 8 weeks old.
     You can begin training a puppy when he is 8 weeks old. You can teach him to "come," "sit," or "fetch." Give the puppy a reward if he obeys your command. Do not punish young puppies if they cannot learn the tricks right away. It takes time for them to learn the tricks.

Answer These Questions:

1. This story is all about _____

2. Puppies begin to walk when they are _____ weeks old.

3. Do puppies see or hear first? _____

4. You should wait until a puppy is 8 weeks old before you begin training him

   because _____

5. "Reward" means _____

6. Do you think you should punish puppies if they cannot learn the tricks? _____

   Why do you feel this way? _____

   _____

Appendix Item 45
Comprehension Skills Test: Level 3

Motivation Statement:
　　Dogs are fun but they also make you work. Read this to find out what you must do to take care of a dog.

Selection:
　　There are many things you must do to take care of your dog. You should feed him every day. There are many different kinds of dog food. Ask your mother to read the label to see what vitamins are in the food.
　　Every once in awhile you should give your dog a bath. Use a little soap, but rinse him carefully. Remember soap removes the natural oil from the dog's hair and skin.
　　Make sure your dog gets plenty of exercise. Let him out in the morning and evening to play and go to the bathroom. Dogs are fun, but you have many jobs when you have a dog.

Answer These Questions:

1. A good title for this story is _____

2. Name three jobs you have when you have a dog. _____

　　_____

3. When should you let your dog out? _____

4. You should use just a little soap when you give a dog a bath because _____

　　_____

5. Another word for "job" is _____

6. Why do most people like dogs even though they are so much work? _____

　　_____

This card is from **The Reading Corner** ©1977 Goodyear Publishing Company, Inc. and Harry W. Forgan, Jr.

Motivation Statement:
Dogs are used in many ways. Read this story to find out how dogs help people.

Selection:
There are many kinds of dogs. Some dogs are hunting dogs that help find birds and other animals. They fetch the animals when they are shot.

Some dogs are good watchdogs because they protect families and stores. Good watchdogs scare most robbers.

Dogs are still used to herd sheep by keeping the flock together.

Guide dogs are very important to blind people because they warn their masters of obstacles.

Sled dogs are used chiefly in the Arctic. They pull sleds over the ice and thus provide transportation.

The favorite kind of dog is a pet. Dogs are very popular pets and are said to be man's best friend.

Answer These Questions:

1. This story should be called _____

2. Name three uses of dogs (a) _____

    (b) _____ (c) _____

3. When do dogs fetch other animals? _____

4. Why are dogs called "man's best friend?" _____

    _____

5. What is an "obstacle?" _____

6. Do you think the favorite kind of pet is a dog? _____ Why do you think this way? _____

    _____

This card is from **The Reading Corner** © 1977 Goodyear Publishing Company, Inc. and Harry W. Forgan, Jr.

Motivation Statement:
Sometimes dogs get dirty. Read this story to find out some important things to remember when bathing a dog.

Selection:
Dogs do not need as many baths as people, but sometimes they get dirty. If you have a dog you should bathe him at least three times a year.

When bathing your dog you should take several precautions. First, put a rubber mat on the bottom of the tub so the dog does not slip. Second, make sure you get a mild soap rather than a detergent. Fill the tub with warm water only as high as your dog's legs.

As you wash your dog be careful the soap does not get in his eyes. Talk gently to him so he will not be afraid during the bath. Have a towel ready to dry your dog so he does not catch cold.

Answer These Questions:

1. A good title for this story is _____

2. How full should the dog's bath water be? _____

3. What is the first thing you should do when you are getting the water ready for the dog's bath? _____

4. Why should you talk gently to your dog when bathing him? _____
   _____

5. What does "precaution" mean? _____

6. Should you ever bathe a dog more than three times a year? _____
   Why? _____

This card is from **The Reading Corner** ©1977 Goodyear Publishing Company, Inc. and Harry W. Forgan, Jr.

Motivation Statement:

Dogs are either purebreds or mutts. Read this selection to learn why they are different.

Selection:

There are well over a hundred different breeds of dogs. A dog is a purebred if his parents, grandparents, and great-grandparents are all of the same breed. A dog whose parents are of different breeds is called a mutt or mongrel.

If a dog is a purebred, he has "papers" that tell the names of his parents and other ancestors. This is called a pedigree. Of course mongrels do not have papers, but this does not mean purebreds are better dogs. Many times mutts are as smart and as friendly as purebreds. The fact is, some people prefer mutts because they say they are better adjusted than purebreds.

Answer These Questions:

1. What is the major point in the selection? _____

   _____

2. When is a dog considered a purebred? _____

3. What should you do before buying a purebred? _____

   _____

4. Why do some people prefer purebreds? _____

   _____

5. What does "ancestors" mean? _____

   _____

6. Do you agree that mutts are better than purebreds? _____

   Why do you feel this way? _____

   _____

This card is from **The Reading Corner** © 1977 Goodyear Publishing Company, Inc. and Harry W. Forgan, Jr.

Category Tic-Tac-Toe

Directions:
Play this game the same as regular tic-tac-toe **except**, before you can put an **X** or an **O** you must name the category and tell one more item that could be in it.

Pencils Paper Crayons Books _____	Chairs Beds Tables Dressers _____	Cereal Hot Dogs Milk Bread _____
Footballs Baseballs Tennis Balls Ping-Pong Balls _____	"The Three Stooges" "Good Times" "The Wonderful World of Disney" "Wild Kingdom" _____	Flowers Trees Bushes Butterflies
Games Trains Race Tracks Dolls _____	Storage Sheds Houses Stores Garages _____	Apples Oranges Bananas Pears _____

This card is from **The Reading Corner** ©1977 Goodyear Publishing Company, Inc. and Harry W. Forgan, Jr.

Follow the Directions

Directions:
Read the directions for each project carefully. You are going to make some interesting things.

Make a Lantern

1. Fold a 9 inch by 12 inch piece of construction paper in half the long way.
2. Cut from the folded side almost to the edge.
3. Open the paper.
4. Paste both end strips together.
5. Tie a string to the top.
6. You now have a lantern.

Spelling Can Be Fun

1. Get an egg carton.
2. Write one letter in each egg cup. Use a, b, c, d, e, f, g, h, i, j, k, and l.
3. Put a marble in the cup with any letter you choose.
4. See if you can flip the marble in the air to another space to spell a word. Make a list of the words you can spell. You get one point for each letter in a word that you spell.
5. Challenge a friend!

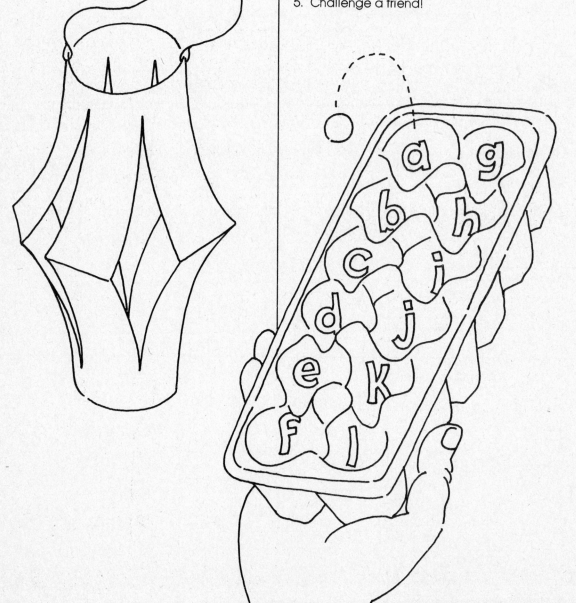

This card is from *The Reading Corner* © 1977 Goodyear Publishing Company, Inc. and Harry W. Forgan, Jr.

Old Black Magic

Directions:
You can be a magician if you follow these
directions carefully.

Can you stab a straw through a potato?

1. Get a raw potato and a paper straw.
2. Examine the raw potato to make sure it does not
   have any holes.
3. Put your thumb over the top end of the straw.
4. Move your straw up and down rapidly. When you
   do so, you force air into the straw.
5. Quickly stab the straw through the potato.
6. Eat the piece of potato in the straw.
7. Discuss what made the paper straw so strong.

Can you fill a balloon without blowing?

1. Get a balloon, a soda bottle, some baking
   soda, and some vinegar.
2. Put two teaspoons of baking soda into an empty
   balloon.
3. Put one inch of vinegar into the empty pop
   bottle.
4. Fit the neck of the balloon tightly over the neck of
   the bottle.
5. Shake the bottle so the soda falls into the bottle.
6. In a few minutes, the balloon will begin to fill with
   air.
7. The soda and the vinegar form carbon dioxide
   gas. This gas fills the balloon.

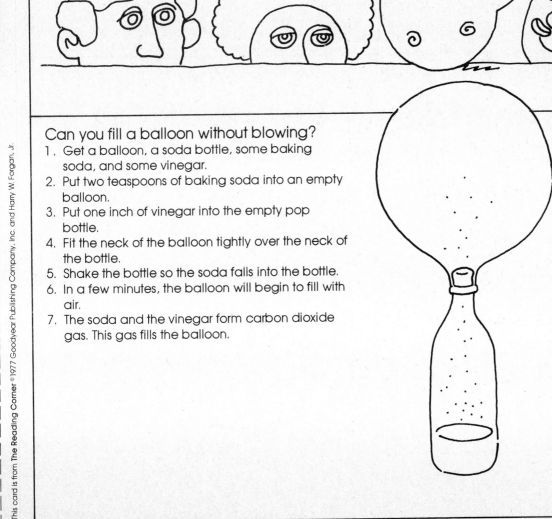

This card is from *The Reading Corner* ©1977 Goodyear Publishing Company, Inc. and Harry W. Forgan, Jr.

Cause 〉Clauses

Directions:
Cut out the cards. Cut each card on the dotted line. Mix the cards and see if you can put the sentences together. Make some of your own phrase puzzles.

The boy lost his dog / and began to cry.

The clouds were so dark / because it was raining.

The school bus was late \ so his mother drove him.

The man has to go to jail \ because he is guilty.

The teacher was angry / because the children were not behaving.

This card is from *The Reading Corner* © 1977 Goodyear Publishing Company, Inc. and Harry W. Forgan, Jr.

Obey the Speed Limit

This card is from The Reading Corner ©1977 Goodyear Publishing Company, Inc. and Harry W. Forgan, Jr.

Move ahead 3 spaces. You are in a hurry to find the main idea.	Move ahead 3 spaces. You are trying to find a name in the telephone book.	Come on! You are in a hurry to finish a pleasure book. Book reports are due tomorrow. Move ahead 3 spaces.
Move back 3 spaces. You were reading so rapidly that you did not understand what you read.	Move back 2 spaces. You are guilty of reading the recipe too quickly and you ruined the cake.	Move ahead 3 spaces. You are in a hurry to find a topic in the encyclopedia.
You are cruising at a normal rate of reading as you enjoy a story. Move ahead 2 spaces.	This joke is pretty good. Move ahead 2 spaces and read at a normal rate to enjoy it.	Good for you! You found the key word in the paragraph. Move ahead 3 spaces.
You are doing fine. This poem requires a normal rate. Move ahead 2 spaces.	You are reading too slowly. Increase your rate when you are reading to find the main idea. Go faster by moving ahead 3 spaces.	You are reading a book with magic tricks. Better read slowly. Move ahead only 1 space.
Slow down. You are reading a social studies book too quickly. Move ahead only 1 space.	Read math problems carefully. Move ahead only 1 space.	Whoops! That is too fast to read directions for putting a model together. Move back 2 spaces.
You are reading a science experiment. Slow down. Move ahead only 1 space.	The directions to the game you want to play are complicated. Move ahead 1 space very SLOWLY.	Go back 3 spaces. You can't read a play that fast. Adjust your rate to the way the character feels.

Name _____

Crack the Code

Directions:
Are you a super spy? See if you can find the symbol or abbreviations for these words. Write the symbol or abbreviation in one column and the secret message word that is with the symbol or abbreviation in the other column. If you are correct, a mystery message will appear.

Word	Symbols Abbreviations	Secret Message Word
add		
subtract		
multiply		
divide		
equals		
is not equal		
less than		
greater than		
cents		
dollars		
inches		
feet		
yards		
ounces		
pounds		
miles		
centimeters		

This card is from **The Reading Corner** ©1977 Goodyear Publishing Company, Inc. and Harry W. Forgan, Jr.

Monster Map Symbols

This card is from *The Reading Corner* ©1977 Goodyear Publishing Company, Inc. and Harry W. Forgan, Jr.

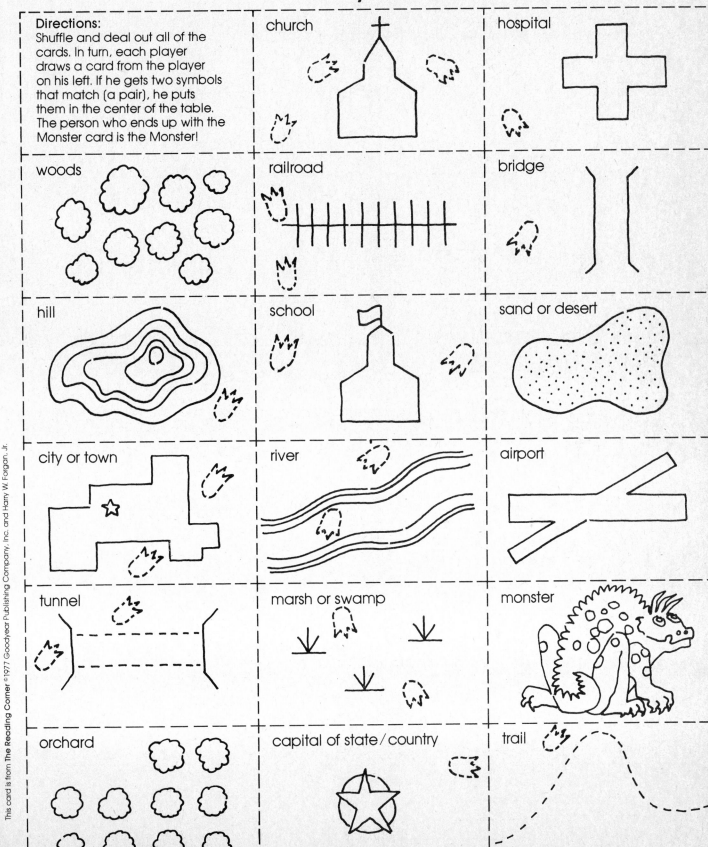

Directions:
Shuffle and deal out all of the cards. In turn, each player draws a card from the player on his left. If he gets two symbols that match (a pair), he puts them in the center of the table. The person who ends up with the Monster card is the Monster!

church

hospital

woods

railroad

bridge

hill

school

sand or desert

city or town

river

airport

tunnel

marsh or swamp

monster

orchard

capital of state/country

trail

Appendix Item **60**
Learning Center Activity Sheet for Reading Graphs

Make a Graph

Directions:
Cut this page on the dotted line and give the bottom half to your friends to complete. Make a separate graph for each question. Write the choices at the bottom of the graph. Color the spaces to show how many children made that choice. Put the correct title at the top of the graph (colors, TV programs, subjects, animals, or bedtimes).

Our Favorite _____

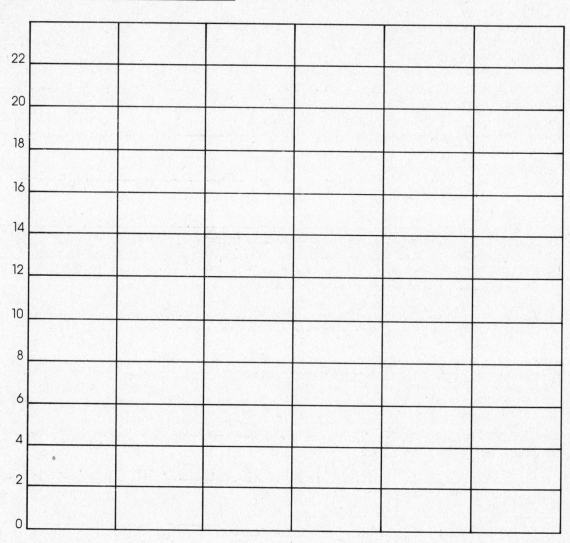

Number of Children

22
20
18
16
14
12
10
8
6
4
2
0

- -

1. Which of the **colors** do you like best?
    orange   red   purple   green   yellow   blue
2. Which **TV program** do you like best?
    "The Three Stooges" "The Waltons" "Good Times" "I Dream of Jeanne" "I Love Lucy" Cartoons
3. Which **subject** do you like best?
    social studies   science   health   spelling   art   reading
4. What **animal** is your favorite?
    cat   dog   horse   fish   bird   turtle
5. What is your **bedtime** on school nights?
    7:00   7:30   8:00   8:30   9:00   9:30

This card is from **The Reading Corner** ©1977 Goodyear Publishing Company, Inc. and Harry W. Forgan, Jr.

This card is from **The Reading Corner** ©1977 Goodyear Publishing Company, Inc. and Harry W. Forgan, Jr.

Name _____

Know Your Book

Directions:
Use your _____ book to answer these questions.

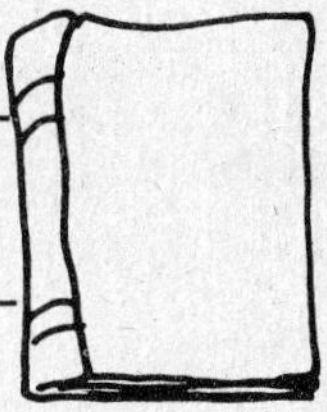

_____

1. What is the title of this book?

_____

2. Who are the authors?

_____

3. When was the book copyrighted?

_____

4. What is a copyright?

_____

5. What company published the book?

_____

6. What edition is this book?

_____

7. Why do some books have more than one edition?

_____

8. What kind of information is in the preface?

_____

9. Give an example of how the table of contents can help you.

_____

10. Is there a list of tables, maps, or diagrams? _____
    How can this help you?

_____

11. How are new words shown?

_____

12. Is there a glossary? _____

_____

13. How can the glossary help you?

_____

14. Where is the index located?

_____

15. When will you use the index?

_____

16. Is there an appendix? _____

_____

17. What information is presented in the appendix?

_____

B Is for Book

Directions:
Get tokens and a spinner. Put the tokens on start and spin the spinner to see who goes first. Alternate turns spinning the spinner and move the tokens the number of spaces shown. If you land on a space that describes a part of a book, you must tell what part it is. If you cannot tell what part it is, you must move backward to the nearest free space. If you land on a Super ? you draw a question card. If you are able to answer the question correctly, you move forward 2 spaces. If not, you stay on the ? mark. The first one to the finish line is the winner.

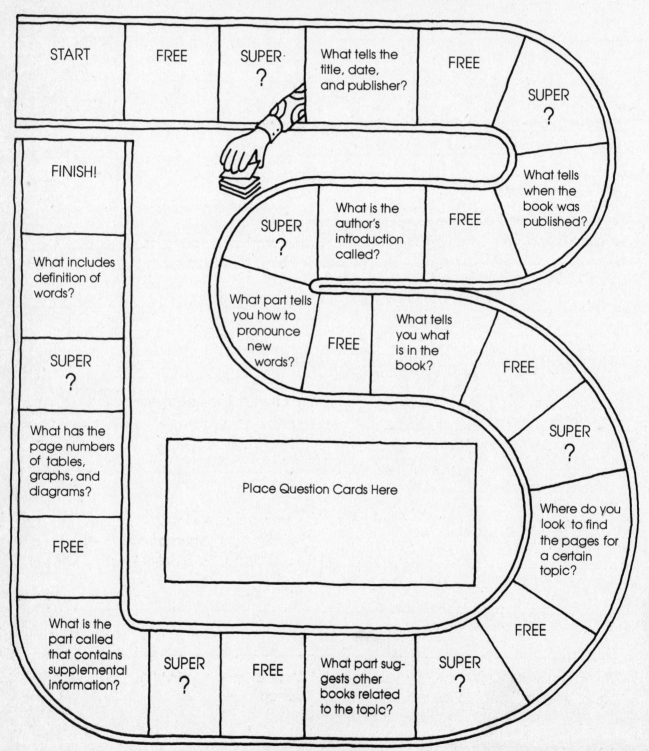

This card is from *The Reading Corner* ©1977 Goodyear Publishing Company, Inc. and Harry W. Forgan, Jr.

B Is for Book

Directions:
Cut out these cards and use them with the "B Is for Book" game.

Why do you want to know the copyright date of a book?	Why are books copyrighted?
What should you do if you can't find a certain topic in the table of contents?	Why do some books have appendices?
If the glossary has two definitions for a word, how do you know which one to choose?	Why do books have a table of contents?
Why do textbooks suggest other activities or questions to answer?	What does "see also" mean in an index?
What is a preface?	Read the page numbers that would be included if these numbers were listed: 12, 14-16, 18, 20-23.
Why do some books have a list of the maps, diagrams, and graphs?	Why do some books have more than one edition?

This card is from **The Reading Corner** ©1977 Goodyear Publishing Company, Inc. and Harry W. Forgan, Jr.

Appendix Item **64**
Skill Test for Reference Materials

Directions:
Listed below are some kinds of information you may
need to obtain. There is also a list of reference
materials that contain information. Match reference
books with the information by placing the letter of
the reference material in front of the information.
You can use the letters more than once. Remember,
sometimes the information might be found in two or
three different types of material, but one would be
the best source.

A. Encyclopedia
B. Atlas
C. Thesaurus
D. Dictionary
E. Telephone Book
F. Almanac

_____ 1. . Pictures of the human body

_____ 2. Address of a friend

_____ 3. Maps

_____ 4. How televisions work

_____ 5. Pronunciation of a new word

_____ 6. Words that mean the same

_____ 7. Where to buy flowers in your
community

_____ 8. Information about animals

_____ 9. Information about the number of
telephones in the United States

_____ 10. Words that mean the opposite

_____ 11. The population of the United
States

_____ 12. Who won the World Series last
year

_____ 13. The telephone number of a store

_____ 14. A map that shows where corn is
grown

_____ 15. To find out what causes bumps
when you hit your head

_____ 16. To find out what stores sell sports
equipment

_____ 17. To find the correct spelling of a
word

_____ 18. To find out what parts of United
States get the most rainfall

_____ 19. To find the high and low
temperatures of different states
in United States

_____ 20. To find pictures of poisonous
snakes

This card is from **the Reading Corner** ©1977 Goodyear Publishing Company, Inc. and Harry W. Forgan, Jr.

Appendix Item **65**
Learning Center Activity Sheet for Reference Skills

Important Telephone Numbers

Directions:
Use the telephone book to list the telephone numbers that are important to you. You may need to ask your parents to tell you some of the numbers.

My home phone number is _____

My dad's telephone number at work is _____

My mom's telephone number at work is _____

The police department's number is _____

The fire department's number is _____

Our family doctor's number is _____

The movie theater's number is _____

The time of day number is _____

My friend _____'s number is _____

My friend _____'s number is _____

My club number is _____

This card is from **The Reading Corner** ©1977 Goodyear Publishing Company, Inc. and Harry W. Forgan, Jr.

Appendix Item **66**
Learning Center Activity Sheet
for Reference Materials

My Favorite Things

Directions:
Use a set of encyclopedias to find your favorite things. Write in your favorites and the
volume and page number so others can locate them.

Favorites	Volume	Page
1. My favorite flag is		
2. My favorite animal is		
3. My favorite sport is		
4. My favorite fish is		
5. My favorite bird is		
6. My favorite flower is		
7. My favorite snake is		
8. My favorite car is		
9. My favorite gem is		
10. My favorite airplane is		
11. My favorite insect is		
12. My favorite horse is		

This card is from *The Reading Corner* ©1977 Goodyear Publishing Company, Inc. and Harry W. Forgan, Jr.

This card is from **The Reading Corner** ©1977 Goodyear Publishing Company, Inc. and Harry W. Forgan, Jr.

Name _____

Appendix Item **67**
Skill Test for Library Skills

Part I — Directions:
In the blank in front of each one of the book titles, write the number of drawer in the card catalog in which you would find the book listed.

_____ 1. **The Great Glass Elevator**   _____ 5. **Secret of the Andes**

_____ 2. **Roller Skates**   _____ 6. **The Witch of Blackbird Pond**

_____ 3. **Daniel Boone**   _____ 7. **It's Like This!**

_____ 4. **Call It Courage**   _____ 8. **101 Ways to Have Fun**

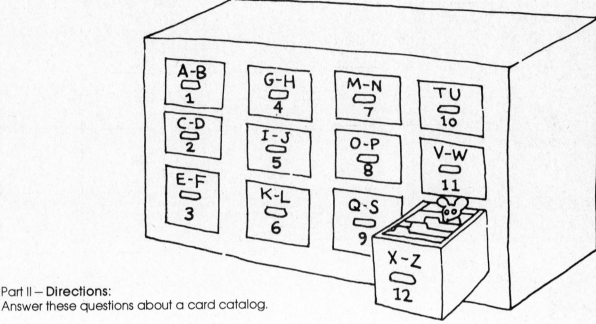

Part II — Directions:
Answer these questions about a card catalog.

1. Why do we have a card catalog? _____

2. Name the three kinds of cards that are kept on every book in the library. After each one put when you would use this card.

_____

_____

_____

3. What does the capital **R** stand for when you see it on a card? _____

4. What does the capital **B** stand for when you see it on a card? _____

5. What do the numbers tell you when you see them on a card? _____

_____

6. If an author's name begins with **Mc**, it is filed as if it begins with what? _____

_____

7. If there are no markings on the upper left-hand corner of the card, this means that

the book is _____

Appendix Item **68**
Learning Center Activity Sheet for Library Skills

Name
_____

Where Do I Belong?

Directions:
Read each of the titles of the books listed below.
Decide whether the book is a reference, biography,
fiction, or nonfiction book. Write the names of the
books on the shelf in alphabetical order.

Reference

Biography

Fiction

Nonfiction

The World Almanac

The Day the Ghost Came to Our Town

The New World Dictionary for
Elementary School Children

The Boys Who Could Fly — The Wright
Brothers

An Atlas of the United States

Hansel and Gretel

Things You Can Do on a Rainy Day

All About Thomas Jefferson

How to Fix Your Bike

How to Increase Your Memory

The Life of President Kennedy

Jokes and Riddles You Will Like

This card is from **The Reading Corner** ©1977 Goodyear Publishing Company, Inc. and Harry W. Forgan, Jr.

Appendix Item **69**
Skill Test for Study Skills and Habits

Directions:
Put a check mark (√) in the column that describes how often you do the following. Be honest. I shall help you learn to study if needed.

	Never	Sometimes	Usually
1. Do you look over what you are going to read before you read it?			
2. Do you form questions about the selection before you read it?			
3. Do you use a slower rate when you are reading your textbooks?			
4. Do you try to pronounce and define words that are in bold print or italics?			
5. Do you read the tables, graphs, and diagrams in your textbooks?			
6. Do you answer questions as you go along?			
7. Do you outline the important ideas and facts as you read?			
8. Do you reread the materials you do not understand?			
9. Do you review what you have read when you have finished?			
10. Do you set a time for study?			
11. Do you have a place to study at home or near your home? Are your supplies ready?			
12. Are you able to concentrate when studying?			
13. If you are doing math problems, do you read them carefully and then reread them to see if your answer is correct?			
14. If you must turn work in to your teacher, are you proud of it? Is it neat and well organized?			

This card is from **The Reading Corner** ©1977 Goodyear Publishing Company, Inc. and Harry W. Forgan, Jr.

Take Five

Directions:
Cut the cards apart and put them in a box. Take turns drawing 5 cards. Read the cards and then add up your score. Put the cards back in the box and shake it for the next player to take 5. After each player has had one turn, the person with the highest score for his 5 questions is the winner.

You forgot to preview. You lose 2 points.	You surveyed before you read. Add 2 points.	Sorry! You recite after reading! Deduct 2 points.
Good for you! You answered your questions after reading. Add 2 points.	How about that! You reviewed what you read! Add 3 points.	Too bad! You forgot to review. You lose 2 points.
You set a time limit for studying. Add 2 points.	You forgot to get all of your supplies ready before beginning to study. Lose 2 points.	You have a place to study with all of your supplies handy. Add 2 points.
You asked certain questions to answer before you read. Add 2 points.	Good for you! You used a slow study type rate of reading. Add 2 points!	You just skipped over the new words. Deduct 2 points.
You are reading without a purpose. Next time remember to ask questions first. Lose 2 points.	You read the material too quickly. Slow down and answer your questions. Deduct 2 points.	Good for you! You stopped to figure out the definitions of new words. Add 2 points.
You outlined the important facts that your teacher asked you to review. Add 2 points.	You didn't outline the important information. Deduct 2 points.	Sloppy work. Subtract 2 points.
Nice job. Your paper is so neat. Add 2 points.	Your parents didn't have to nag you to study. Add 2 points.	Your parents had to keep reminding you to study. Subtract 2 points.

This card is from **The Reading Corner** ©1977 Goodyear Publishing Company, Inc. and Harry W. Forgan, Jr.

This card is from *The Reading Corner* ©1977 Goodyear Publishing Company, Inc. and Harry W. Forgan, Jr.

Name _____

Interest Inventory

Appendix Item **71**
Skill Test for Recreational Reading (Part I)

Directions:
Answer the following questions that tell me about you!

1. Who are the people in your family? _____

_____

2. Write the ages of your brothers and sisters after their names.

3. Do you ever read to your parents? _____ What? _____

4. What is your favorite television program? _____

5. Do you ever go to the library? _____

6. What makes you happy? _____

7. Do you get any magazines at home? _____ Which ones? _____

8. What is your favorite animal? _____

9. Do you have any books of your own at home? _____ What kinds? _____

10. Do you have a pet? _____ If so, what is it? _____

11. What do you wish for? _____

12. What would you like to be? _____

13. What do you like to do after school? _____

14. What do you like to do on the weekends? _____

15. Do you ever read? _____ When? _____

16. Do you collect anything? _____ What? _____

17. Do you have any encyclopedias at home? _____

18. If you could have any toy you wanted, what would it be? _____

19. If you could have your choice of games to play, what games would you like to

play? _____

20. What hobbies or interests do you have? _____

21. What do you like most about school? _____

22. What do you like least about school? _____

Appendix Item **72**
Skill Test for Recreational Reading (Part II)

Checklist of Recreational Activities

Directions:
This is a list of things some children like to do. Read each one and if you like to do it, or think you would like it if you tried, put a check mark in front of it. If you do not like the activity or think you would not like it, leave it blank.

I LIKE TO _____

_____ 1. Finger-paint
_____ 2. Play some musical instrument
_____ 3. Play with trucks and cars
_____ 4. Climb ropes
_____ 5. Play cowboys and Indians
_____ 6. Play store
_____ 7. Paint
_____ 8. Play checkers
_____ 9. Play football
_____ 10. Go bowling
_____ 11. Play marbles
_____ 12. Play pick-up-sticks
_____ 13. Work with leather
_____ 14. Sew
_____ 15. Play with trains
_____ 16. Play with blocks
_____ 17. Do puzzles
_____ 18. Plant things
_____ 19. Play with sponges, boxes, cans
_____ 20. Make jewelry
_____ 21. Play bingo
_____ 22. Play in the sand
_____ 23. Ride horses
_____ 24. Jump rope
_____ 25. Go swimming
_____ 26. Listen to music
_____ 27. Work with a woodburner
_____ 28. Read comic books
_____ 29. Read about animals
_____ 30. Read mystery stories
_____ 31. Read about famous people
_____ 32. Collect shells or rocks
_____ 33. Visit relatives
_____ 34. Play hockey
_____ 35. Watch television

_____ 36. Make airplanes
_____ 37. Ride bicycles
_____ 38. Color
_____ 39. Play with puppets
_____ 40. Play dolls
_____ 41. Play with magnets
_____ 42. Play tic-tac-toe
_____ 43. Play basketball
_____ 44. Go roller skating
_____ 45. Play dominoes
_____ 46. Model clay
_____ 47. Weave
_____ 48. Play table games
_____ 49. Play with boats or water toys
_____ 50. Play with pets
_____ 51. Play shuffleboard
_____ 52. Paste things into a scrapbook
_____ 53. Fly kites
_____ 54. Work with a chemistry set
_____ 55. Play tag
_____ 56. Go camping
_____ 57. Play baseball
_____ 58. Wrestle
_____ 59. Go to a museum
_____ 60. Go to movies
_____ 61. Build model planes or cars
_____ 62. Make fudge, candy, or popcorn
_____ 63. Read about sports
_____ 64. Read about cowboys
_____ 65. Read fairy tales
_____ 66. Read about science
_____ 67. Collect coins, stamps, cards
_____ 68. Visit friends
_____ 69. Play tennis
_____ 70. Other _____

This card is from **The Reading Corner** © 1977 Goodyear Publishing Company, Inc. and Harry W. Forgan, Jr.

Appendix Item **73**
Learning Center Activity Sheet
for Recreational Reading

In the News

Directions:
Use a copy of your local newspaper to answer these questions. Compare your answers with
your friend's answers.

1. If you had $10 to go shopping today, what would you buy? _____

   _____

2. If you could choose a job from the classified advertisements, which one would you

   want? _____

   _____

3. If you could go to a movie, which one would you like to go to? _____

   _____

4. If you could eat at a restaurant, which one would you select? _____

   _____

5. What is the best cartoon in the paper today? _____

   _____

6. What is your horoscope? _____

   _____

7. What is another headline that could be in today's newspaper? _____

   _____

8. What is the most expensive new car? _____

9. What car would you like if you could have any you choose? _____

10. Find a happy story in the newspaper. What is the headline? _____

    _____

11. Find a sad story in the newspaper. What is the headline? _____

    _____

12. Find the menu for the school cafeteria. What is your favorite lunch? _____

    _____

13. Cut out all the articles that deal with schools. How do these articles affect you? ___

    _____

14. Circle the TV programs you would like to watch tonight.

15. Cut out the picture you think is the best picture in the paper. Write a

    different story for some picture.

This card is from **The Reading Corner** ©1977 Goodyear Publishing Company, Inc. and Harry W. Forgan, Jr.